GOVERNING THE BBC

ASA BRIGGS

Governing the BBC

BRITISH BROADCASTING CORPORATION

Published by the
British Broadcasting Corporation
35 Marylebone High Street
London W1M 4AA
First published 1979
© Asa Briggs 1979

ISBN 0 563 17774 8

Printed in England
by Jolly & Barber Ltd., Rugby

FOREWORD

All but the last section of this essay was written before the publication of the Government's White Paper Cmnd 7294 (1978). The historical sections set out to explore changing relationships, not simply to point the way to the present and the future. In the record of the past I have not gone beyond the autumn of 1978.

The essay could not have been written at all without the invaluable help at every stage of Leonard Miall and Pat Spencer. They are solely responsible for preparing the appendices.

Asa Briggs
Worcester College
April 1979

CONTENTS

LIST OF ILLUSTRATIONS

INTRODUCTION
HOW CAN ONE *GOVERN* THE BBC?

Many questions of social importance can be asked about broadcasting, a relatively new phenomenon in history. The first organised sound was broadcast in 1922; the first organised vision, for
a privileged minority, in 1936. The questions are of varying
degrees of importance and range from the structure and scale
of broadcasting organisation through the volume and quality of
broadcasting output to the reception and impact of different
types of programme and the general significance of the media,
particularly television.

It is impossible to understand the current structure of British
broadcasting, a unique structure within the world context, without comparing it with other broadcasting structures and without
tracing its origins back to the 1920s. This essay concentrates on
the second task.[1] Before the BBC became a public corporation in
1927, it had already developed a sense of public service. After its
monopoly was broken in 1955, the new and competitive Independent Television Authority drew on notions of responsible
control which were already associated with an established tradition.[2]

The scale of the broadcasting enterprise has changed dramatically. There were 2,395,183 wireless licences in 1927: in 1977
there were 8,098,386 monochrome television licences and
9,957,672 colour television licences. A huge sound broadcasting
public was built up over a twenty-eight-year period, with the
peak figure for sound licences alone (11,875,566) being reached
in 1950, while the growth of the television public was even more
rapid. It took nearly a quarter of a century for the number of
sound licences to pass the ten-million mark in 1946: it took only
thirteen years from the post-war resumption of television for the
number of television licences to pass that figure in 1960.

Achieving this build-up before and after the end of the mon-

[1] For the first task, see my *BBC Lunch-time Lecture*, 'The BBC in World Perspective'
Eleventh Series, 8 March 1977, and W.B. Emery, *National and International Systems of
Broadcasting, their History, Operation and Control* (1969).
[2] See George Wedell, *Broadcasting and Public Policy* (1968), for the argument that the
British system is in fact a single system with variants, not a dual system.

Sir John Reith

opoly provided the BBC with increasing licence income. Yet it involved detailed planning, frequent new initiatives in programme policy and heavy capital expenditure. Unlike the Independent Broadcasting Authority, the name of which was changed (from ITA) in 1972 when commercial local radio stations began to operate, the BBC *makes* programmes. And the scale of programme making has changed dramatically also. The BBC now provides 160 hours of television a week, some 2240 hours of domestic sound broadcasting, and through its External Services – an exclusive responsibility – 704 hours in 39 languages. No one can watch or listen to all this vast output. Nor, even if it were thought to be desirable, could the whole output be sifted or controlled 'in advance'.

As audience numbers and programme output have grown, the size of the BBC staff has grown with them. In 1922, when the

British Broadcasting Company was set up, it had a staff of four: in 1927, when it was replaced by the British Broadcasting Corporation, there was a staff of 989. Ten years later, just before the first and still the best-known of the BBC's Director-Generals, John Reith, left the BBC, the staff was 3673. In 1929 it was 5100 and in 1945 10,727. Ten years later it was 13,524. By June 1978 it had risen to 26,041.[1]

Such increases in staff figures can be paralleled in the records of other organisations; and their implications for management and control are obvious. From the 1930s onwards 'hierarchy' troubled the BBC, and already there were many complaints of 'bureaucracy'. During the late 1960s and particularly during the 1970s new issues emerged with the growth of 'professionalisation' and 'increasingly effective' unionisation.[2] In a 1977 message from the Chairman of the Governors to all BBC staff the key distinction Sir Michael Swann felt that he had to draw was not one between 'creative' and 'administrative' people, the favourite division of the 1930s, or one between engineers and programme makers, an even older division, but one between 'weekly' and 'monthly' grades.[3]

So many people are now involved in broadcasting as a professional career and so huge is the output designed for scattered home and overseas audiences (catered for through different and to some extent competing BBC services) that it is right to pose as the first of many questions in this essay 'How can one *govern* the BBC?' One former Director-General, Sir Ian Jacob, is on record as saying that 'governing the BBC is a very greatly more difficult job than it was in my comparatively peaceful days'.[4]

From 1927 the BBC has had a Board of Governors, appointed in the public interest, to direct the Corporation. The numbers have varied from five at the beginning, to nine in 1952 and twelve in 1979. For a time during the Second World War there were only two. They have always been headed by a Chairman who speaks

[1] See Appendix IV.
[2] Sir Charles Curran, 'Broadcasting, the Executive Function', *BBC Lunch-time Lectures, Ninth Series*, 11 March 1973, p.7. 'It is clearly right that any management or operational decision which has an effect on the lives of a work force should come to them through their unions, as well as through management channels.' (p.8).
[3] Message from the Chairman to all BBC staff, 10 Aug. 1977.
[4] Letter to Leonard Miall, 19 March 1979.

in public on their behalf. During the first fifty years of the BBC's history there were 85 Governors in all, 67 men and 18 women, headed by 13 Chairmen, all of them men. During the same period there have been nine Director-Generals. [1]

The Governors, more in the limelight since the 1960s than before, have always been encouraged both to voice their own praise or blame for particular programmes and to respond to public praise or blame. But they have never been able to deal with the whole range of programme details, even though some of them on occasion have thought it desirable to do so. What they have tried to do, often forcefully, is to maintain balance and to watch quality. Yet they have sometimes been criticised on this count, or on the more serious count that they 'do not govern'. [2]

Oversight of programmes is only one part of their task. Constitutionally the Board *is* the BBC. It holds the legal title to BBC property, and it is responsible for policy and for oversight of management. As the 1939 *BBC Handbook* put it, without seeking to define the difficult word 'control', 'the Board of Governors, to whom the Director-General is immediately responsible, controls BBC policy'. [3] However much it is the case that they have the power to review, to deal with complaints and to some extent 'to help create a climate of opinion, in broad matters of programme policy', [4] nonetheless they have always had to show trust in the people who plan and make programmes.

BBC policy is by its nature many-sided, and some of the most important decisions the Board has taken have dealt more with development than with routine matters. In these matters, too, it has been guided by Director-Generals and other senior officials in the Corporation, particularly perhaps in engineering matters since the Board has included only a few knowledgeable people in this field. The development has been striking – the pioneering Regional scheme for sound broadcasting of the late 1920s; the

[1] See Appendix II.

[2] Mary Whitehouse, *Cleaning Up TV* (1967), Ch. 8, 'Governors who do not Govern'. Cf. R. Bevins, *The Greasy Pole* (1965), p.116, 'A curious thing about the BBC is the apparent inability of the BBC Governors to exert any real influence.' See below, p.119.

[3] *BBC Handbook, 1939*, p.94.

[4] Sir Michael Swann, 'The Responsibility of the Governors', *BBC Lunch-time Lectures, Ninth Series*, 29 Oct. 1974, pp.10–14.

beginning of the 'Empire broadcasting' scheme in 1932 and of world broadcasting from 1938 onwards; launching the first regular high-definition television programmes in the world in 1936; the new approach to minority broadcasting, the Third Programme in 1946; a Ten-Year Development Plan for Television in 1953, and ultimately second-channel television which began transmissions in 1964; and the fostering of new technologies, the latest of which is CEEFAX. Although the knowledge and the drive in each branch of development have come from the Director-General and his staff, the Board as a whole has always been involved in critical questions of costing, priorities, timetabling and, above all, relations with Government. The last have often been difficult, as in the case of issues as different, for example, as the first Empire broadcasting, a Reithian idea, the maintenance of post-war External Services, very much a preoccupation of Sir Ian Jacob, the speed and financing of television development, the presentation of news (the BBC was attacked from outside on these latter two issues), and the fixing of the size of licence fees. The licence fee problem is the most topical, but it is not a new one. Two factors have increased its importance – inflation and the build-up of the television audience to a point of almost maximum coverage. Only the continued increase in the proportion of colour television licences allows for growth of income from licence fees.

The word 'Governors' does not have a very wide range of reference in the English language. Governors, indeed, who used to be associated with colonies – the BBC's first Chairman, the Earl of Clarendon, went on with no break to become Governor-General of South Africa in 1930 – are now usually associated with schools, hospitals, banks or prisons. The *Oxford Dictionary* most generally, but very unhelpfully, defines a governor as 'one who governs (Middle English)', going on to give the seventeenth-century usage as 'statesman, pilot, captain' and the chief modern usage as 'an official title'. Neither definition quite fits the governors of schools, hospitals, banks or prisons. Nor does either fit the Governors of the BBC. The governors of schools and hospitals have to work through headmasters, teachers, health administrators and doctors. Neither type of institution could function if they were called upon to 'control', and the same is true of BBC

THE EARL OF CLARENDON.   *George Belcher*

Here is the Head of the Corporation
That casts abroad to the British nation;
And, when it decides exactly what
Is good for our ears to hear or not,
Its choice is bound to be based upon
"The Constitutions of Clarendon."

MR. PUNCH'S PERSONALITIES.—XXXIII.

Governors, if not entirely true of governors of banks or prisons.

'What is the function of a Board of Governors of an Independent School?', a witty and successful headmaster was once asked. 'To appoint and never to disappoint a Head' was his reply. [1] There have been times in BBC history when this might have seemed to be the main role of its Governors; and it has always been a matter of the utmost importance that they have had the power to select successive Director-Generals and their key staff without consulting government. 'Far more important than anything else in a body like the BBC,' the present Chairman has said, 'is the making of senior appointments. The Board itself makes the top thirty or forty of them, down to the level of controller, and it takes the job very seriously indeed. For in the long run, it is the choice of these men and women that determines what sort of body the BBC is.' [2]

Yet this has never been the whole story, and there have been periods in the history of the BBC when the choice of many of the senior appointments (though not, of course, that of the Director-General) has had little to do with the Board. They have been made 'from within'; and because the pull is always to make appointments from within, 'junior' appointments procedures are important. Neither school nor hospital raises the same controversial questions of general public policy as the BBC, although the Bank of England sometimes has done; and 'independence' means something quite different in the context of a school or hospital and the context of a broadcasting organisation. Broadcasting penetrates homes, and, given perceptions of its power, possibly exaggerated, a further *Oxford Dictionary* definition of 'Governor' may sometimes have seemed more appropriate – 'a self-acting contrivance for regulating the passages of gas, steam, water, etc., especially in order to ensure an even and regular motion in a machine'.

Although the phrase occurs nowhere in the Royal Charter of the BBC, the members of the Board of Governors have traditionally been charged with acting (as the Crawford Committee put it in 1926) as 'trustees of the national interest in broadcasting'. 'We have no purpose but to serve the public,' one distinguished

[1] Joyce Waley-Cohen, 'What are Governors for?', in *Conference*, June 1973, p.23.
[2] Swann, 'The Responsibility of the Governors', p.8.

former Chairman, Lord Normanbrook, remarked in 1965, 'and if we fail to serve them, or allow ourselves to serve some other interest, we forfeit our right to guide and influence this national service.'[1] *The Guardian* was less sure. 'When it comes to exercising the office "trustee of the national interest" . . . the ITA leaves the Governors floundering. It is not that the Authority is more censorious it is simply more efficient.'[2]

The first difficulty, of course, is that however 'jealous' the Governors may be of the trust committed to them – another word used by Normanbrook – it is not easy to interpret 'the national interest'. During the period of his own Chairmanship – with Sir Hugh Greene as a reforming Director-General – there were fierce debates inside and outside the BBC about whether the line of action followed by the Director-General (and its underlying philosophy) was really in the public interest. Was it compatible with a public corporation financed from licence fees? Some thought it 'corrupting', others 'subversive'. The critique was not sharpened when A.J.P. Taylor demanded that 'the Governors of the BBC must satisfy public taste or make way for those who can'.[3]

The conception of the public interest has changed considerably since the 1920s, even since 1965. It was defined most clearly in war-time, when the powers of the Governors were least, when there was one national goal, and when controversy was restricted. Yet it became difficult to define between 1945 and 1951 and even more difficult when to economic and political differences were added differences in approaches to 'traditional morality'. Asked what was the biggest change after 1945, Phillip Whitehead, MP, one of the members of the Annan Committee, the latest committee to concern itself with the structure of broadcasting, singled out the fracturing of 'an everlasting consensus arranged around the centre' as it was conceived before 1939 and during the Second World War.[4]

Sir Michael Swann has stressed the polarities of the critics. 'There are those who still complain that the governors exercise all

[1] Lord Normanbrook, 'The Functions of the BBC's Governors', *BBC Lunch-time Lectures, Fourth Series*, 15 Dec. 1965.

[2] *The Guardian*, 22 Dec. 1965.

[3] *Sunday Express*, 28 Feb. 1965. Mrs Whitehouse quotes the passage in op. cit., p.96.

[4] Quoted in Alastair Clayre, *The Impact of Broadcasting* (1973), pp.33–4.

Sir Michael Swann

too little control over the broadcasters. But there are others . . .
for whom . . . the governors are a matter of no great moment,
and who believe that society would be better served if the BBC
were dismembered, financed directly by government, and controlled in new ways by the broadcasters themselves.'[1] The second
set of critics draw their models from publishing.

Certainly the operations of broadcasters themselves influence
the changing conception of national interest, particularly,
perhaps, in an age of television. There is disagreement, however,
as to how much.[2] Milton Shulman wrote that after seven years as
Director-General, Greene could feel that he had 'helped push the
BBC right into the centre of the swirling forces that were changing life in Britain. And that, by its interest, the BBC was not

[1] Swann, 'The Responsibility of the Governors', pp.3–4.
[2] See Philip Schlesinger's criticism of Anthony Smith's view that television is 'the
principal form of social regulation' in *The Times Higher Education Supplement*, 22 Sept.
1978. Schlesinger mentions schools, unions and political parties also. Yet there are
critics of the view that television 'regulates' more than it 'disturbs'. See A. Smith, *The
Shadow in the Cave* (1973), Chs. 2 and 3, and *The Politics of Information: Problems of Policy
in Modern Media* (1978); and N. Garnham, *Structures of Television* (1978).

merely reflecting and recording these changes, but was helping to agitate them as well'. [1] Yet not all the forces swirled. Phillip Whitehead admitted in the same year, as most historians would admit, that he did not know the answer to the question whether broadcasting had helped to cause what he called the fracturing or whether, more simply, it was merely that the 'national mood' had changed. [2]

By debating the term 'national interest' free from short-term political or, equally important and more neglected, economic pressures, the Governors may help to clarify it: they will also draw others into the debate. Yet as Oliver Whitley, a distinguished former member of the BBC staff once put it, 'the nation divided always has the BBC on the rack'. [3] The BBC does not exist in a vacuum; broadcasting covers every activity of society. The Governors, none of them full-time, cannot escape the influences of their own background, education and occupation. They bring to broadcasting their own conception of society and of the 'national interest'. 'Mass communication ordinarily does not serve as a necessary and sufficient cause of audience effects', one of the best-known American sociologists of communications has written, 'but rather functions among and through a nexus of mediating factors and influences'. [4] Concerned as he mainly was with the United States, where the market has dictated the evolution of broadcasting policy, he did not add that 'mediating factors and influences' can affect broadcasters, and in Britain Governors, just as much as they affect audiences. This essay considers parts of the nexus.

There have been times when it has seemed that Government and BBC have been related elements in a unified political, social and cultural 'system', dominated by an 'Establishment'. [5] At such

[1] M. Shulman, *The Least Worst Television in the World* (1973), p.102.

[2] Quoted in Clayre, op. cit., p.34.

[3] Whitley coined the phrase in the first draft of *Broadcasting and the Public Mood*, see below p.43. Sir Huw Wheldon quoted it in his *Richard Dimbleby Lecture* 'The British Experience in Television', Feb. 1976, p.10, adding 'on controversial matters one man's programme meat can very easily be another man's programme poison'.

[4] J.T. Klapper, *The Effects of Mass Communication* (1960), p.8.

[5] See Henry Fairlie, 'The BBC: Voice of the Establishment', in *Encounter*, vol. 13, No. 2, Aug. 1959. While criticising the BBC's 'dependence on authority', Fairlie questioned the use of the term Establishment. 'It is a pity, one sometimes feels, that it was ever popularized and there is much to be said for the view that it should have been left to ferment in the more obscure vats of A.J.P. Taylor's writings.'

times it has seemed as if Government had settled through the Charter for 'remote control of broadcasting' through Governors it could trust, saving itself from close fire on both trivial and basic issues. There have been other times, however, particularly since 1964, when Government (or Parliament) has been suspicious of all 'non-elective centres of power': the Governors and Members 'have undertaken that *Hansard* is made available at the meetings of the ITA and the BBC', Anthony Wedgwood Benn, then Postmaster-General, told the Commons in 1965.[1] 'All controls outside themselves should be resisted by those in charge of broadcasting', Sir William Haley, then Director-General, argued in 1948:[2] 'Broadcasting is really too important to be left to the broadcasters', Wedgwood Benn argued twenty years later.[3]

Out of the intermittent dialogue passing through different phases – with Mrs Whitehouse once accusing the BBC of being a 'deaf adder'[4] – agreement has most been reached on the need for 'public accountability'; yet it is important to emphasise that by the Royal Charter that accountability is to Parliament, not to Government or to a particular department of state, like the Home Office. The Governors have always had to take account of changes in Government, sometimes at crucial moments in broadcasting history. They have always found it necessary – but often difficult – to try to work out independently, as the Charter enjoins them to do, how they can best establish the accountability of the Corporation. Their worst moments have been when they seemed to be suspicious of outside criticism and have become far too defensive.

If accountability is a criterion – and it is certainly not the only one – the Governors of the BBC have proved most effective in two quite different guises – first, when they have been varied in their outlook and able to argue fiercely with each other in the light of complementary or even of conflicting experience; and second, when they have spoken with one voice, sometimes an awkward voice as far as the Government of the day is concerned.

[1] *Hansard*, vol. 712, col. 511, 12 May 1965.
[2] Sir William Haley, *The Central Problem of Broadcasting* (1948), p.9.
[3] *The Times*, 19 Oct. 1968. See below, pp.III/10–11.
[4] Whitehouse, op. cit., Ch. 7: 'They are like the deaf adder that stoppeth her ear: which will not hearken to the voice of charmers, charming never so wisely. (Psalm 58, v. 4–5)'. For a later autobiography see *Who Does She Think She Is?* (1971).

On both occasions they have shown initiative as well as trustee-ship. And despite the arguments, by no means new, that they should be more 'representative', they have in general benefited from not being tied to representative formulae. Two new devel-opments involving representation were, however, the formal decision to appoint 'national' Governors to 'represent' Scotland, Wales and Northern Ireland from 1952 onwards and the infor-mal conventions under which from 1956 one Governor has had a trade-union background, and from 1962 another has come from diplomacy. A similar convention that normally at least one Governor should have experience in finance and another in education dates from the very first Board.

The formal powers of the Governors have been laid down in five successive BBC Charters, which came into effect in 1927, 1937, 1947, 1952 and 1964. At each of these scattered dates there was a constitutional crystallisation, sometimes after a period of un-certainty; and it is interesting to note that already there has been a greater time lag between the last Charter and the present year, 1979, than there had been between any previous two Charters.

The very first BBC Charter laid down the main constitutional points, fixing a five-year period of office for the Governors and allowing for their number to be increased 'from time to time'.[1] It also included a clause about remuneration, setting out only the maxima – for the Chairman £3000 per annum, for the Vice-Chairman £1000 per annum, and for the other Governors £700 per annum. These were not insignificant sums in the 1920s, when the Postmaster-General was paid £2500 and a judge £5000. They compared favourably, indeed, with the sums paid to non-executive directors of most business concerns.

To the four grounds for disqualification of a Governor set out in the first Charter the second Charter of 1937 added a fifth – 'if he holds any office or place of profit in which his interests may in the opinion of Our Postmaster-General conflict with the interests of the Corporation'.[2] All five grounds for disqualification have subsequently survived in all Charters, although their order has changed. The first is straightforward termination by the King-in-Council of the appointment without reasons necessarily being

[1] Cmd 2756 (1926), *Wireless Broadcasting*, Article 10(iv).
[2] Cmd 5329 (1936), *Broadcasting*, Article 12(b).

given, although such termination has never in practice been carried through. The second is unsoundness of mind or bankruptcy, and no Governors have ever been displaced for this reason. The third is resignation, and over the years ten Governors have resigned, some after a very short period of office. The fourth is absence from meetings continuously for three months without the consent of the Corporation. In this last case it is the Corporation itself which resolves that the office be vacated. There was one difficult case in 1950 when Marshal of the Royal Air Force Lord Tedder, a new Governor, applied for one year's leave of absence. The Governors approved, but the Vice-Chairman, Lady Reading, dissented.[1] The second Charter removed one awkward ambiguity about reappointment. 'A retiring Governor shall not be eligible for reappointment unless Our Postmaster General shall certify to Us that it is in the public interest that he should be reappointed.'[2] The fourth Charter stated more simply, however, that 'a retiring Governor shall be eligible for reappointment'.[3]

In general, the second Charter was more explicit about organisation than the first. Thus, a clause was inserted in it about a quorum, which was to be set by the Postmaster-General, although the Charter did not specify the number, and it laid down also that decisions should be taken by majority vote.[4] There have been periods in the history of the Governors when there were votes on almost every issue and periods when there have been few. Many votes were taken during the early years of Lord Hill's Chairmanship (at his own choice), but in only a few cases (and then probably at the request of the Governors) has the size of the votes been recorded.[5] There has never been any need for elaborate rules of procedure.

The second Charter stated also that 'there shall be a Chairman of the Corporation who shall be entitled to preside at the meetings thereof', 'that the chief executive officer of the Corporation shall be called the Director General' – this term went back to January 1927 – and that 'the Corporation may appoint persons

[1] Board of Governors, *Minutes*, 11 May 1950.
[2] Cmd 5329 (1936), Article 10(iii).
[3] Cmd 8605 (1952), *Broadcasting*, Article 8(1).
[4] Cmd 5329 (1936), Article 8(i).
[5] For Hill's Chairmanship, see below, pp.129–36. There were 11 issues on which Governors divided between January 1968 and November 1970.

or Committees to advise them with regard to all or any matters connected with the Broadcasting Service and the business operations and affairs of the Corporation' (along with sub-Committees). [1]

Such obvious formalities suggest that there was a stronger sense of organisational complexity in 1937 than in 1926. And although the salary of the Chairman remained the same, that of the Governors was fixed at £1000 per annum, not because of inflation, but on grounds of increased responsibility. The Labour Government reduced the figure to £600 in 1946, [2] a mistake, and it was not restored to £1000 until 1959. The 1946 White Paper, which preceded the first post-war enquiry into the BBC, stated more fully than it had ever been stated officially before that it was 'on the Governors that the Charter places the responsibility for developing and exploiting the service "to the best advantage and in the national interest"', and that it was to them that 'the Director-General and all other officers of the Corporation are responsible for their actions'. 'In exercising this responsibility', the White Paper went on, 'it is the Governors' duty to take an active interest, not only in the programmes, but also in the financial and staff policy of the Corporation.' 'The best possible talent' was necessary to discharge these tasks. [3]

The third Charter of 1947 added nothing. [4] The fourth, however, in July 1952 set out the names of the Governors at the time of publication, provided for National Governors for Scotland, Wales and Northern Ireland, and laid down precise salaries. National Governors for Scotland and Wales were to receive £1000, other Governors £600, the Vice-Chairman £1000 and the Chairman £3000. [5] The naming of the Governors was for political not for constitutional reasons. This was a Charter drafted in the knowledge that there would soon be changes both in the pattern of broadcasting and, above all, in the composition of the Board. Within a month there was a new Chairman and soon there was virtually a new Board. Yet the Charter was clear enough to last until 1964, when the fifth Charter was published, the Charter which is still in force.

---

[1] Cmd 5329 (1936), Articles 6(i) and (v) and 9.
[2] Cmd 6852 (1946), *Broadcasting Policy*, para. 23.
[3] Ibid.
[4] Cmd 6974 (1946), *Broadcasting*.
[5] Cmd 8605 (1952).

This latest Charter mentioned no names, set out no details of remuneration, and provided no pattern of meetings.[1] It elaborated, however, on the position of the National Governors, allowed for sub-Committees, and gave guidance about voting.[2] As far as the National Governors were concerned, each person appointed was to be selected 'in virtue of his knowledge of the culture, characteristics and affairs of Our People in the country and his close touch with opinion in that country'.[3] They were, of course, to be full members of the Board of Governors also, and the Board as a whole was permitted to meet in Scotland, Wales and in Northern Ireland 'at such intervals as may to the Corporation seem appropriate, regard being had to its representative function'.[4] Despite inflation, the basic salaries of the Governors remain the same as they were in 1959, although the salary of the Chairman has increased to £10,764 and those of the Vice-Chairman and the National Governors for Scotland and Wales to £2000.

The Charters deal only with formal powers. As in all kinds of government, conventions matter as much as rules and are sometimes more binding; and personalities – and balances of personality – influence policies in striking ways. There is always an intricate interplay of personal and social forces. I approach all my own questions in this essay as a historian studying situations, not as a constitutional lawyer searching for precedents. Economists, who can conceive of quite different broadcasting models from that of the BBC, models based on a market or set of markets with no 'gubernatorial function', would have different interests.[5] So, too, would political scientists, who can conceive of broadcasting systems dealing in propaganda, popular mobilisation and

[1] Cmnd 2385 (1964), *Broadcasting*, Articles 6(5–7).

[2] Cmnd 2385 (1964). Article 7(3)(d) was interesting procedurally. Before the Chairman or the Vice-Chairman dealt with urgent questions on his own he had to consult 'if and so far as may be reasonably practical with the other Governors or each of them as may be accessible to him.' He also had to report such decisions.

[3] Ibid., Article 5(3).   [4] Ibid., Article 7(3)(a).

[5] Anthony Smith has pointed to the American belief, somewhat overstated, that 'a society has no right to make policy choices in the mass media through its elected representatives'. 'Elsewhere,' he goes on, 'it is axiomatic that the allocation of spectrum and the establishment of cultural policies in the broadest sense . . . are part of the same governmental process.' He relates the 'gubernatorial process' as he calls it to the demands not of government but of 'society in some suitable manifestation' ('American Television' in *Daedalus*, vol. 107 no. 1, winter 1978).

social development with no belief in the 'independence' of the broadcaster. Nonetheless, as a historian, I am used to drawing on some of these different disciplines, and above all I am looking for evidence wherever I can find it – through a study of the arts and processes of programme making, for example, and of the sciences and technologies which on occasion propel and which always sustain all broadcasting organisations.

This study of BBC Governors and their *relationships* with Director-General, management and government – the word *relationships* is crucial – supplements, therefore, the brief account of the subject which I have given in the four volumes of the *History of Broadcasting in the United Kingdom*. It brings that account almost but not quite up-to-date, carrying it on beyond 1955, the terminal point of Volume IV. The focus of this essay is different, of course, from that of the *History*, since the essay deals with complex issues from one angle only. Such a one-angle approach, however, is not new. Attempts have been made on several occasions inside the Corporation to set out 'in plain terms', as Lord Hill put it in 1971, 'the role of the Governors in the work of the BBC',[1] while parallel attempts have been made from outside, notably by official committees of enquiry from Crawford (1926) to Annan (1977).[2] There have been five of these in fifty-three years, along with two separate reports (not based on an inquest) on television policy – the Selsdon Report (1935) and the Hankey Report (1943)[3] – in addition to the Sykes Report of 1923, the first inquest on the original British Broadcasting Company.

The committees of enquiry, like the BBC 'insiders', have devoted almost the same amount of attention to the role of the Director-General and 'Boards of Management' – the official name 'Board of Management' was new in 1947[4] – as to the Governors; and it is interesting to note that the Governors were not mentioned at all in the two BBC papers submitted to the

[1] 'The Role of the Governors: a Note by the Chairman', 10 Dec. 1971.

[2] Cmd 2599 (1926), *Report of the Broadcasting Committee*; Cmnd 6753 (1977), *Report of the Committee on the Future of Broadcasting*.

[3] Cmd 4793 (1935), *Report of the Television Committee; Report of the Television Committee, 1943*. Selsdon was 57 years old in 1935 and Hankey 66 years old in 1943.

[4] It was part of a basic Haley reorganisation and held its first meeting on 5 January 1948, when it was agreed that the different Directors (of which Television was not then one) would attend the meetings of the Board of Governors 'in turn' to deal with any points arising out of their written reports covering ten weeks of broadcasting. See below, p.87.

The Board of Governors, April 1979.

L to R: Lord Allen of Fallowfield, Sir John Johnston, George Howard, Lady Faulkner (N. Ireland), Ian Trethowan (Director-General), Sir Michael Swann (Chairman), Mrs Stella Clarke, Lady Serota, Gerard Mansell (Deputy Director-General), Philip Chappell, Roy Fuller, Hon. Mark Bonham Carter (Vice-Chairman), Dr G. Tegai Hughes (Wales)

Ullswater Committee in 1935. Very little was said in Parliament about the Governors in the debates which followed the Report, although one MP complained in 1936 of the age of Governors. [1] Two perhaps more pertinent points are first that the chairman of the Ullswater Committee investigating the BBC was himself 80 (Lord Beveridge was 70 when he took on the same task after the Second World War), and second that the average age of Director-Generals has been younger than that either of Committee members or Governors – 46 on appointment and 52 on retirement.

The most remarkable statements both about Governors and their key relationships have been made outside Committees of Enquiry. It is possible, indeed, to produce an anthology of *obiter dicta*, superficial and profound, from many sources. Among the most remarkable is ex-Director-General Sir Hugh Greene's *dictum* that 'if the Governors started to try to run the BBC them-

[1] *Hansard*, vol. 311, cols. 999–1000, 6 July 1936.

selves from day to day there'd be an awful breakdown in no time'.[1] Another *dictum*, worthy of F.M. Cornford's *Microcosmographica Academica* or even the Little Red Book of Chairman Mao, is a comment in a letter *to* Reith in 1923 (from Field-Marshal Sir William Robertson), 'Committees are never any good to anyone, I know them well'.[2]

Memorability and management do not necessarily go well together, and it is dangerous, in any case, to pull pithy maxims of principle or precept out of their context. Relationships, actual or possible, can seldom be treated in terms of a formula or set of formulae, if only because 'the beginning of administrative wisdom is the awareness that there is no one optimum type of management system'.[3] I have drawn in places in this essay on studies of management and of organisational theory, wryly noting some of the changes of fashion.

The grounds for my historical approach are rather broader than the relevant and valid argument that a knowledge of 'the past and the very recent past is essential to anyone who is trying to perceive the here-and-now of . . . organisation'.[4] The BBC as an organisation – examined in terms of its size, management structure, formal and informal, efficiency and adaptability – cannot be understood at any point or during any period in its history without careful attention being paid to the politics, society, culture and often the economy of Britain. It is doubtless generally true, as the theorists point out, that an organisation cannot 'evolve or develop in ways which merely reflect the goals, motives or needs of its members or of its leadership', since it must 'bow to the constraints' imposed upon it by the nature of this 'relationship with the environment'.[5] The word 'environment' is an awkward one, and in the case of the BBC the relevant 'environment' is the whole of politics, society and culture.

[1] See the report of an interview with Kenneth Harris in *The Observer*, 22 March 1964 and Greene's book *Third Floor Front* (1969), pp.84–5.

[2] Letter of 22 Aug. 1923 (Reith Papers).

[3] Professor Tom Burns, quoted in D.S. Pugh, D.J. Hickson and C.R. Hinings, *Writers on Organizations* (1964), p.2.

[4] Another statement of Burns, quoted ibid., p.17.

[5] P.J. Sadler and B.A. Barry, *Organisational Development* (1970), p.58. Cf. S.A. Culbert, *The Organization Trap* (1974), p.9. Part of what we attribute to a 'system' or even to its underlying technology can be understood only in terms of 'experience' in 'the social, economic and political spheres of society'.

The changing position of the Governors can be understood only if their role and that of their Chairman, the latter an increasingly important one as the Governors themselves have realised, are related both to internal and to external forces – to the range of experience and knowledge represented in the Board and to the balance of personalities in it; to the personality and ability of the Director-General; to the size, composition and organisation of the BBC's professional staff; to the attitudes and relative strength in Parliament of Government and Opposition; and to the spectrum of public opinion and pressure groups. The 'system' is seldom in equilibrium – every element in it has changed since the 1920s – and each of the forces must be considered in turn.

The Governors are often thought of as a 'team'. Indeed, this is the way the Press has always described them.[1] They only meet once a fortnight, however, and have only rarely been photographed together. Other observers have described them as being like a Board of Directors. Robert Foot, the war-time Director-General, always spoke in this vein:[2] so, too, did Lord Aldington, the Chairman of the BBC's General Advisory Council, who referred, in 1977, to a 'commercial analogy' which the Annan Committee had not grasped. By that analogy, the Governors were Directors 'and once that distinction was understood, there could be no fear of the Board becoming too interventionist in management'.[3]

Yet such a fear has often been expressed, and not every Governor has understood the analogy. It all depends on the background of experience. Lord Beveridge, who thought in political, not business terms, used a memorable phrase when he spoke of the importance of Governors appearing to be 'completely masters in their own house', a phrase not picked up by Pilkington or Annan. His Committee also spoke of their looking 'into every detail'.[4] Lord Normanbrook in his classic 1965 statement emphasised the Board's concern with 'values as well as with

[1] See below, Chapter III.
[2] See below, pp.78–81.
[3] Report of General Advisory Council Conference at Ditchley Park, 13–15 May 1977, on the theme 'Annan's Future for the BBC. Do we like it?', Report on the Fourth Session: 'Governors, Management and the Creative Task of the BBC'.
[4] Cmd 8116 (1951), *Report of the Broadcasting Committee, 1949*, para. 554, p.166. See also T. Burns, *The BBC, Public Institution and Private World* (1977), p.30.

efficiency', using this as an argument, not entirely convincing, for not having hitherto included 'anyone engaged in the business of broadcasting': 'it need not include', he adds, 'anyone with practical experience of the professional techniques of broadcasting'. [1] His talk of 'conscience', if not of 'soul', raises moral, rather than business or political issues. Sir Michael Swann has rightly identified a 'quiltwork of styles' inside the BBC's management structure. [2] It does not stop there.

It is necessary at every given stage in the history of the BBC to examine which 'team' or 'Board' or 'conscience' or 'structure' we are talking about, bearing in mind that there have been very strange breaks in continuity, as Appendix II shows. Thus it was a relatively new Board which had to deal with the campaign for commercial television – with a virtually new Director-General [3] – and when McKinsey's, the management consultants, were invited in 1968 to produce a report on the BBC, the Board, which had been increased in size to twelve at the beginning of that year, included in the words of one critical ex-Governor, 'few who knew any other regime than that imposed by Lord Hill'. [4] There are not many Boards of Directors of companies – even of nationalised industries – which have undergone such internal changes of balance, except when in the case of the former there have been takeover bids.

The characteristics of the 85 Governors who served during the first fifty years of the BBC's history are described in Chapter II of this study. Taking them as a group, 56 of them had a university education, 40 at Oxford or Cambridge. Twenty were products of Eton, Harrow or Winchester. (One of the first had been a Winchester headmaster, and two of the Chairmen have been ex-University Vice-Chancellors.) There has always been a natural tendency, therefore, to draw analogies neither from business nor politics but from education. When Edward Heath invited Sir Michael Swann to become Chairman, he told Swann that 'he had come to the conclusion that the BBC, as an institution, was

---

[1] Normanbrook, 'The Functions of the BBC's Governors', p.5. Two subsequent Governors, Sir Ralph Murray and Sir Hugh Greene, had had this professional experience.

[2] Swann, 'The Responsibility of the Governors', p.7.

[3] See below, p.100.

[4] Robert Lusty, 'Inside Story', in *Books and Bookmen*, Oct. 1977, p.13.

most like a university'.[1] It had a large number of potentially wayward and contrary 'creative' people in it. Swann agreed, but he soon came to the conclusion that it resembled the armed services also with its 'clear cut network of people, all doing their jobs in a tightly controlled way'.[2]

The political experience in the Board has come mainly from the House of Lords, although there were nineteen former Members of Parliament (at Westminster or Belfast) in the first 85. Only in war-time were two Governors serving Members of Parliament at the time – by the House of Commons Disqualifications (Temporary Provisions) Act.[3] One of them, Sir Ian Fraser, who had served as a member of the Crawford Committee, claimed that he was the first Member of Parliament to take an interest in broadcasting.[4] When Mary Agnes Hamilton became a Governor in 1933, she 'informally agreed' with the Postmaster-General that in the event of her becoming a candidate for Parliament 'she would place her office as Governor in the hands of the Postmaster-General of the day'.[5] Of the politically active Governors, nineteen were Conservatives or Unionists; one 'Liberal and Conservative' ('the Radio Doctor', a broadcaster long before he became Chairman); seven Liberal (including one ex-Speaker of the House of Commons, who became the second Chairman); one National Liberal; one a former Liberal MP who had become a Labour Peer; one a National Labour MP (although he switched his political convictions more than once); and eight were Labour.

The peers were allowed to take part in debates on broadcasting in the House of Lords, although two Governors (including the then BBC Chairman, Lord Simon of Wythenshawe) were once 'discouraged from taking part' in a particular debate under the so-called 'Addison rules', which were designed to ensure that members of public boards should not seek to answer for the

[1] Sir Michael Swann, 'A Year at the BBC', an Address to the Royal Society for the Encouragement of Arts, Manufactures and Commerce, Jan. 1974. Beveridge had the same approach, and Annan himself was a member of the Committee of Vice-Chancellors and Principals.

[2] Swann, 'The Responsibility of the Governors', p.7.

[3] The Law Officers of the Crown had ruled in 1937 that a Governorship of the BBC was an 'office of profit' under the Crown. See Board of Governors, *Papers*, 'Governors and Parliamentary Candidature: Note by the Director-General', 15 Oct. 1951.

[4] Sir Ian Fraser, *Whereas I Was Blind* (1942), p.158.

[5] Note by Sir Kingsley Wood, 5 Dec. 1932 (Post Office Archives).

Government or impinge on the responsibility of Ministers. [1] They stayed silent, although the BBC Board resented the BBC being treated as just another nationalised industry, and Sir William Haley issued a powerful counter-statement in which he claimed that 'it would be to the public good that Governors of the Corporation should from time to time give their fellow Peers authoritative information about the BBC's activities, should explain matters which may not be clear, and correct misconceptions. The House of Lords is predominately a place where acknowledged authorities speak on their own subjects.' [2] The Board affirmed on 9 November 1950 that Governors who were peers should have the right to speak on BBC matters, but that no Governor should exercise this right without the concurrence of his colleagues. [3]

The Governors also agreed a month later on a set of standing orders, codifying various documents concerning their conduct, and stating firmly that while the Chairman during his term of office should 'cease to be an active member of any political party', other Governors should be 'completely free to speak on any subject, however controversial, including Party politics, so long as the BBC is in no way involved'. If speeches on BBC affairs by any of the Governors, including the Chairman, involved matters of policy, they should be made only with the consent of and in the name of the Board. This order was to apply also to speeches on BBC matters in the House of Lords by those Governors who were members of that House. [4] Governors were not normally to broadcast while they were in office, except officially on matters affecting the Corporation, when the rule set out previously would apply, and if they did broadcast, they were to have the consent of their colleagues and to be paid no fee.

Since then, the standing orders on broadcasting have been modified to allow *inter alia* for a Governor to broadcast 'in circumstances and on matters wholly arising out of his or her non-BBC activities and in no way related to his or her Governorship

---

[1] The Addison Rules, set out in 1951 by the then Leader of the Labour Party in the House of Lords, dealt with Members of Public Boards. 1951 was the date of their final formulation (*Companion to the House of Lords Standing Orders*, section (xv), p.92). See below, p.189.

[2] Board of Governors, *Papers*, 'Governors' Speeches in the House of Lords: Note by the Director-General', 6 Sept. 1950.

[3] Board of Governors, *Minutes*, 9 Nov. 1950.   [4] Ibid., 7 Dec. 1950.

or to the BBC'.[1] If this sensible rule had existed during and after the Second World War, it would have permitted Harold Nicolson and Barbara Ward, two distinguished Governors of the BBC, to continue to contribute to broadcasting output as well as to policy-making and organisation.

Business experience has been a less potent influence on the Board, perhaps, than education or politics, although 21 Governors out of the 85 had made their careers principally in finance or business, while six had trade-union backgrounds. One of the latter, Dame Anne Godwin, was Chairman of the TUC in the year she was appointed. The professions were prominent. Thirteen Governors had spent most of their time in social services of various kinds, while eleven had held major posts in diplomacy or the Civil Service. Seven were primarily known as authors, six were journalists, five were lawyers, and another five had been professional members of the armed services. Two only were former members of the BBC staff. Sixteen had shown considerable interest in the arts, and eight were outstanding sportsmen. Two were blind.

Several Governors had distinguished themselves in more than one profession. Sir Arthur fforde, Chairman for seven years, had been both a solicitor and a headmaster. Learie Constantine had worked at different times as an author, a journalist, a social welfare official and a lawyer as well as a professional cricketer, a High Commissioner and a Life Peer. Some had family connections: Mark Bonham Carter's mother was a Governor. Gerald Coke's father-in-law had been Chairman (Sir Alexander Cadogan). On the death of Lord Bridgeman (who had been promoted to the Chairmanship only five months previously) his widow was appointed to the Board.

Just under half (36) of the Governors were reappointed for further terms or to complete a normal span when the end of a Charter had intervened. Nine were reappointed for a third term, Professor Barbara Wootton for a fourth, and Sir Robert Lusty had altogether five terms of service. The longest serving Governor was one of the least well known, C.H.G. Millis, Managing Director of Baring Brothers.

Seven Governors were promoted during their service on the Board to become Vice-Chairman or Chairman. Only Sir James

[1] Board of Governors, *Standing Orders*, July 1976.

Duff formally served in all three capacities, although Sir Robert Lusty was Governor, Vice-Chairman and Acting Chairman. Lord Clydesmuir was already on the Board when he was appointed the first National Governor for Scotland. Nineteen of the Governors failed to complete their terms of office, either through death or resignation. The resignations were usually for private reasons, but in the case of Lord Inman (after less than four months as Chairman) it was to join the Cabinet, and in the case of Lady Plowden, it was to become Chairman of the IBA.

The Members of the ITA (later the IBA) and the Governors of the BBC have quite different functions but similar characteristics, although the life of the former has been far shorter. Thus 69 per cent of IBA Members have had a university education as against the BBC's 67 per cent. Yet there has been a greater IBA input from commerce and the city (37 per cent against 24 per cent). They have each had the same proportion of lawyers (6 per cent) and public servants (19 per cent), although education and science have been more strongly represented on the IBA (33 per cent as against 20 per cent) and the arts more strongly represented on the BBC (19 per cent as against 13 per cent). The average age on appointment has been (only slightly) higher in the IBA than the BBC – 57 as against 54.

Turning to the Chairmen, six of the thirteen were peers. Clarendon, Whitley, Bridgeman and Hill had all held political office, while Norman, Powell, Inman and Simon had all seen action in public affairs on the fringes of politics. Cadogan and Normanbrook had headed the Diplomatic and Civil Services respectively. fforde, Duff and Swann came from the world of education. Their average age on appointment was 61 and the average term of office for those who completed it was five and a half years. One Chairman, at least, thought this was too short.[1] He was comparing his own tenure with that of two Director-Generals – Reith, sixteen years, and Haley, six.

The tenure of all subsequent Director-Generals has been longer than the average tenure of Chairmanship, but Lord Hill spent nearly ten years in the Chairmanship first of the IBA and then of the BBC. He more than any other person has had the

[1] Lord Simon of Wythenshawe, *The BBC from Within* (1953), p.63. See below, pp.93-4.

Lord Hill of Luton

opportunity, which he has taken, to reflect on the differences
between the two organisations, and (more controversially) on
the proper relationship between Chairman, Governors and
Director-General. His interpretation of personalities, relationships, events and trends is – and has been – open to
criticism. Yet he was right to insist that the main reason why his
years in the chair of the IBA were more 'serene' than his years at
the BBC was that 'the former was supervising and transmitting
television and employing 800 people, while the BBC was
programme-making in radio, television and radio overseas and
employing 25,000 people'.[1] It is interesting to note, too, that the
final paragraph of his book deals neither with the BBC nor
with Government but with 'a disturbed, uncertain and divided
society'. 'In a world of such conflict,' he exclaimed in similar
language to that of Oliver Whitley, 'the BBC is on the rack.'[2]
The Corporation, which had been created in the 'national interest', had itself become a 'national target'.[3]

[1] Lord Hill, *Behind the Screen* (1974), p.260.
[2] See above, p.20.   [3] Hill, op.cit., p.271.

Sir Charles Curran

Before turning to the BBC, Government (and successive Prime Ministers quite deliberately chose Hill for each of his two posts) and the changing spectrum of public opinion, it is necessary to explore more fully the relationship between Chairman and Director-General and the effect of change in the size, composition and organisation of the BBC's professional staff. The relationship between Chairman and Director-General is crucial, whatever the size, composition and organisation. When the relationship is discordant, there are bound to be difficulties, some of which will bring in 'the staff'. Moreover, there is a triangular relationship – as Harman Grisewood has called it[1] – between Director-General, Chairman and Governors. The Chairman sees more of the Director-General than of the other Governors, but he always has to pay attention to the attitudes of the Governors as well when he is dealing with the Director-General. If there is outside criticism – and there has never been any absence of it – Chairman and Director-General have to assess it together and decide how to deal with it, for some of it may be reflected in the Board itself.

[1] Note by Harman Grisewood, 17 March 1979.

There have been nine Director-Generals during the BBC's history. Of the eighth, Sir Charles Curran, the poet-Governor Roy Fuller wrote genially in 1977 (on Curran's retirement):
'He listened here – he travelled there,
Like Ariel, mastering the air.'[1]

Reith, the first Director-General, an exceptional Director-General, who was little influenced by his Board,[2] left his mark on more than one subsequent Director-General – of different mould. It was difficult to forget about him while he was alive, and Robert Foot, who had never previously met him, was amazed to receive a telephone call from him (the first telephone call he received in his BBC office), when he took over an enquiry before becoming Director-General. Greene thought Reith one of the two 'greatest men' he had known and when he was asked in 1964 whether any of his predecessors had any influence on the way he was running the BBC, he replied 'Yes, Reith. Directly or indirectly he still influences everybody who works there.'[3]

As late as 1977, an independent writer, Professor Tom Burns, while critical of Reith personally, was still pitting Reith's concept of the BBC as a mission-orientated institution (stressing that a sense of purpose offers a means of dealing with conflicting values and purposes inside the Corporation) against later versions of the BBC based on the 'professionalisation' of an enlarged staff and a confessedly managerially orientated Board of Management. The former was the only concept, he said, which made 'political and economic sense'.[4] There is substance in this view in that the management model by itself is quite inadequate. It was a management magazine which stated memorably, 'Blessed be he that hath a firm set of corporate objectives to lead him to the promised land – and cursed be he that hath none. The BBC management deserve sympathy for being rooted firmly in the purgatory of the latter category, to which it has been condemned for ever by the nature of its job and its Royal Charter. The public expects the BBC to be all things to all men.'[5]

[1] Roy Fuller, 'The Souvenirs of S.O.G.', 21 Sept. 1977. See also *BBC Handbook 1979*, p.6.
[2] See below, pp.55 ff.
[3] Kenneth Harris, *Conversations* (1967), p.97.
[4] T. Burns, op.cit., p.296.
[5] *Management Today*, May 1979.

Yet Burns's arguments have been sharply criticised. 'The answer is [not] to return the BBC to the rule of the saints', Anthony Howard wrote in a review of Burns. 'I'd rather be in the hands of the professionals.'[1] There are difficulties in drawing such a sharp contrast since by no means all the professionals have looked for a management model. 'Professionalism' indeed expressed itself not only in the diffusion of the philosophy that 'broadcasters know best', so sharply criticised by Anthony Wedgwood Benn in 1968,[2] but in attacks on 'the system' and demands for workers' control. 'Politicisation' plays its part in this story, yet 'professionalism' has gained in significance also as a result of completely non-political factors, like the movement of 'professionals' from BBC to commercial companies and vice versa. The kingdom of means is increasingly shared, if not the kingdom of ends. The issues are complex: some of them are dealt with by T. J. Johnson in his *Professions and Power* (1972).[3]

Although Greene admired Reith – and even after Reith broke with him, never minimised the importance of a 'philosophy' of broadcasting – he emphasised more than any Director-General before him the role of 'professionals', treating as one of the major tasks of the Director-General 'delegation at all levels'. The 'independence' of the producer was for him as necessary as the 'independence' of the Corporation. 'Through training and experience', Greene argued, 'producers should get the instinctive feeling of the limits of their freedom and of the occasions when they should go to the next chap up and say "Is this really all right?"' There should be no written directives, only a 'framework of general guidance which arises from the continuing discussion of programmes by themselves, their seniors, myself, my fellow Directors on the Board of Management, and the Board of Governors'.[4]

[1] A. Howard, 'Inside the Goldfish Bowl', in the *New Statesman*, 2 Sept. 1977.

[2] *Financial Times*, 19 Oct. 1968, reporting Benn's critique at a Bristol Labour Party meeting of the BBC's 'enormous accumulation of power'. 'With the exception of government itself, there is scarcely any other body in Britain enjoying as much power as the BBC.' The *Daily Telegraph* (19 Oct. 1968), describing Benn as 'a member of the Government which, in the last resort, holds the BBC purse strings', complained that 'the new technologist looks very like the old politician, writ large'.

[3] For contributions of broadcasters to a discussion of this question, see Grace Wyndham Goldie, *Facing the Nation* (1977) and P.H. Newby, 'Broadcasting – A Professional View', *The Haldane Memorial Lecture* (1977), which argues the case for a large 'quality' broadcasting organisation with a level of staffing and resources sufficient to provide 'the critical mass that generates good broadcasting'. See also Burns, op.cit., esp. pp.139–40.   [4] Harris, op.cit., pp.99–100.

One of the implications of such an approach was that the 'creative staff' of the BBC should become responsible for financial control of programmes. There was a change of structure, therefore, as well as a change of style. By 1973, all thirty-seven of the BBC's top managers (with engineering, finance and personnel management as exceptions) had served as producers. [1] There was also a shift inside the organisation towards news and current affairs, again with Greene taking a lead. [2] Among the implications were the possibility of friction with the Governors, including the Chairman, the increased likelihood of friction with the Government, and the certainty of hostility in the country from sizeable minorities and at times the majority.

Even if Director-Generals and their Chairmen agreed, there was often a danger that such implications would threaten the BBC, which remained dependent on the income derived from licence fees set at particular levels by the Government in the light of its assessments both of the needs of the BBC and of the balance of party and public opinion. There were times, however, when Director-General and Chairman were out of sympathy with each other, as during the short Greene/Hill regime from 1967 to 1969. The circumstances of Hill's appointment were not propitious – he was transferred from the ITA, itself a controversial move, at a time when the Prime Minister was known to be highly critical of the BBC – and Greene cannot have been made easier by such newspaper headlines as 'Hill leaves ITA to run BBC'. [3] As Director-General, Greene had enjoyed an excellent working relationship with fforde, in his view 'perhaps the best Chairman the BBC ever had', and with Normanbrook. And his opinion of Hill as Chairman was far lower than Hill's of himself as Director-General, even though – or perhaps because – Hill acknowledged that as Chairman he was 'an amateur' working with 'professionals'. [4] Nor was there an easy relationship between Hill and Curran, when the latter took over in 1969.

---

[1] See Lord Annan, 'A Corporation and its Discontents', in *The Times Literary Supplement*, 7 Oct. 1977.

[2] Burns, op.cit., pp.155–210; H. Greene, op.cit., p.127. Greene said of the News Division which he took over when he was appointed Director of News and Current Affairs in 1958: 'To me as an old journalist the whole system was incredible. I changed it.'

[3] Hill, op.cit., p.73. See below, pp.128–30.

[4] See his review of Hill in the *New Statesman*, 20 Sept. 1974.

'Tired of getting Government complaints, Sir Hugh?'

Hill has insisted upon the fact that while he wanted to be 'an active chairman', he did not want to assume 'the management responsibilities of the Director-General'. He has stated, moreover, that the relationship with Curran was 'friendly and frank', with the two of them enjoying 'our daily exchanges'. Yet he carved out a distinctive approach of his own and expected his experienced Director-Generals to display qualities which he did not possess.[1] The analogy which he himself drew between Chairman and Director-General on the one hand and Minister and Permanent Head of a Civil Service Department on the other was misleading. A Director-General is not the Permanent Head of a Civil Service Department: as Hill in his more reflective moments recognised, he is managing a creative enterprise almost every aspect of which is in public view.

Curran himself was correct in the way he put his own version of the relationship, and he did not seek to minimise the 'strength' of his position. 'One must, as Director-General and Chief Executive, have a respect for the authority of the Governors. One must

[1] Hill op.cit., esp. Ch. 31.

also maintain the professional standards which are necessary for the effective conduct of broadcasting. It is the reconciliation of those two factors which is the most testing of a Director-General's responsibilities. The Board of Governors is there, in the words which have been applied to the constitutional Monarch, to advise, to encourage and to warn. The Director-General is there to make things work and to take proper notice of the advice and encouragement which he may receive from the Board.'

Curran rejected the view, therefore, that he was a kind of Permanent Under-Secretary. 'I see the role of the chief executive as being authoritative in a way in which it would not be proper constitutionally for say a Permanent Under-Secretary to be authoritative,' he explained. 'It is a very heavy responsibility and I remember saying at the time when my appointment was being considered that what was needed in the BBC was a minor resurrection of the authority of the Board of Governors which Reith, having invented, promptly buried in order to make the operation work at all.'[1]

Given even this brief sketch, it should be clear that it is just as difficult to generalise about the relationships between Director-Generals, Chairmen (and Vice-Chairmen) of Governors and the whole Board as it is to generalise about management patterns. The same Director-General has often had different relations with different Boards of Governors – Reith provides an example, as this essay will show – and the same Chairman has often had different relations with different Director-Generals. Hill had to deal with Greene and Curran. Sir Allan Powell had to deal with Ogilvie, Foot, Graves and Haley. Board, Chairman and Director-General, however, have had to cope separately or together with the huge increase in the size of the BBC – its staff and its operations, with the concomitant change in its composition, organisation and attitudes, and with changes in Government and society.

The 'minor resurrection of the Board of Governors', which Curran hoped to see, must be examined in such perspectives. Curran saw that in the conditions of the late 1960s and early 1970s there was 'no area of programmes' in which the BBC

[1] C. Curran, 'Speech to the Third Overseas Broadcasting Management Conference', 28 Sept. 1972.

would 'be free from political interest – and indeed political pressure'. Even light entertainment could produce dynamite. 'Drama in the permissive society offers an excellent opportunity for the moralising politician to beat his breast publicly for the sins and omissions of the broadcaster. But most of all, of course, the public affairs programme will be the target of political comment. And in replying to criticisms the Director-General must re-member that in maintaining freedom to broadcast programmes which have a critical approach to society he is, at the same time, making more difficult his own task of persuading the State to furnish him with the money to produce those programmes.' 'In a longer term and more general sense' it was also true that 'a Director-General who maintains the principle that his broad-casters are free to produce critical or independent programmes will be adding to the problems which he faces in persuading the State authorities of his capital investment needs, and particular developments involving the technical consent of Government may be made the more difficult to argue.' [1]

The more difficult the BBC was to govern, the more indispens-able were the Governors. Curran referred mainly in this par-ticular statement to programming and capital expenditure. He might also have referred to the continuing suspicion of poli-ticians, Government and, above all, Prime Ministers, and some-times their resentment towards a separate centre of power and influence. Already during the 1960s, the BBC was increasingly thought of outside Television Centre, Broadcasting House and Bush House not so much as a large organisation – possibly as over-large – but as a powerful – probably over-powerful – institution, a self-appointed 'investigator in chief of ineptitude and inefficiency in politics, industry, and commerce'. [2] The Select Committee on Nationalised Industries in 1972 referred to what it called a 'shift' in emphasis, from people considering the media solely in terms of the programmes produced by the media to one in which BBC and IBA were seen as 'powerful institutions in their own right, whose whole style of decision making and action profoundly affects the community'. [3] The Committee

---

[1] Ibid.

[2] G. Scott, 'Mr Benn and the BBC', in the *Sunday Times*, 20 Oct. 1968.

[3] *Second Report from the Select Committee on Nationalised Industries*, House of Commons Paper 465, 1972, para. 145, p.lxii.

greatly exaggerated the recent extent of the shift. [1] Nonetheless, it is just because of the coincidence of external concern (expressed both in official committees of enquiry, of which Annan is the latest, and elsewhere) and of internal ferment inside the BBC that the Governors have been drawn into a review of their own role.

As this essay will show, Hill certainly grossly exaggerated the extent to which the Governors had been 'ciphers' since Reith's days. He may have wanted a 'less impotent' body of Governors, but he knew little about those he had got, and it could scarcely have been reassuring to any of them, if they believed in their 'independence', that the Prime Minister told him on his appointment that there would soon be three extra Governors. [2] At least one Governor, the Acting Chairman Sir Robert Lusty – and the man to whom the surprising news of Hill's appointment had been communicated by the Postmaster-General – thought Hill's version of history a travesty. [3] Hill exaggerated also when he claimed that he had introduced 'tighter financial control by the Board' through a new Finance Committee (carried by five votes to three in a then rare vote in the Board): the Board had often discussed finance to great effect, had been well advised, and from before the Second World War had always had one Governor specialising in the subject. Yet there is, nonetheless, a sense in which there has been rather more than a 'minor resurrection' in the role of the Governors.

Hill himself found Normanbrook's 1965 lecture 'a clear and detailed description of what the Governors are required to do'. In 1968, however, soon after taking office, he got Oliver Whitley, then Chief Assistant to the Director-General, to draft a subsequently much revised and ultimately undiscussed paper, *Broadcasting and the Public Mood*. [4] He encouraged more 'stock-

[1] For very early evidence of a sense of the BBC as an 'institution', see statements by the Archbishop of Canterbury in the *Radio Times*, 17 Dec. 1926, when he referred to broadcasting becoming 'a well-assured factor in our national life', and Lord Gainford, first Chairman of the British Broadcasting Company, in the issue for the following week. 'It has been remarked that the growth of National Institutions is commonly measured in decades or even centuries. The Directors of the BBC have had the stewardship of a great public service for only four years, during which broadcasting has [become] an accepted and essential part of the machinery of civilization.'

[2] Hill, op.cit., p.70.

[3] R. Lusty, *Bound to be Read* (1975), Ch.19.

[4] See above, p.20 n.3.

taking of general policy on programme matters', like a two-hour Governors' 'debate' in 1971 on 'the perennial problems of taste, language and sex in our programmes', some of the debate taking place informally with staff outside Board meetings. And in the same year he invited the Board fully to discuss its own activities, present and future, in the light of proposals then being mooted and which Hill did not like, to create a new 'external body', 'a Council for Broadcasting' to do the job of the Governors – and possibly of the Members of the IBA – for them.[1]

Undoubtedly, 'the minor resurrection' was speeded up by 'attacks on the BBC' which had multiplied during 1971. At the same time how best to deal with 'creative people' inside the BBC itself was also an issue, and the two issues were interconnected in that some of the 'attacks on the BBC' were inspired by disgruntled 'creative people' inside. Hill's successor as Chairman, Sir Michael Swann, who took over in January 1973, was to argue that 'the control of creative people can only be on a loose rein',[2] and Hill argued in 1971 that although the handling of 'creative people' was especially delicate and difficult, yet 'the creative spirit was the engine of broadcasting'.[3]

For Hill, the Board meeting of 13 January 1972 was the most interesting that he had ever attended. 'What was interesting was the way in which most Governors sought to strengthen the Governors' role in one way or another. More information, more opportunity to discuss controversial or likely to be controversial decisions in advance, and so on.' An exclamation followed: 'How long it has taken to strengthen the role of Governors! Wilson and Short may have expected that my appointment would briskly lead to a more effective Board. If they did, they have had to wait an awful long time for it.'[4] What 'more effective' meant is uncertain. Before ending his chapter Hill added a further post-script. Around the same time he received a letter from 'only one of hundreds of thousands', including the sentence – 'You have no control over the BBC staff and programmes'.[5]

The years of the chairmanship of Hill's successor have been associated with the Annan enquiry, which opened in 1974 and

[1] Hill, op.cit., pp.92 ff., p.206, pp.213–14; 'Role of the Governors: a Note by the Chairman', 10 Dec. 1971.
[2] Swann, 'A Year at the BBC'.
[3] 'Role of the Governors: a Note by the Chairman', 10 Dec. 1971.
[4] Hill, op.cit., p.215: Diary note of 18 Jan. 1972.   [5] Ibid., p.216.

concluded in 1977, by financial pressures, and by continued technological advance against a completely different national background from that of the hectic 1960s. During the 1960s all institutions, old or new, were subject to internal strain and external attack. During the 1970s, with no comparable sense of *élan*, they have continued to feel strained and threatened. The two decades were bracketed in the history of the BBC by the protracted and often bitter discussion about *Broadcasting in the Seventies* and its aftermath. It was during this last decade, moreover, that some of the youthful rebel voices of the universities of the 1960s became older voices of the media. And it was during this last decade also that there were signs of a backlash against permissiveness and of a reaction against drama in politics. The mood has changed from that described by Hill in 1968, although there has always been a danger of polarisation.

The interest in the role of the Governors remains alive. Indeed, it has increased somewhat since the publication of the Annan Report and the Government's 1978 White Paper. Hill's resistance to a Broadcasting Council was consolidated and proved successful, and the (divided) Annan Committee repudiated also all ideas of a 'representative' Board of Governors or of direct staff representation. The Committee went on, nonetheless, to remark that much of the evidence which it had collected revealed 'a growling ill-humour that the Governors were both judge and jury in their own cause, trying to combine the regulatory function with the managerial decision-taking needed to produce good programmes'. It is not clear whether the last sentence of this charge relates to the evidence or is an Annan judgement. 'As a result their role had become hopelessly confused.'[1] Certainly the sections of the Report which follow are not without their own confusion.

Even in Reith's time, the Governors had always been more than 'an advisory committee to the executive', Hill's description, as this essay will show. And no Governor of the BBC in 1927, 1937, 1947, 1957 or 1967, and no Director-General, would have disputed Annan's punchline: 'The buck stops at the Governors'.[2] The difference between 1977 (and possibly 1967) and earlier

[1] Cmnd 6573 (1977), para. 9.61, p.118.
[2] Ibid., paras, 9.63, 9.64, p.119.

"Can you fix it so I CAN'T
get BBC?"

years is that at the most recent dates more emphasis was being placed inside and outside the BBC on the difficulties in making this simple statement of fact both operative and manifest.

One way to deal with the difficulties was to follow the Annan Committee in shifting the focus of emphasis further towards the public face – 'accountability' – and further away both from the 'public interest' and the managerial function. Indeed the only positive recommendations relating to the Governors in the Report were that the size of the Board should be reduced from twelve to nine – in line with much past BBC thinking; that the Governors should be provided with their own secretariat; and that there should be an increase in the number of joint meetings with members of the Board of Management.

Other students of BBC history have talked in what David Riesmann has called an 'inner-directed way' of the role of the Governors in terms of moral imperatives, acquired experience and testable judgement. Annan concluded with the radar-like sentence 'it would do worlds for the reputation of the BBC with the public if the Governors were seen to govern.'[1] The same has often been said of Government itself since the 1960s, and it is salutary to recall that Sir Harold Wilson, never completely in charge himself, is probably the first Prime Minister to ask a Governor 'Are you in charge?'[2]

---

[1] Ibid., para. 9.66, p.120.
[2] Statement by Lord Fulton, Vice-Chairman from 1968 to 1970.

This essay deals first with Governors' powers and performance; turns second to the characteristics of BBC Governors during the first fifty years of its history; and considers only third 'the public eye' – what the public, enlightened and uninformed, has made (if anything) of Governors and their role. Since there is room for scepticism about general formulae, the fourth chapter examines in rather fuller detail a number of case histories of difficult (and sometimes controversial) situations in which Governors have found themselves. The fifth chapter, which was written after the publication of the Government's White Paper on broadcasting (Cmnd 7294) in the summer of 1978, considers the sense of an uncertain future.

In his review of Professor Burns's *The BBC, Public Institution and Private World*, Lord Annan reflected that 'when you ask a sociologist to recommend rather than analyze and explain, he is likely to answer . . . that whatever action you take will have the defect of its merits'. And he will reinforce rather than shift attitudes by demonstrating that 'every reorganization or reform, every intention to improve conditions or halt a deterioration in relations, is certain to bring in its train consequences which cannot be foreseen; or, if they can, only in the dim, obscure and ominous form in which oracles in ancient times foretold the future'.[1]

If all this happens when you ask a sociologist, it is refreshing to note that when you ask a historian the most you can expect is to have the complexities identified and the perspectives established. Once that is done, of course, it may become possible to draft an agenda for the future.

---

[1] Annan, 'A Corporation and Its Discontents'.

CHAPTER ONE
POWERS AND PERFORMANCE

When the British Broadcasting Company was created in October 1922, it was a commercial organisation subject to exceptional rules and restrictions. The Company was formed by Licence, not as the result of an official report but rather of a meeting of interested parties held at the invitation of the Postmaster-General.[1] In the background was fear of broadcasting falling into anarchy. There was little talk of the inherent possibilities of a medium, much of the wizardry of invention and the delights of a new toy. Yet J.C.W. Reith, who was appointed General Manager in October 1922 and took over in December, was full of high hopes. He had a consciousness of mission, and as he put it simply, he was from the start 'in full control of the staff' and 'responsible to the Directors'.[2]

Two official reports on broadcasting followed – the Sykes Report of 1923, which recommended future control of broadcasting by the Postmaster-General aided by a 'Broadcasting Board', and the Crawford Report of 1926, which recommended the establishment of a public corporation, 'acting as Trustee for the national interest', with a monopoly of broadcasting.[3] These were Reports which were to set a pattern. The former forecast that the number of wireless licences, then 170,000, might soon increase to half a million and reach saturation point at a million or two. The latter, concerned with what to do with broadcasting after the Company's two-year Licence came to a close, recommended that five or seven 'Commissioners' should be nominated by the Crown for a five-year tenure: their 'prestige and status' should be 'freely acknowledged and their sense of responsibility emphasised'.[4] Together they would constitute a new authority.

They should have some business experience, but they should

---

[1] Cmd 1822 (1923), *Licence by the Postmaster-General to the British Broadcasting Company, Ltd, for the establishment of eight radiotelephonic stations and the transmission therefrom of broadcast matter for general reception.*

[2] Reith to Sir William Noble, a key figure on the Board, 20 Dec. 1922 (Reith Papers). See also J.C.W. Reith, *Broadcast over Britain* (1924), said to have been published at the request of the Broadcasting Company's Board of Directors.

[3] Cmd 1951 (1923), *Report of the Broadcasting Committee, 1923*; Cmd 2599 (1926), *Report of the Broadcasting Committee, 1925.*

[4] Cmd 2599 (1926), para. 16.

not represent specific interests as the Sykes Committee had suggested. They should also possess 'the maximum of freedom which
Parliament is prepared to concede', described in an alternative
phrase as 'the greatest possible latitude in regard to the conduct
of their own affairs'.

As a result of the Sykes Committee's recommendations, there
had been in existence for a short time a representative Broadcasting Board, chaired by Sykes, including members from the Post
Office, the newspapers, the wireless trade, the Radio Society and
the Trades Union Congress. All 'complaints and proposals relating to broadcasting' were to be referred to it. It had met only six
times, however, and the Postmaster-General who had supported
its creation never attended any of its meetings. [1] Reith, who did
not mention it in his autobiography, regarded its concern with
broadcasting as at the same time superfluous and inadequate.

Crawford had been told, therefore, that the enquiries of his
Committee should be 'in no way dependent on previous enquiries', and after his Report had been accepted the Board
disappeared. The new 'broadcasting arrangements' were to be
'entirely in the hands of the Corporation', the new body which
was to replace the Company. [2]

The reason why the Crawford Committee proposed 'the greatest possible latitude' in regard to the conduct of BBC affairs was
that in its view 'the progress of science and the harmonies of art'
would be 'hampered by too rigid rules and too constant a supervision by the State'. The argument was as trenchant as – and
more fully explained than – the argument for monopoly. 'The
aspirations and the public obligations of Broadcasting can best be
studied by a body appointed *ad hoc*, endowed with adequate
tenure, and concentrating on this particular duty.' [3]

This was the origin of the Board of Governors, soon hailed as
'a peculiar British expedient . . . supported by a peculiarly British argument – the undoubted fact that it works'. 'Its curiously
undefined and elastic framework,' Hilda Matheson, a devoted
BBC official who had a mind of her own quite independent of
Reith's, wrote in 1933, 'is wholly in keeping with the British

---

[1] All the meetings took place between April and July 1924.
[2] The Postmaster-General to Sykes, 15 Nov. 1926. The Board held a farewell lunch
party that month.
[3] Cmd 2599, para. 16.

constitution, and it is more and more common to find it quoted as a possible model for the management of other national services for which private control and direct State management are equally unsuitable.'[1]

The basic recommendations of the Crawford Report owed much to a memorandum submitted by the Secretary of the Post Office, Sir Evelyn Murray, and read and commented upon by Reith.[2] 'Public service', based on a 'high conception of the inherent possibilities' of broadcasting, mattered more to Reith than any of the diverse economic interests represented on the first Board of the Company,[3] and he was strong enough to ensure that it was his own approach which prevailed. 'I am quite sure that if I had been categorically in favour of a continuation of the Company,' he wrote in 1926, 'this would have been achieved.'[4] Since he was not in favour of such a continuation, the Postmaster-General (the fourth with whom Reith had had to deal since 1922) and the Government accepted the relatively untried idea of a public corporation, and it won the full support of Parliament.

In so far as any fears were expressed in Parliament, they were not that the Corporation might be 'irresponsible' but that it might be too subservient to Minister or Government, and this was the view expressed also in many sections of the Press. 'The shadow of the Postmaster General lies heavy on the scheme', the *Star* complained.[5] *The Economist* was clearest in seeing the advantages. The 'dangers of bureaucracy in Departmental control' had been avoided. Yet a monopoly had been taken out of the hands of shareholders 'who have admittedly a particular interest in the sale of wireless apparatus'. A corporation had been set up 'from which all question of private profit is eliminated to act as a trustee and steward for the public in the maintenance and de-

---

[1] H. Matheson, *Broadcasting* (1933), p.34.

[2] Crawford Committee, *Minutes of Evidence*, File I, Paper I.

[3] *Broadcast over Britain*, p.32. Andrew Boyle, *Only the Wind Will Listen* (1972), p.170, calls the Directors of the Company 'convenient stepping stones over a turbulent river which Reith could not have crossed unaided'. Yet in asking Lord Gainford to become Chairman in August 1922, Noble had conceived of the Chairman's job in a quite different context – 'to hold the balance evenly between the companies' making up the BBC consortium. (Noble to Gainford, 22 Aug. 1922).

[4] Reith Papers. 'Even those who are most definite in their appreciation of the Company's attitude, recognise the desirability of its being a public service, not only in deed but in constitution.' See also *BBC Hand Book 1928*, pp.31–5.

[5] *Star*, 6 March 1926.

velopment of a new element in national life of great social and economic value'. [1]

The only parallel ventures before 1939 were the Port of London Authority, the Central Electricity Board and (after 1933) the London Passenger Transport Board, although the word 'parallel' may suggest greater affinities than were usually recognised. As one of the first writers on public corporations put it, 'The BBC exists to perform a function so unique in character that it may well be doubted whether its political and administrative features can usefully be compared with those of other existing or hypothetical semi-independent Public Corporations.' [2]

It could never be treated *merely* as a 'utility', and that was one reason why Parliament itself was kept at something of a distance. The Postmaster-General stressed two years after the founding of the Corporation that while he recognised that he must take 'a certain measure of responsibility . . . over matters of general policy', he would not and could not deal in 'details'. Nor would he – or the Speaker – allow questions on output to be put at Westminster. 'In the ordinary matters of detail and of day-to-day working' the Governors were to be 'absolutely masters in their own house'. [3]

The new instrument of a public corporation was devised to apply to what came to be called 'public administration', yet it had its antecedents less in the civil service than in 'commercial enterprise', in the intricate history of the joint stock company. [4] There were five necessary elements in a public corporation according not only to Reith but experienced commentators like Sir

[1] *The Economist*, 13 March 1926.

[2] T.H. O'Brien, *British Experiments in Public Ownership and Control* (1937), p.96. The best work on the subject is Lincoln Gordon, *The Public Corporation in Great Britain* (1938). Ch. IV deals with the BBC. For Herbert Morrison's belief in this kind of institution, see H. Morrison, *Socialisation and Transport* (1933).

[3] *Hansard*, vol. 219, cols. 2495–6, 12 July 1928. The Speaker ruled that 'to put questions to Ministers on matters in regard to which they have no responsibility would be futile' (Ibid., vol. 233, col. 246, 10 Dec. 1929).

[4] Gordon, op.cit., p.3. A.V. Dicey forecast in 1905 that the time would come when 'every large business may become a monopoly, and [when] trades which are monopolies may wisely be brought under the management of the state' (*Lectures on the Relation between Law and Public Opinion* (1905), p.248). The British Broadcasting Company had not been a typical joint stock company. It had been brought into existence under Post Office sponsorship and its dividends were limited to $7\frac{1}{2}$ per cent. 'The Company will have no business to secure,' Gainford was told by Noble, 'as it will simply [sic] have to provide broadcast programmes.' (Noble to Gainford, 22 Aug. 1922.)

Henry Bunbury – public, not private, control over major policy; absence of public interference in management; choice of the right field of operation; disinterestedness; and expertness.

The last of these was eventually to become identified with 'professionalism', but it was the second, perhaps, to which Reith himself attached most importance. Already, indeed, by 1926, before the first element was assured in the form of a new public corporation, Reith had succeeded in becoming master within his joint stock company house to an extent at least as great as – and probably greater than – most of his counterparts in private industry. The detail and the day-to-day management structure of both old and new BBC depended directly upon him. Noble had told him before the first meeting of his Board in 1922, 'We're leaving it all to you. You'll be reporting at our monthly meetings, and we'll see how you are getting on.' [1] Reith was in no sense like a senior civil servant dealing with a Minister, therefore, not even like the powerful Secretary of the Post Office, whose Ministers came and went with such frequency.

From January 1924 onwards, the internal management structure of the BBC had consisted of a five-man Policy Control Board (with Reith himself as Chairman), Rear-Admiral Charles Carpendale as 'Controller', and three Assistant Controllers, complemented after May 1924 by a Programme Board. (There was then only one Assistant Controller in charge of Programmes.) It was a clear sign of the extent of Reith's control before 1926 that the Directors of the Company submitted no joint evidence to the Crawford Committee: Reith spoke for the Company in his own name. Another sign was that during the last weeks of 1925 one of the Directors complained mildly to Reith that since the question of programme policy had never been considered by the Board, it ought to figure on the next agenda. [2]

A style had already been set, therefore, as well as a structure, by the time that the Company gave way in January 1927 to the Corporation – with very little public discussion and with no changes in internal management, except for the notepaper. When the *Evening News* held an epitaph competition in January 1927 to celebrate the end of the Company twelve readers inde-

[1] J.C.W. Reith, *Into the Wind* (1949), p.88. Lord Simon quoted this passage in his *The BBC from Within* (1953), pp.49–50.
[2] W.W. Burnham to Reith, 7 Dec. 1925.

pendently submitted the simple lines 'The BBC is dead, long live the BBC'. [1]

The *rationale* behind such a management structure was to be developed further by Reith inside and outside the new Corporation between then and his great 'reorganisation' of 1933, when after going into retreat he introduced a triumvirate consisting of himself, Carpendale, renamed Controller of Administration, and a newly appointed Controller of Output. [2] Reith continued to stand by this structure long after he had ceased to be Director-General. Throughout, he drew sharp distinctions between the management group and Board of Governors. He felt that the Governors would appreciate the fact that what was recommended to them came not only from the Director-General, but from the Control Board.

There was a change in January 1927 in the Board of the new Corporation as compared with the old Company. The nine members of the Board of the Company gave way, with little recognition, [3] to a smaller five-member Board of Governors for the Charter-based Corporation, and it was in the new Board as a corporate body that the property and powers of the Corporation were vested. There was a new Chairman, the sixth Earl of Clarendon, but the Chairman of the old Company, Lord Gainford, who became Vice-Chairman of the new, gave an immediate 'assurance of effective continuity'. As outgoing Chairman he paid a tribute to 'the zeal, ability, attention to and pride in their work which have been shown by our executive colleague, Mr Reith and by our staff'. [4]

Appointments of the new Governors (perhaps significantly

[1] *Evening News*, 4 Jan. 1927. The writers of the more fanciful epitaphs misunderstood the nature of the change. The tersest epitaph was the best: 'Well earthed'. The same newspaper (26 Jan. 1927) referred to the members of the BBC's Programme Board as 'the seven gods of the BBC' but added that Reith always had the last word: 'Everything he bans just disappears.'

[2] BBC Internal Memorandum No. 233, 29 Aug. 1933. For the new structure and the *rationale* behind it, see below, pp.60-1.

[3] The Treasury was grudging in its acceptance of their entitlement to an honorarium (R.A. Dalzell to Reith, 7 Feb. 1927), even though, as Reith pointed out, they had 'subordinated their trade interests and permitted the Company to be run as a public service'.

[4] *Radio Times*, 24 Dec. 1926, 'A Message from Lord Gainford'. 'I believe', he concluded, 'that, under the Corporation, we shall have greater power, greater freedom and greater resources wherewith to extend what has been built by the Company.'

they were not called Commissioners) [1] were made by the King in Council on the recommendation of the Prime Minister and the Postmaster-General, [2] and the names were announced while Reith was still arguing with the Postmaster-General about what he considered fundamental financial and constitutional issues. [3] The fact that the Governors did not back him between their appointment and their first formal meeting persuaded him of the new Chairman's 'spinelessness'. According to Reith, Clarendon had yielded to a threat by the Postmaster-General to find five new Governors as a replacement. [4] The history of the Board begins, therefore, with one of the most dramatic episodes in the whole story – a threat of dismissal *en bloc* and a behind-the-scenes capitulation.

Reith became quickly aware, too, at least as soon as the first formal meeting of the new Board in January 1927, of internal strains between the members. In particular, Clarendon and Mrs Snowden were temperamentally opposed. The one was cold and reserved, the other demonstrative and rhetorical. Moreover, neither had been told exactly what they were expected to do as 'Governors', and there was nothing in the Charter to guide them. It had been hinted to Clarendon that three-quarters of his time would be needed for his duties as Chairman and to Mrs Snowden

[1] For the possible significance, see T. Burns, *The BBC, Public Institution and Private World* (1977), p.28: 'The term [Commissioners] carries with it the connotation of direct appointment and direct responsibility to Parliament. Mitchell-Thomson's [the Postmaster-General] preference for "Governors" must have been deliberate, and is therefore important.' This statement, on which a large part of Professor Burns's subsequent argument depends, is wrong in that the word 'Commissioner' does not and did not necessarily carry either connotation. He may be right, however, in suggesting that the term 'Governor' deliberately left many points vague.

[2] The appointment of Clarendon was announced first early in October. The other names were published at the end of the month. 'Most of the appointments were decided a considerable time ago,' *The Scotsman* noted on 6 Oct., 'but the secrets in this case have been well kept.' The fact that the Prime Minister took the initiative, not a Departmental Minister, distinguished the BBC from the Central Electricity Board. The members of the London Passenger Transport Board (like the present independent members of the Press Council) were appointed by 'trustees'.

[3] The issues included the size of the Corporation's share of future licence fees, its borrowing powers and the governmental 'ban' on controversial broadcasting which Reith wished to have lifted. 'The constitution was to be changed to admit more scope and more autonomy,' Reith complained to Clarendon in a letter of 15 Nov. 1926, 'but none of these has materialised.'

[4] C. Stuart (ed.), *The Reith Diaries* (1975), pp.139–41: 'What a sickening affair it is. Clarendon is so weak and stupid that he immediately accepted the terms. This confirms my suspicions of his appalling weakness.'

Wireless Magazine December 1926

Members of the British Broadcasting Corporation

IN CONTROL
OF BRITISH
BROADCASTING
FROM JANUARY 1
ONWARDS.

At present Managing
Director of British
Broadcasting Co., Ltd.,
Mr. J. C. W. Reith
(seen above) will on
January 1 become
Director-General of the
British Broadcasting
Corporation. He was
formerly connected with
an engineering firm.

Distinguished both as a scholar and an
athlete, Mr. Montague Rendall (above), who
from 1911 to 1924 was Headmaster of
Winchester School, will be another member
of the new Corporation.

Another member of the
British Broadcasting
Co., Ltd., will become
associated with the new Corporation.
That is Lord Gainford (below), who is
Chairman of the present B.B.C.

Chairman of the new British
Broadcasting Corporation,
Lord Clarendon (seen above)
has had a distinguished career.
He has been Under Secretary
of State for Dominion Affairs
and Chairman of the Overseas
Settlement Committee.

Mrs. Philip Snowden, wife of
the ex-Chancellor of the Exchequer, will look after women's
interests in broadcasting.

Sir J. Gordon Nairne
(above) is a Director
and late Comptroller of
the Bank of England.
He is an officer of the
Legion of Honour.

that she would be 'almost fully occupied'.[1] Both versions of the extent of possible commitment caused Reith an immense amount of anxiety, even making him contemplate resignation. 'I have always functioned best,' he wrote, 'when responsibility for decisions rested wholly and solely on me.'[2] Now, for a time, it did not. And although for some months the tension between Clarendon and Mrs Snowden prevented them from co-operating against the Director-General, by 1928 they had come to the same conclusion that 'the Board were kept in the background' and that the BBC's staff 'did not appreciate what the Board's duties and responsibilities were'.

The staff point was a sensitive one. The Governors had been given powers under the Charter to 'appoint such officers and staff as they may think necessary', but Reith did not like them 'poking their noses' too much into staff matters. A letter from Mrs Snowden to Gainford would have infuriated him had he seen it, 'My method of learning about an organisation is perhaps unorthodox, but it is satisfying to me. It is perhaps a woman's method. I am less concerned with masses of facts in the first place than with personnel.'[3]

At a Board meeting in July 1929 Clarendon wanted to insert a rebuke into the minutes about the Director-General's behaviour. 'Unfortunately,' he told Gainford, 'he has given us all the impression that he wants – if he does not agree with the Board – to over-ride us.'[4] By then the Governors were lunching together as a group after Board meetings at the Savoy Hotel, and infuriating Reith by never inviting the Director-General to join them. They were also prepared to issue ultimata. They demanded the right to

---

[1] *Into the Wind*, p.117. For the 'unspecific' nature of the first Charter, see O'Brien, op.cit., p.118.

[2] *Into the Wind*, p.260. For Mrs Snowden's side of the story, see letters quoted in Boyle, op.cit., p.218. One particularly sharp letter of Mrs Snowden to Reith has been preserved (20 Feb. 1930). It ended 'I do not particularly want to broadcast, but neither am I prepared any longer to tolerate the amazing inconsideration and positive rudeness which you and (catching their tone from you) certain members of your staff have so frequently exhibited towards myself.' Reith sent a copy of the letter to Clarendon. See also Board of Governors, *Minutes*, 26 Feb. 1930.

[3] 1 May 1927, quoted in Boyle, op.cit., p.218. Cf. Lady Simon's activities, below, p.93. It should be added that Reith's ways with staff always required independent scrutiny. (See Boyle, op.cit., pp.227 ff.)

[4] Gainford Papers, quoted in Boyle, op.cit., p.221. Cf. Board of Governors, *Minutes*, 3 Sept. 1927. 'The Board concurred with this request, but Mrs Snowden recorded a personal protest.'

attend all advisory meetings, to call on heads of departments 'collectively or in pairs' and to ratify all appointments and resignations. When Reith objected to this approach, Clarendon read the terms of the Charter to him. 'The Charter makes absolutely clear the supremacy of the Board of Governors,' he exclaimed. 'Like the commander-in-chief on a battlefield, their status and powers were unquestionable.' 'Surely,' Reith replied, 'the Board held an equivalent authority to the Cabinet, with the chief executive in the position of commander-in-chief.' [1]

Rt Hon. J. H. Whitley

Neither interpretation was helpful, either constitutionally or psychologically, and the position inside the BBC would have deteriorated further had not Clarendon been made Governor-General of South Africa in February 1930. The vacancy was filled by J. H. Whitley, recently Speaker of the House of Commons. This appointment was certainly not made to propitiate Reith, for the Labour Postmaster-General, H. B. Lees-Smith, thought Reith neurotic and megalomaniac. MacDonald, who knew Reith better, had asked him whether he had 'anyone in mind' for the Chairmanship, but had told him, when Reith replied that the name of Gainford came to mind, that Gainford 'would not do'. As it was, Whitley's appointment ushered in a period of peace. Thereafter, at least as far as the Director-

[1] See *Into the Wind*, pp. 118 ff.

General was concerned, all was 'light, understanding and excellent wisdom'.[1]

There was certainly order, for in 1932, the year when the BBC moved from Savoy Hill to Broadcasting House, Whitley and Reith drafted a document defining the rights and duties of the Board of Governors which was to remain definitive for more than thirty years. The text was not published, but successive Governors were all presented with it on appointment by the responsible minister:

The Governors of the BBC act primarily as trustees to safeguard the broadcasting service in the national interest. Their functions are not executive. Their responsibilities are general and not particular. They are not divided up for purposes of departmental supervision. The suggestion sometimes made that Governors should be appointed as experts or specialists in any of the activities covered by the broadcasting service is not regarded as desirable. The Governors should as far as possible be persons of wide outlook and considerable experience of men and affairs, preferably with previous public service of one kind or another; and there should be included also a person or persons with financial and commercial experience. They are, subject to the duties laid upon the Postmaster-General by Parliament in the Royal Charter, responsible for seeing that the many purposes for which broadcasting was established, and which in 1926 were reviewed in the Royal Charter, are carried out. With the Director-General they discuss and then decide on major matters of policy and finance, but they leave the execution of that policy and the general administration of the service in all its branches to the Director-General and his competent officers. The Governors should be able to judge of the general effect of the service upon the public, and subject as before mentioned, are finally responsible for the conduct of it.[2]

This document was not seriously challenged either by the Chairman of the Board or by the Governors until 1947 when Lord Simon of Wythenshawe became Chairman.[3] Meanwhile BBC internal 'reorganisation' in 1933 was carried out according to a 'Reith' plan in which the Governors played only a minor

[1] Ibid., p.127. Whitley's first letter to Reith (3 June 1930) expressed pleasure at 'being associated with you in the great work of which you are the creator'.
[2] For the document, see A. Smith, *British Broadcasting* (1974), pp.60–1, and a paper by Oliver Whitley, Whitley's son and later a distinguished BBC official, 'The Whitley Document', 8 March 1976.   [3] Simon, op.cit., p.51.

part. They played no part in the Control Board, Reith's management group, which from 1933 to 1935 was actually called the
Director-General's Meeting. Reith thought of the key job in the
reorganisation – that of Controller (Output) – as being in his
own 'gift', and no document was drafted covering his own
powers.[1] There was, indeed, little doubt about his authority
during the 1930s, either in the Board of Governors or the Control
Board, although by 1938 he was anticipating an increase in the
responsibilities of the Control Board vis-à-vis the Director-
General, and throughout the 1930s he encouraged Governors to
intervene in matters of administrative detail.[2]

After the Second World War Reith, long absent from Broadcasting House, was to tell a newly appointed Governor that
'whatever Governors may be prepared (under safeguards) to
leave to the Executive, they must decide and direct policy; and
they must have a lively, comprehensive, and continuing care for
the product of the organisation they are appointed to govern'.[3]

There seems to have been little discussion by the Governors
during the 1930s, however, about what might be called 'broadcasting strategy' – the increase in the number of licences; the
wider regional coverage; the place of regions within the broadcasting system. And they backed Reith uncritically – rather than
probed his assumptions – when he pursued a carefully formulated
programme policy, 'deriving from a sense of responsibility –
general and specific'. This included a Sunday policy, which was
very strongly criticised in most sections of the Press, and a
restrictive policy in broadcasting news.[4]

Garry Allighan, an early radio journalist, recounted in his
biography of Reith a public challenge to the austere Sunday
programme policy. During a press conference in 1935 Cecil
Graves, the new Controller of Programmes, declared there was
no demand for lighter fare on Sundays. Allighan urged him to ask
how many of the sixty national journalists present wanted dance
music and variety on Sundays. There was a unanimous vote in

---

[1] *Into the Wind*, p.117, for a discussion between Reith and Lord Blanesburgh about
the desirability of such a document. Blanesburgh told him that no document would be
satisfactory to him and acceptable to the Governors.

[2] Reith, *Diary*, 5 April 1938: 'Controllers' Meeting will do far more than in the past
so still less for D.G. to do which is as it should be.'; *Into the Wind*, p.301.

[3] Lord Reith showed me a copy of this letter written in 1952.

[4] Ibid.

favour. This so disconcerted Graves and Sir Stephen Tallents, the Public Relations Controller, that they begged the newspaper men not to report the event. Surprisingly they obliged. [1]

Whitley would never allow an announcement to be made to the Press in the name of the Board of Governors. 'We are one body,' he maintained, 'Governors, Director-General and staff. The Corporation; the BBC.' [2] This was a sensible policy when Reith was at his best, but Reith's personal interest in broadcasting flagged considerably after the reorganisation. These were 'the golden years of wireless', but he himself did not feel 'fully stretched'. Management became increasingly a matter of routine. Not only did the senior executives (under Reith) supervise administration or 'manage', as we would now put it; they initiated 'legislative policy' as well. The Board supported them as a matter of course and would reverse them only on 'an absolutely fundamental question of principle'. [3]

After Whitley's death in 1935, indeed, the Board concentrated mainly on Reith and his problems. 'We talked and thought too much about the D.G.,' said Mary Agnes Hamilton, who replaced Lady Snowden as a Governor in 1933, 'and too little about broadcasting.' [4]

Not surprisingly, there was an undercurrent of public criticism of the BBC during the early 1930s, often fanned by disgruntled BBC employees. Since successive governments followed the conventions laid down by the Postmaster-General in 1928, it seldom reached the floor of the House of Commons. [5] Commentators on the BBC's constitution during the 1930s were aware, however, of the fact that the Governors were not 'masters' of their house in quite the sense that Sir William Mitchell-Thomson, the then Postmaster-General, had suggested. Their importance and the weight of their responsibility, it was sensed, 'lay more in their

[1] G. Allighan, *Sir John Reith* (1938), pp.227–8.

[2] *Into the Wind*, p.176.

[3] Gordon, op.cit., p.195.

[4] M.A. Hamilton, *Remembering My Good Friends* (1946), p.285.

[5] For a reiteration of the former policy on the part of the Postmaster-General, see *Hansard*, vol. 318, col. 2738, 17 Dec. 1936. A 1933 debate (ibid., vol. 274, cols. 1807–66, 22 Feb. 1933) ended with a resolution that it would be 'contrary to the public interest' to 'subject the corporation to any control by Government or by Parliament other than the control alrady provided for in the charter and the licence'.

reserved *de jure* powers than in those [which they] ordinarily exercised'.[1]

After 1934, Reith was less in daily charge – by choice – than he had been before, and he talked often of the need for devolution and of necessary distinctions between *de jure* and *de facto* in the Control Board too. Nonetheless, he was always unmistakably at the summit of his own organisation, and he generalised his philosophy of public broadcasting in speaking to audiences in other parts of the world. 'The generation of tomorrow will judge us not just in terms of the amusement we have given, but by what we have stood for.'[2] In the United States, he complained, the 'best men' lacked 'much idea of their responsibility to the public' because there was no 'institution' like the BBC;[3] and he always encouraged British Dominions overseas to copy the BBC pattern. Thus he told the Prime Minister of the Union of South Africa in 1934 that:

Assuming that the Members of the Board of Governors are individuals of high standing in the community, experienced in dealing with men of affairs and of wide general interest, they would engage and largely depend on, their experts in particular fields, and they should be able to devolve in large measure upon their Chief Executive. In fact, without derogation from the supreme and absolute authority vested in them, they should, in terms of their confidence in the Chief Executive and his expert staff, be able to function as trustees, able to intervene in any way, at any stage and on any matter. But a great deal is bound to depend upon the Chief Executive.[4]

During the middle 1930s Reith, whose salary was more than twice that of the Chairman of the Governors, continued to have more difficulties with his own growing organisation (and with the Press, which picked them up) than with his Governors or with Parliament. Since authority was 'focused' at the top, there were always rumblings from below. He was successful in 1934 in convincing the political parties of his *bona fides*,[5] but a year later complaints percolated through to the Ullswater Committee

[1] Gordon, op.cit., p.194.
[2] Notes for a Blattnerphone Record on Broadcasting (1931).
[3] Reith, 'Broadcasting in America' in the *Nineteenth Century*, Aug. 1931.
[4] *The Union of South Africa – Broadcasting Policy and Development*, Nov. 1934, para. 39.
[5] Reith, *Diary*, 2 Feb., 10 May 1934.

which was reviewing broadcasting problems. Reith, who disliked the presence on the committee of Mitchell-Thomson, raised to the peerage as Lord Selsdon, was once again reassured, however, to learn that 'it was not in the least inclined to turn the world upside down'. [1]

Reith would have preferred to have had the BBC's Charter renewed in 1936 without another major enquiry, but instead the terms of reference of the committee under the chairmanship of eighty-year-old Lord Ullswater, like Whitley a former Speaker of the House of Commons, were extremely broad – to consider not only 'the constitution, control and finance of the broadcasting service' but the Empire Service, television and wireless exchanges. It began its hearings (in secret) in May 1935 and reported – favourably for the BBC – in December.

Governors were to remain as they had been – neither specialists nor representatives of particular interests and localities – and they were to continue to leave the execution of policy to BBC officials. After cuts in the early 1930s, they were to be paid £1000 a year, and the Chairman was to receive £3000. They were to exercise 'joint responsibility', with their major task being that of judging 'the general effect of the broadcasting service upon the public'. The Ullswater Committee had been made fully aware, however, it stated, of 'widespread strictures upon the personnel of the Board' and in their Report the members of the Committee 'trusted' that 'full attention' would be paid to 'width and variety of outlook' in the appointment of Governors. 'It is well that there should be, within the Board of Governors, knowledge of men and affairs and experience both of public service and of financial and commercial matters; but we think it important that any undue homogeneity of age or opinion should be avoided.' [2]

In a note of reservation Clement Attlee, then Leader of the Opposition, went further. It was 'undesirable', he said, that Governors should be drawn exclusively from persons whose 'social experience and background is that of the well-to-do classes'. He advocated retirement at sixty and pointed to 'the desirability of including . . . persons who share the outlook of the younger generations'. [3] He was well past that

[1] Quoted Boyle, op.cit., p.266.
[2] Cmd 5091 (1936), *Report of the Broadcasting Committee, 1935*, para. 12.
[3] Ibid., pp.48–9.

stage himself, and his Chairman was twenty years older.[1]

With Reith's blessing (and probably on his initiative) the Ullswater Committee suggested also that responsibility for 'the cultural side of broadcasting should be transferred from the Postmaster-General to a Cabinet Minister in the House of Commons, preferably a senior member of the Government, and free from heavy Departmental responsibilities'.[2] Although in 1936 both Attlee and Clement Davies, the Liberal leader, supported the idea of a transfer, it did not formally take place until 1974, and the Home Secretary, though senior, had heavy departmental responsibilities. Reith chafed under the Post Office regime, which he felt needed greater governmental scrutiny. While he argued firmly that 'control should only be felt' when the Board was 'not carrying out its obligations'.[3] Government spokesmen stated in 1936 that they felt the Ullswater proposal to be 'inconsistent with the preservation of independent management by the Corporation'.[4]

Reith did not get his way either on the question of the number of Governors, which on the recommendation of the Ullswater Committee was increased 19from five to seven in face of BBC opposition. 'Collective wisdom does not grow with numbers,' Reith argued, 'and a small Board is generally more efficient than a large one.' The argument cut no ice with the government. Nor did a second argument on which he placed just as much emphasis – the fact that the number five had been endorsed by MacDonald and the Postmaster-General in discussions with Whitley in 1933.

Whitley had a new Vice-Chairman to assist him after January 1933, Ronald Norman, a younger brother of the Governor of the Bank of England, and it was he who became Chairman in 1935 soon after Whitley's death (in February of that year) and the

[1] See Attlee's speech in Parliament, 6 July 1936 (*Hansard*, vol. 314, cols. 972–6). For complaints that Governors represented only 'age, safety and respectability', see L. Woolf, 'The Future of British Broadcasting' in the *Political Quarterly*, vol. 2 (1931), p.177, and W.A. Robson in ibid., vol. 6 (1936). Both these critics came from the same (Fabian) stable. See also Robson's *Public Enterprise: Experiments in Social Ownership and Control in Great Britain* (1937). See also above, pp. 30–4 and below p.113 and 152.

[2] Cmd 5091 (1936), para. 53. For Reith's views on the subject see *Into the Wind*, p.187. *The Times*, 17 March 1936, assumed that the Committee had in mind the Lord President of the Council.

[3] Reith, 'Business Management of the Public Services', a paper read to the Institute of Public Administration, Jan. 1930.

[4] *Hansard*, vol. 314, cols. 866, 927, 6 July 1936.

L to R: R.C. Norman (Chairman), G.C. Tryon (Postmaster-General), Lord Selsdon with Jasmine Bligh at Alexandra Palace.

death (in August) of his immediate successor, Viscount Bridgeman.[1] The newspapers had quipped in 1932 – as they were to do in later years when the announcement was made of the names of new Chairmen – that Norman seemed to be qualified 'by possession of a wireless set'.[2] Yet Norman brought to the BBC considerable knowledge of men and affairs, and, if not quite 'light, understanding and excellent wisdom', at least 'his own blend of charm and realism'.[3] His extended term of service with the Corporation 'covered perhaps the most striking period of expansion in the BBC's history'.[4]

In fact, Norman's appointment was a crucial one, for it was he who had to deal with the (final) resignation of Reith – he may, indeed, have played the part of 'prime mover' in engineering it[5] – and the appointment of a successor, Professor F.W. Ogilvie, in

[1] 'In neither of MacDonald's appointments to the chair', Reith noted, 'had he chosen a member of his own party' (*Into the Wind*, p.216). For the atmosphere of a Board meeting in 1933, see his *Diary*, 11 Jan. 1933: 'Norman came in and spent two hours asking all kinds of questions . . . He is very pleasant indeed. The Board meeting was almost rowdy, certainly quite amusing.'

[2] *Reynolds News*, 18 Dec. 1932, on his appointment as Vice-Chairman.

[3] Boyle, op.cit., p.269.   [4] *BBC Handbook, 1940*, p.11.

[5] See Boyle, op.cit., pp.289 ff. Boyle's account is a little more firm in its outlines than the impressions I derived myself from a day's talk with Norman, but it is undoubtedly on the right lines.

June 1938. This was the first time the Governors had had the chance of carrying out what has often been called the most important of all the tasks committed to them. They set important precedents. Thus, Reith was asked *not* to be present at a crucial meeting of the Board on 29 June, and he had nothing thereafter to do with the appointment, the secrets of which Norman carefully guarded in retirement. Reith had hoped, too, that it might be possible for him to continue to sit on the Board, but Norman made it clear to him that one or two of the Governors were opposed to this.[1]

Reith switched off the Droitwich transmitter and generating plant on the night of 30 June, his last act for the BBC, signing the visitor's book 'J. C. W. Reith, late BBC'. It was not until 10 July, however, that Ogilvie's name was announced, and not until October that he took up his post. In a brilliant poem by Sagittarius, 'The Air Presumptive' asked

'Breathes there a being fit to sway
Reith's self-made Empire of the air?'[2]

Norman took full responsibility for the appointment, regretting later on that Ogilvie had every qualification except one – that of being able to manage a large organisation. Reith from the start had no doubts: Ogilvie was 'a man of fine character and outlook', but 'I was quite sure he was not the man for the BBC'.[3]

He was certainly not the man to deal with the complex problems of war, and war figured prominently on the possible agenda in June 1938, even if neither Norman nor Ogilvie talked much of it. As early as 1935, indeed – before the publication of the Ullswater Report – Reith had been a member of a secret subcommittee of the Imperial Defence Committee which planned the wartime role of a Ministry of Information, and in the early summer of 1938, just before he left the BBC, he had negotiated with the Post Office – without disclosure to the Governors – a scheme whereby in the event of war (when the new Ministry would be 'responsible for censorship control of all BBC programmes') the Director-General and the Deputy Director-General would be made Chairman and Vice-Chairman of the

---

[1] Reith told me that he was hurt by this. He had been taking soundings with his new employer Imperial Airways as to whether it would change its rule that its Chairman could not serve on other boards (*Diary*, 3 June 1938).

[2] *New Statesman*, 16 July 1938.

[3] *Into the Wind*, p.318.

Board while retaining their executive posts and responsibilities. The Board as a whole would go 'out of commission'. [1]

The members of the Board knew nothing of these plans until the Munich crisis of September 1938 – they were told at their meeting on 28 September 1938 [2] – by which time Reith had moved to another Empire of the Air, Imperial Airways. The Board took no action then, but in July 1939 on the initiative of Sir Ian Fraser, who had prepared a paper called 'The Control of Broadcasting', further discussions with Government were held, this time with the full participation of the Board. It was agreed after these discussions that in the event of war the Board should be reduced to two – the existing Chairman and Vice-Chairman. 'The Board realise,' the Governors stated, 'that in time of war control of broadcasting so far as it has any bearing on the conduct of affairs must be the responsibility of the Government and that this would necessitate such change in number and personnel of the Governors or in procedure as will ensure the smooth and speedy carrying out of Government decisions which in time of emergency will call for prompt action.' [3]

There was a new Chairman by then, Sir Allan Powell – who took over in April 1939 with the memorable words, 'I know nothing of radio. Frankly I don't know how many valves my set has got.' [4] Powell had been a member of the Import Duties Committee, Mayor of Kensington, and Clerk to the Metropolitan Asylums Board, and Jimmy Maxton asked the Prime Minister in Parliament 'which of these bits of experience' qualified Powell 'to arrange variety programmes?' [5] The same might have been asked about his Vice-Chairman C.H.G. Millis, who by then had had nearly two years' experience in the post.

Whatever they knew about radio or the BBC, Powell and

[1] Note of 27 July 1938, 'The BBC and the Ministry of Information'; Board of Governors, *Papers*, particularly 'Memorandum by the Chairman on War-time Relations between the Government and the BBC', 16 April 1941; Notes prepared for the Director-General by G.R. Barnes, 4 April 1949.

[2] Board of Governors, *Minutes*, 28 Sept. 1938. The Postmaster-General had explained the plan to Ogilvie and Graves the day before (Draft letter by Ogilvie to *The Times*, 24 Oct. 1939).

[3] 'Memorandum on the Administration of the Broadcasting System in War' prepared by Powell and Millis and approved at Board Meeting on 6 July 1939.

[4] *News Review*, 18 Dec. 1941.

[5] For the discussion in Parliament during which Chamberlain refused to explain the specific reasons why he had chosen Powell, whom he called 'eminently suitable for the position', see *Hansard*, vol. 345, cols. 31–2, 13 March 1939.

Sir Allan Powell

Millis had one immediate advantage. They knew Neville Chamberlain (and Chamberlain's confidant, Sir Horace Wilson, whom they met in 'deputation' on 21 July), and they, too, kept Chamberlain's confidence when perhaps the best-known of the Governors, H.A.L. Fisher, expressed doubt about the rearrangements on the outbreak of war, saying that while he did not object to there being only two Governors 'for the duration', he did not approve of making BBC executives members of the Board.[1] They also kept the confidence of Churchill after 1940. Although the new Director-General, Ogilvie, was to 'resign' in 1942 – he himself used the quotation marks[2] – and there were to be large-scale changes in the internal structures (and finance) of the BBC, both Chairman and Vice-Chairman survived.

Fisher's 1939 protest has been described as 'the last voice of Gladstonian liberalism resounding in a rapidly expanding desert'.[3] 'If the Charter is suspended and the BBC placed under a Ministry of Information,' Fisher exclaimed, 'it is highly unlikely

---

[1] Millis wrote to Sir Horace Wilson on 1 August 1939 agreeing to the rearrangements and Powell wrote to Lord Macmillan on 5 September accepting the direction of the Government 'in all matters pertaining to the war effort'. Attlee, who asked Chamberlain in September 1939 to reconsider the reduction in the number of Governors, justified the reduction later (*Hansard*, vol. 361, col. 412, 28 May 1940) on the grounds that it was 'to ensure a rapid and effective direction of policy under wartime conditions'. 'In the present circumstances,' he added, 'I can see no justification for altering present arrangements.'

[2] Letter from Ogilvie to A.P. Ryan, 10 March 1942. 'I "resigned" from the BBC with keen regret – even in order to "facilitate reorganisation", as the phrase was.' (Letter passed to me by A.P. Ryan.)

[3] D. Ogg, *Herbert Fisher* (1947), p.129.

that the regime of liberty will ever be restored.'[1] Fisher certainly carried some, at least, of the Governors with him, when Ogilvie was asked to retire from their meeting in July 1939: the Conservative Fraser, for example, believed in 'the most vigorous protest' and pointed out that 'we had been set up by Royal Charter by the express will of Parliament', and 'that our independence ought not to be taken away from us without the express will of Parliament'.[2] Although Millis wrote to Ogilvie expressing full confidence in his capacity – 'with the BBC's future in the hands of you and Graves [his Deputy Director-General] to assist you, I haven't a qualm in the world'[3] – he passed on to Sir Horace Wilson the views of those Governors who felt that 'the chief executive officers, so far from gaining increased freedom of action by doubling the role of Governor and executive, might be hampered thereby'.[4]

Not every wartime Minister of Information was as inadequate as Chamberlain's first choice, Lord Macmillan, who told the House of Lords three weeks after war had started that he 'believed' the Board 'had been more or less suspended and that the Chairman and Directors are in charge'. He added that he did not know exactly what the system of control was. Reith, who succeeded him as Minister in January 1940, knew too well – at least about his own version of what control implied – and was told by Chamberlain to be 'gentle' with the BBC 'and not to use my knowledge of it to do things that another Minister would not do'.[5] It was wise advice, for it was an exaggeration to say that the BBC had been placed *under* the Ministry of Information. It still retained more independence than Fisher believed possible. The control which was applied varied from time to time, but it was never absolute.

The Governors, however, do not seem to have played a major part in any of the critical discussions about control policy then or later, when Duff Cooper (and later Brendan Bracken) succeeded Reith at the Ministry, even though Ogilvie consulted the retired

[1] Ibid. Ogilvie sharply criticised Fisher for writing to *The Times* in September 1939. In his letter, not published until 23 October 1939, which Ogilvie said 'lacked something both in accuracy and taste' (Note of 24 Oct. 1939), Fisher had revealed Reith's earlier plan to do without the Governors altogether.

[2] I. Fraser, *Whereas I Was Blind* (1942), p.163.

[3] Millis to Ogilvie, 17 July 1939.   [4] Millis to Wilson, 27 July 1939.

[5] *Into the Wind*, p.352.

Governors from time to time in 1939 and 1940 'on programme questions'.[1] There was no formal discussion, for example, of the difficulties which followed the appointment of Frank Pick to the Director-Generalship of the Ministry in August 1940: he wanted substantial power for a Broadcasting Division within the Ministry and told Ogilvie in November 1940 that the Government would end by 'taking over the BBC'.[2] It was to Ogilvie that Pick's more genial successor, Sir Walter Monckton, wrote in December 1940 – on New Year's Eve – telling him that the War Cabinet had decided that two official Advisers should be appointed to the BBC and asking him to pass on the letter to Powell.[3] Powell expressed fears that the Advisers would be able to range freely and without check over the whole field of BBC administration and operations,[4] and it was he and Ogilvie who had to pursue further discussions on the issue.

The situation was difficult. When one of the two new Advisers, A.P. Ryan, who had already worked in the BBC, wrote to Ogilvie in April 1941 asking him to send him Control Board minutes 'as you agreed', Ogilvie replied tersely 'I agreed to no such thing'.[5] Yet Powell and Millis were claiming during the spring of 1941 that the Minister of Information had always 'received the Governors' representations with great consideration' and that he had made it clear that the Government was not prepared 'to take over the BBC'.[6]

It was during this same spring that Duff Cooper decided to reinstate the Board of Governors. Powell and Millis were now joined by Fraser, Mallon, Lady Violet Bonham Carter and Arthur Mann, the last two new members of the Board.

This was not the first time that the issue of reinstatement had been raised after the outbreak of war. As early as October and November 1939, indeed, A.P. Waterfield, the Deputy Director-General of the Ministry of Information, was asking Ogilvie what he thought of the reduction, and Sir Horace Wilson was summoning him for discussions on the grounds that the matter was

[1] Note of a Telephone Conversation between A.P. Waterfield and Ogilvie, 10 Oct. 1939.
[2] Note by Ogilvie, 22 Nov. 1940.
[3] Note by Sir Walter Monckton, 1 Jan. 1941. (Public Record Office INF 1/869.)
[4] Note by Powell, 4 Jan. 1941.
[5] Ryan to Ogilvie, 3 April 1941: Note by Ogilvie in red ink.
[6] Memorandum by the Chairman, 16 April 1941, loc.cit.

'coming to the forefront again for political reasons'. It was Ogilvie then – not the Government – who urged that there should be no increase. 'If the pre-war system were re-introduced in its full beauty,' he told Wilson, 'I could confidently predict a breakdown either of the system or of broadcasting efficiency.' 'Reinstatement of the Governors,' he added in a memorable phrase, 'would be jam for Goebbels.' [1]

During the early summer of 1940, when the pace of the war had quickened and Holland, Belgium and France fell, the political situation was transformed, and Duff Cooper declared himself satisfied that machinery existed whereby he could 'exercise complete control over the BBC'. Two months before the reinstatement, he told a group of senior BBC officials that the Government had avoided 'any change in the status of the BBC so that as soon as the war was over normal relations could be resumed'. [2] The new fact in the situation in April 1941 was that he was more confident about an extended BBC Board than he was about the Director-General. The decision to reinstate the Governors was in fact a challenge to Ogilvie, and events were soon to prove that Duff Cooper and his successor Brendan Bracken were not afraid that sacking a Director-General might offer even thicker and richer jam for Goebbels.

It is interesting to note that in July 1941, after the reinstatement of the Board, when Duff Cooper was once more criticising the BBC for failing to carry out Ministry of Information directives – he cited twenty instances [3] – he thought of making the Director-General a Ministry of Information official. Whether he would have wished at that stage of the war to keep Ogilvie as the first Director-General to serve as a Ministry of Information official or whether Ogilvie would have been willing to serve is not clear. What is clear is that the new Board very quickly established its independence. It dismissed the suggestion as both 'unworkable' and 'unacceptable', [4] and when Ernest Thurtle, Bracken's Parliamentary Secretary, made a foolish statement in the House of Commons in October 1941 that the BBC's Governors were concerned only with culture and entertainment – not with the

[1] Report by Ogilvie on a Conversation with Sir Horace Wilson, 29 Nov. 1939.

[2] Quoted in the Memorandum by the Chairman, 16 April 1941, and in Barnes Memorandum, 4 April 1949.

[3] Board of Governors, *Minutes*, 10 July 1941.   [4] Ibid., 17 July 1941.

BBC's contribution to the war effort, Powell and the Board protested so strongly that Bracken replied that in future Thurtle would not be allowed to answer questions about the BBC. Even this did not satisfy them. 'We are not content with this,' a new Governor wrote, 'and point out that if what Thurtle said was really BBC policy, then we are not worth collectively £7000 a year of Government money.' [1]

The Board of Governors during World War II.

L to R: Dr. J.J. Mallon, Sir Ian Fraser, Lady Violet Bonham Carter, R.W. Foot, Sir Allan Powell, Sir Cecil Graves, Hon. Harold Nicolson, A.H. Mann

The new Governor was Harold Nicolson, whose Government post had been taken over by Thurtle. He was disappointed at losing his post and doubtless joined the Board as a second best. The rest, however, were delighted. Mann, former editor of the *Yorkshire Post*, who was told by Duff Cooper that he might be of 'particular service' in helping the BBC with its news policy, warmly welcomed the chance: he was perhaps the first Governor to be told to take an interest in a specific responsibility. [2] Lady Violet Bonham Carter, a friend of Churchill, was happy by contrast to 'rove' everywhere. 'Can a bloody duck swim?' she remarked after having been asked by Churchill to join the reconstituted Board, and she later described her work as 'enthralling,

[1] H. Nicolson, *Diaries and Letters, 1939–1945* (1967), p.187, entry for 9 Oct. 1941. Duff Cooper had already replied to a questioner at the time of the reinstatement of the Governors in April 1941 that they would be allowed 'to exercise genuine freedom' (*Hansard*, vol. 370, col. 991, 2 April 1941). For Thurtle's views on the BBC, see his autobiography *Time's Winged Chariot* (1945), Ch. 22.

[2] Letter from Arthur Mann to Powell, 2 May 1943.

though it involves a vast amount of homework in the way of reading listener-research reports, monitoring, etc.'[1]

Lady Violet was then 53 years old, and Mann was 64. Nicolson, who was 54, was an experienced broadcaster, and probably knew more about the BBC than any previous Governor. Press fears were expressed that fresh from the Ministry of Information he might turn out to be 'a pro-Bracken Fifth Columnist in the BBC camp',[2] but these were completely unfounded. Neither he nor Fraser as MPs had to resign their seats on becoming Governors. Fraser had had to do this when he first joined the Board in 1936, but under wartime rules they could serve both in Broadcasting House and in the Commons.[3]

Bracken was looking for allies rather than for a fifth column among the Governors, and with his close access to Churchill he ensured that the BBC felt far more 'secure' than ever before. At the first Board meeting which he attended in August 1941, he at once made conciliatory noises. 'He was satisfied,' he said, 'that it was undesirable in the national interest for the BBC to be taken over by the Government, and that the more freedom the Corporation could have in the conduct of its affairs, the better it could serve the national interest.'[4]

Many years later in 1949 an interesting post-war paper on the wartime position was prepared by George Barnes. 'If Government is prepared to take and exercise control,' he wrote, 'it only needs a D.G. to give these orders to. If, having taken the necessary powers, it wishes to influence and is prepared to persuade, it needs the Board, reduced if necessary in numbers, as in peacetime. Excessive control kills itself by becoming unworkable.'[5] The Board had now been restored, a sign that the Government considered 'influence' and 'persuasion' to be both feasible and effective. The problem which remained was that of the Director-

---

[1] Filmed interview with Kenneth Harris, 14–17 Feb. 1967; *The Leader*, 4 Nov. 1944. The *Daily Express* noted in 1941 (4 April) that she was then a member of the governing body of the left-wing '1941 Committee' which had complained that the Governors had banned Michael Redgrave and others from broadcasting. In 1944 she became the first woman President of the Liberal Party.

[2] *Truth*, 1 Aug. 1941.

[3] Fraser's case was covered by an Order in Council, 25 April 1941. See also *The Times*, 26 April 1941.

[4] Board of Governors, *Minutes*, 14 Aug. 1941. Bracken, like Duff Cooper, occasionally attended Board meetings. So, too, did Monckton and Radcliffe.

[5] Memorandum by Barnes, 4 April 1949.

F.W. Ogilvie

General. When Ogilvie had been appointed in 1938, a writer in
Punch, noting four wrinkles in his face, had called them
    'The wrinkles of a broad-based policy
    That understands the democratic will'. [1]
By 1941 the wrinkles were wrinkles of care and concern, and
understanding of 'the democratic will' had come to mean something quite different from what it had meant in 1938.

    The Governors, supported by Bracken, decided in January
1942 that 'the chief executive control of the BBC under wartime
conditions . . . called for different qualities and experience from
those suited for peacetime control.' [2] And a solution seemed in

---

[1] *Punch*, 3 Aug. 1938.
[2] Board of Governors, *Minutes*, 21 Jan. 1942. There had been a number of arguments
inside the BBC not only about finance but about programmes, notably about a
broadcast birthday greeting to the King of Italy in a Christopher Stone record
programme. The financial position of the Corporation (especially a gap between
estimates and expenditure) was investigated from November 1941 onwards by R.
Kettle of Deloitte, Plender, Griffiths & Company. The Kettle Report lay on Ogilvie's
desk when he retired.

R.W. Foot and Sir Cecil Graves

sight after October 1941, when Robert Foot was brought in from outside the BBC – from the Gas Light and Coke Company, at Bracken's suggestion – to consider ways of dealing with parlous BBC finances. This was a different dose of 'understanding and excellent wisdom', and this time of light too. Foot's title was General Advisor on War-time Organisation – and it was he and the veteran BBC executive, Sir Cecil Graves, who had joined the BBC in 1926, who replaced Ogilvie in January 1942 in an unprecedented 'diarchy' of Director-Generals.

The idea of the diarchy – based on a combination of BBC and outside experience – seems to have emerged in the Governing Body. Certainly it won the approval even of those Governors who had a 'soft spot' for Ogilvie. 'To Grosvenor House,' wrote Harold Nicolson in his *Diary*, 'where we have a hush meeting of the BBC Board. We decide to retire Ogilvie, and put Graves and Foot as joint Director-Generals in his place. I am sure this is right, as Ogilvie is too noble a character for rough war work. Yet I mind deeply in a way. This clever, high-minded man being pushed aside. I hate it, but I agree.'[1]

Reith, who had lost all connections with the Ministry of Information in 1941, argued from the sidelines that it was not only Ogilvie who should go, but Foot and the Governors as well, leaving Graves, whom he had always favoured as his successor, at the Director-General's desk.[2] And he told Bracken that all would have been well if his own version of broadcasting control had been accepted in 1939. Sir Cyril Radcliffe admitted that 'the reconstitution of the Board which Mr Duff Cooper achieved' had 'made for a dual responsibility which is not, I think, really fair to either', but told Reith, perhaps to placate him, that 'ultimately, I think, we are getting back towards the plan you originally recommended'.[3]

The double use of the 'I think' raises suspicions. In fact, Bracken put the matter more accurately in the House of Commons, when he told members that they could not have it both ways. 'Either they want the Governors to have a certain amount of independence or they want the BBC to be an appendage of the Ministry of Information, which would be a very bad thing.'[4] It was a 'substantial independence' which was left for the rest of the war. Yet it rested as much on the warmth of the relationship behind the scenes between Bracken and Foot as on the energy and determination of what was perhaps the most distinguished Board of Governors the BBC has ever had.[5]

Unlike Ogilvie, who was to become an influential post-war critic of the BBC, Foot left on paper his own account both of what had happened in the winter of 1941–2 and of his subsequent relationships with Bracken and the Government and with Graves and the Governors. 'Before our appointment there is no doubt that whatever Ogilvie's personal ideas and hopes may have been, the BBC was drifting nearer and nearer to control by the Government, and if the change had not been made the drift

[1] Nicolson, op.cit., p.207, entry for 26 Jan. 1942. A year earlier Churchill had told the House of Commons that he did not think it necessary to amend the Charter of the BBC in order to secure a form of administration suitable for war conditions. (*Hansard*, vol. 368, col.25, 21 Jan. 1941.)

[2] Letter from Reith to Cyril Radcliffe, Director General of the Ministry of Information, 5 Jan. 1942 (Public Record Office INF 1/869).

[3] Letter from Radcliffe to Reith, 10 Jan. 1942 (Public Record Office).

[4] *Hansard*, vol. 377, cols. 1165–6, 4 Feb. 1942.

[5] Board of Governors, *Minutes*, 10 Sept. 1942: Foot reported that matters with the Ministry had 'improved so much in recent months that all would be well'.

The Control Board during World War II.
L to R: R.W. Foot, Sir Cecil Graves, B.E. Nicolls, Miss K. Fuller, I. Kirkpatrick, Sir Noel Ashbridge

would undoubtedly have continued simply because the BBC's own internal organisation was not sufficiently strong and efficient to enable it to manage its own affairs, whether financial or otherwise, without any considerable interference.'[1]

Thereafter, according to Foot, all worked well. Bracken never put any pressure on him when he (and, at first, Graves) saw him twice a week. Graves was a loyal friend as well as colleague until the diarchy came to an end in 1943. Graves dealt with 'output', Foot with 'administration', but both worked together on such questions as the future of the monitoring service, one of the issues which had precipitated Ogilvie's downfall.[2] 'So far as I was concerned,' Foot commented later, when Graves had decided to resign on grounds of ill health, 'I would have been perfectly happy to repeat the joint control provided we got the right man to be my partner. But the Chairman and Governors took the opposite view very strongly and insisted that under the new arrangement the final executive control must rest with me, and with me alone.'[3]

---

[1] Typescript of Foot Autobiography, p.141.
[2] Foot reported to the Governors in April 1942 that he and Graves had visited Monitoring Headquarters at Evesham and 'there had been no signs of restlessness or of anything wrong' (Board of Governors, *Minutes*, 9 April 1942).
[3] Foot Autobiography, p.180.

There had already been a substantial reorganisation involving the abolition of Reith's old Administrative Division, set up in 1933, the subdivision of the old Control Board into three Committees, and an increased element of decentralisation.[1] The Governors seem to have had little to do with this, but they strongly supported the idea of finding an Editor-in-Chief, the first BBC position filled by the future Director-General, William Haley, who joined the BBC from the *Manchester Guardian* and *Evening News* Ltd. Haley, then forty-two years old, was 'in no way a nominee of the Government', Powell told the Controllers, and Foot had been fully concerned with all the new arrangements.[2]

'The Governors and I,' Foot wrote later, 'had by this time been working for a considerable time together . . . and I knew that they had complete confidence in me . . . We naturally had many discussions on contentious matters, almost entirely on what I will still call the programme side, and sometimes disagreements, but they did not detract in any way or disturb the mutual confidence which they had in me and I had in them.' Lady Violet Bonham Carter, in particular, had written to him in 1943, expressing full confidence, after having voiced, as was her wont, many criticisms of particular programmes.[3]

In a passage which is revealing precisely because it displays a certain innocence about earlier BBC history, Foot went on:

The relative positions and responsibilities of the Board of Governors and of the Director-General have from time to time throughout its history given rise to a certain amount of doubt and comment both inside and outside the BBC. Who was really the 'boss' – the Governors or the

[1] In the spring of 1938 a distinction had been drawn between Controllers' Meetings at which detailed operational matters were discussed and Control Board at which major matters of policy were on the agenda, but the last separate Controllers' Meeting was held in May 1939. This last body was revived in 1942 in the form of a weekly meeting of Director-Generals and Output Controllers. The other two new Committees were a weekly Director-Generals' meeting and a fortnightly Controllers' Conference. For later changes, see below, pp.87–8.

[2] Statement by Powell at the Controllers' Conference, 1 Sept. 1943. Foot had been given Haley's name by Christopher Chancellor of Reuters and met Haley at a Reuters dinner, when he had no doubt that 'he was the man we had been looking for'. He immediately suggested the name to Bracken, who approved. 'Why ever didn't I think of him myself?' Bracken asked. (Typescript of Autobiography.)

[3] Ibid. He quoted a letter from her to this effect, dated 8 May 1943. The Governors' *Minutes* reveal how many questions Lady Violet Bonham Carter raised about particular programmes.

Director-General? Where do the responsibilities of the former end and of the latter begin?

When I arrived on the scene, or more accurately, when I became Director-General I was warned both from outside and inside the BBC that I must always be on my guard to see that the Governors did not try to usurp or infringe upon the executive authority of the Director-General. From the outside the warning came particularly, and indeed I think only, from Brendan Bracken. I can remember him now so distinctly saying to me on my appointment 'Don't you let those Governors butt in on your authority – you are the boss and you mustn't let them interfere.'

And inside the BBC one or two, or possibly more of the senior executives, particularly those whom I may, without disrespect call the old hands, who had been there both in Lord Reith's and Mr Ogilvie's time, went out of their way to impress the same warning on me.

For two reasons – both of them good ones – these warnings were quite unnecessary so far as I was concerned.

The first reason was the composition of my Board, as I have already called it, and the complete understanding by its Chairman and its Vice-Chairman of what should be the proper relationship between the Board and the Director-General, and between the Director-General and the rest of the Corporation.

Foot could remember only one occasion when 'a movement was started by one or two members of the Board which, if it had been successful, would have had the effect of interfering with or undermining the absolute authority of the Director-General as the Chief Executive of the Corporation'. Soon after he and Graves became Joint Director-Generals, a suggestion was made that Sub-Committees of the Board should be set up with responsibilities direct to the Board, 'and in that sense by-passing the Director-General over certain specified aspects of the activities of the Corporation'. They would make 'direct and official contact with the various Controllers and Heads of Departments on the programme side'. As their work would have been confined to 'the programme side', Foot did not feel very strongly about the proposal. Cecil Graves, did, however, 'and he was of course right'. 'And so with the complete support of the Chairman and without any difficulty or ill-feeling, the proposal was turned down.'

'The intentions behind the proposal,' Foot reflected later, 'were of course excellent, and beyond criticism. Individual members of the Board quite rightly felt that they had contributions to make in the planning of our programmes, but as a matter of principle the only place for these contributions to be made was at the Board Meeting itself, at which Cecil Graves (while he was still active) and I were always present, and to which any of the Controllers could be, and very often were, summoned when any particular question affecting their work was under discussion.'

The second reason why Foot felt that the warning was quite unnecessary in his case was that as a Chief Executive with the Gas Light and Coke Company 'with a Board composed of Directors of high standing and of great experience in various directions with no executive functions or individual responsibilities in the Company', he had been fully prepared for his post as the Chief Executive in the BBC.

'The road between the Chief Executive and his Board in large organisations like the Gas Light & Coke Co. or the BBC, both of which carried important responsibilities to the public is or certainly should be a very short one,' he remarked, 'and should be regarded both by the Board and the Chief Executive as being specially designed and always available for two-way traffic, with the traffic from each end coming always rather more than half-way along the road. If in these circumstances the Board and the Chief Executive are both fit for their respective jobs and therefore understand and make full allowance for the responsibilities, duties and if you like the temperaments and personalities of each other, the whole thing will work extremely well. It has certainly always done so with me.'

Foot concluded by insisting, as later Director-Generals were to insist, first that 'under the Constitution of the BBC' the Governors were 'in fact the "bosses", or to put it legally . . . "the Corporation",' and second that it was 'absolutely right and essential that they should be'. 'It is they and not the Director-General,' he added, 'who carry the final responsibility on all important matters of policy' and it was for the Director-General 'to put the policy into effect and to make it successful'. If on any really important matter there was a serious difference of opinion on policy between the Board as a whole and the Director-General, the final word had to lie with the Board, and the

Director-General would either have to accept the decision 'in the right spirit and do his best to make a success of it' or – and this was the only alternative – 'make way for someone else'.

How far was Foot's account of his relationship with the Governors corroborated by the Governors themselves? There had been remarkably few private statements by pre-war Governors – at least few have survived – concerning how they saw their own personal role since the days of Lady Snowden, who told Reith plainly that 'your policy from the beginning has been to keep your Governors in the background as much as possible'.[1]

Only H.A.L. Fisher, who admitted that he had done little listening until he became 'an invalid', from time to time made remarks on his role, conscious of the fact that he was 'a former member of the House of Commons' as well as a Governor.[2] He received occasional protests from members of the public and occasionally wrote to the Postmaster-General.[3] He also 'ruminated' at length on the 'vexed question' of the appointment of a Deputy Director-General of the BBC in 1937, concerned that if Graves rather than Sir Stephen Tallents secured the post it would be difficult ever to make him Director-General because he was a Roman Catholic. 'I think it would be quite impossible that the supreme executive control of one of the most important organs of public education in this country should be placed in Roman Catholic hands.'[4]

After the appointment of Foot as sole Director-General and Haley as Editor-in-Chief in 1943, several of the Governors set down their views on 'the functions and organisation of the Board of Governors' and the question as to whether they should be given 'more precise definition'.[5] Nicolson foresaw that any post-war Government considering the renewal of the 1936 Charter would not meet in 'the atmosphere of comparatively calm detachment' which had characterised the Ullswater discussions.

[1] Lady Snowden to Reith, 20 Feb. 1930. During Lady Snowden's last two years on the Board Reith felt their relations had been 'entirely friendly' (*Into the Wind*, p.117).

[2] Fisher to Norman, 6 May 1936; Fisher to Norman, 23 July 1936.

[3] Fisher to Reith, 4 July 1935, referring to 'a long and vehement letter' from Dr G.G. Coulton protesting against a broadcast by G.K. Chesterton; Fisher to Sir Kingsley Wood, the Postmaster-General, 25 Nov. 1937, suggesting that Norman might continue as Chairman.

[4] Fisher to Norman, 22 Feb. 1937.

[5] Board of Governors, *Papers*, 'The BBC Board, Its Functions and Organisation: Memorandum by Harold Nicolson', 9 Sept. 1943.

There would be 'acute criticisms' and they would have party undertones. 'The Conservatives feel that the BBC has given too great prominence to left-wing tendencies; the Socialists complain that the BBC has been too cautious in its handling of the essential economic and social controversies of the day. There are many men on both sides of the House who believe (rightly or wrongly) that the BBC has not maintained its original standards and has declined into cheapness and vulgarity.' The Board of Governors would have to take a stand, if only because it was less likely that monopoly as such would be challenged than that the attack would be on 'the present composition, powers, functions and efficacy of the Board itself'. [1]

Nicolson, whose general views were supported by Lady Violet Bonham Carter, [2] drew attention to four kinds of 'incoherence' – in any estimates of the 'powers' of the Governors, their 'purpose', their 'approach', and their 'method'. As far as the first were concerned, the 'incoherence' went back to the beginnings. 'Whereas the Postmaster-General has laid it down that our duties cover general policy only, and not administration, the Charter expressly empowers us to appoint and dismiss members of staff.' [3] It was impossible in practice to draw a sharp line between 'policy' – for the Governors – and 'administration' – for the Executive. Yet the Governors would be incapable of devoting 'intense and hourly application' to the affairs of the BBC, and the discipline of the staff would be weakened were they 'to look to the Board or even worse to individual Governors, as the arbiters of their punishments and awards'. In Nicolson's view, the Governors often wasted the time of the Director-General by 'discussing at length matters of administration'. Nonetheless, a future Parliamentary Committee 'so far from wishing to diminish the powers of the Board' would seek to increase them, probably by making the Board more 'representative'.

The Board on which Nicolson sat was remarkable in its willingness to discuss fundamental matters of principle, although Nicolson felt that members should never disagree openly with each other in the presence of Controllers and that they should

[1] Ibid. Foot disagreed strongly with this forecast. He thought that the attack would be on monopoly (Note of 12 Oct. 1943).

[2] Note by Lady Violet Bonham Carter, 13 Sept. 1943.

[3] For Tom Burns's comments on the initial 'incoherence' and its effects, see above p.55 n.1. Cf. E.G. Wedell, *Broadcasting and Public Policy* (1968), pp.110 ff.

prepare policy directives.[1] He detected a division, which may have been healthy at that time – although Lady Violet Bonham Carter did not think so [2] – between those Governors who felt 'that in anything we do we should have as our main purpose to raise the standard of public education, morals, enlightenment and taste' and those 'who feel that we should please the public and avoid giving them new and disturbing ideas'. Although Nicolson may have exaggerated, there was a policy issue here, often revived later. 'There is no consensus of opinion in the Board, for instance, as to whether we should emulate *The Times*, *The Manchester Guardian*, *The Telegraph*, *The Daily Express* or *John o' London's Weekly*. There is no consensus of opinion even as to our target audience. Do we, for instance, aim mainly at the educated, the half-educated, or the uneducated?'

The wartime Board, imbued with a Churchillian zest, was obviously seeking to provide a united leadership. 'The drive, impetus and conviction which are essential to the direction of a great enterprise,' Lady Violet exclaimed, 'cannot be born of compromise. They can only spring from unity of aim and purpose.' And Arthur Mann, the former editor of the Conservative *Yorkshire Post*, who demanded 'positive qualities in everything we put out on the air', concurred. 'If the microphone is to exert a healthy and inspiring influence upon the nation in a period of history when leadership, imagination and vision are most urgently needed there must be sound and far-seeing leadership and clear thought within the Corporation itself.'

Mann, who argued for a strong central Executive, composed of the Editor-in-Chief with two or three Assistant Editors and with the Director-General as *ex officio* Chairman, went into detail about sad lapses in talks, discussions, variety programmes and the standard of spoken English. He also urged far more news programmes. 'Our leadership and influence on the national life will depend entirely upon the degree to which our output commands both the respect and confidence of the people.'[3]

---

[1] Nicolson would have disputed the willingness of the Board to discuss principle. 'We are apt', he wrote, 'to drop a discussion of detail in the moment that it threatens to raise a matter of principle.'

[2] 'We do not, in fact, by our differences complement one another,' Lady Violet wrote. 'We tend instead to neutralize one another, to cancel one another out.'

[3] Board of Governors, *Papers*, Memorandum by Arthur Mann, 'Broadcasting as an Instrument of Democracy', 3 Oct. 1943.

Mann's interest in the internal structure of BBC committees went further than that of any other Governor. He argued forcefully, winning no support from his fellow Governors, that it was wrong that 'the present set-up leaves the D.G. in almost complete control' and that while 'in theory the Board of Governors decide higher policy, in practice we have become little more than figureheads'.[1] Graves had told him, he said, that 'no one man can carry the direction of policy and detail of the BBC', and he himself thought it was necessary to create 'a Central Executive composed of men free from departmental duties'.[2] The Governors then could take full account of what this Central Executive said.

At the same time, Mann's interest in such arrangements was related to his conception of the role of the BBC in national life. If it extended its news services, as he believed was essential, it would become increasingly vulnerable. The 'question of news presentation has an important bearing on the wider issue of control over broadcasting. Whether positive or negative, the influence of the BBC on the national life is already enormous, and is destined to increase still further as new techniques of short-wave transmission and television are developed.'[3]

This prescient comment preceded the return of post-war television. And Mann went on to relate change inside the BBC to change in society as a whole. While quoting the example of Churchill, he placed emphasis on changes in 'the character and outlook of the people' during the Second World War. Politicians were suspect, particularly if they dealt in slogans. There was criticism of anything that smacked of complacency, wishful thinking or cocksureness. The BBC should make war on cynicism, however, and should engage in 'friendly rivalry' with the Press.[4]

Mann's analysis of public taste did not go quite deep enough, but he recognised the need for innovation in programming as well as for responsibility. In this sense, too, he went further than some of the other Governors, although they were all prepared to back Haley in 1944 in seeking (against Churchill's inclinations)

[1] Mann to Powell, 4 March 1946.
[2] Mann to Powell, 14 March 1946; Mann to Powell, 4 March 1946.
[3] Mann to Powell, 4 March 1946.
[4] Mann, 'Broadcasting as an Instrument of Democracy', 3 Oct. 1943.

to extend 'controversial' broadcasting.[1] If the Governors did not support this, Lady Violet Bonham Carter argued, 'the responsibility will rest with us alone and it will be justly laid at our door'.[2]

Fraser had been reluctant at first about 'stirring up opinion' in wartime, and he was on his own in suggesting that if 'the only way to get television' was commercial sponsoring he would have been in favour of it. The Governors had explicitly rejected this approach on the eve of the war in 1939,[3] when the case against sponsoring had been made most forcefully not by a Governor or by the Director-General but by B.E. Nicolls, a senior BBC official. 'The question of sponsoring in Television', Nicolls maintained, 'raises that of sponsoring in Sound, and that in turn raises the far wider and ultimately more important issues of the comparative prestige abroad of the present "incorruptible" system as against the sponsoring system . . . The estimate of the revenue to be anticipated from sponsoring does not affect the principle but it may influence the decision.'[4]

Mann does not seem to have been particularly interested in this issue, but he continued to press the case for substantial internal reorganisation of the BBC after Foot had resigned, Haley had taken his place as Director-General, and the war had ended. Indeed, he had an acrimonious correspondence in 1946 with his Chairman. Powell, a Chamberlainite, and staunch anti-appeaser Mann can never have been close, and Mann was prepared to criticise Haley too. He even passed on to Powell a newspaper comment by a 'quite intelligent' radio critic that he had yet to hear of the Governors doing 'anything positive or useful for British radio', adding that 'the galling verdict' was justified 'because practically every suggestion for improving programmes made by a Governor is resisted or ignored or treated

[1] Board of Governors, *Minutes*, 15 June 1944; Programme Policy Meeting, *Minutes*, 1 Aug. 1944.

[2] Memorandum of 12 June 1944.

[3] A secret Treasury paper had been prepared supporting this for the Cabinet Committee on Overseas Broadcasting in February 1939 (Post Office Archives, A.B.C.(37)26). The Television Advisory Committee took the same line, although it noted the BBC's reservations. Some officials of the BBC, including the Chief Engineer, Sir Noel Ashbridge, were not hostile to sponsoring, and in a memorandum of 29 Jan. 1942 Gerald Beadle, later to be Director of BBC Television, envisaged that television shall 'be partly, at least, commercial'.

[4] B.E. Nicolls, Note on Sponsoring for Television, 17 Aug. 1939.

Sir William Haley

with contempt by the Executive'.[1] Mann's only criticism of
Haley was that 'he had set his face against the original Central
Executive scheme'.[2] If the Board had felt that Foot as Director-
General was overworked when he had Haley at his side as Editor-
in-Chief, how much more overworked must Haley be in 1946
when he had no Editor-in-Chief beside him.[3]

By the end of 1947 Haley was working with a new Board.
Mann left the Board, along with Lady Violet Bonham Carter, in
April 1946. Nicolson followed in July and Powell in December,
the latter to be succeeded briefly as Chairman by Lord Inman, a
member of the Labour Party.[4] Inman in turn was succeeded in
June 1947 by Lord Simon of Wythenshawe. It reads almost like a
Biblical genealogy. The other new members included an ex-
Conservative minister, Geoffrey Lloyd, and the youngest Governor to be appointed, Barbara Ward, at the age of 31. Lord Simon,
who decided almost from the moment of his appointment that he
would write a book on broadcasting, felt that Clement Attlee in
inviting him to serve was 'vague about the relation between the

[1] Mann to Powell, 4 March 1946.
[2] Mann to Powell, 25 March 1946.
[3] Mann to Powell, 16 March 1946.
[4] See below, pp.II/6–7. Inman stayed just long enough to have his name inserted in
the *BBC Year Book* for 1947 and deleted in an erratum slip.

Board and the Director-General'.[1] When Haley told him about 'the wisdom and importance of the Whitley Document' he was completely unconvinced. 'From the beginning I found it quite impossible to accept this view.'[2] Haley, who had known Simon in Manchester, wrote little publicly about their relationship;[3] Simon, as we shall see, wrote at length.[4]

It was Simon and Haley together who had to deal with a new Labour Government – with a huge majority until 1950 – with the first stirrings against the monopoly and the subsequent noisy campaigns against it, and with the long awaited official enquiry into broadcasting. In fact, the enquiry under the direction of one of the most prominent of wartime figures on the Home Front, the Liberal Lord Beveridge, did not begin its work until the autumn of 1949. Simon was at pains to tell Beveridge that the Whitley Document should go. The question was not without its interest to Beveridge, but to him there was a prior question which had to be settled: should the BBC's monopoly go? Both Simon and Haley were subject to tough questioning on the subject.[5]

Before the Committee met, the BBC's Charter was renewed in 1946 for a further five-year period, and it was explicitly stated by the new Government that 'the Government intend to ensure that the Governors of the Corporation are as representative as possible of the public which they serve'. 'It is on the Governors', the relevant White Paper declared, 'that the Charter places the responsibility for developing and exploiting the service "to the best advantage and in the national interest" and it is to them that the Director-General and all other officers of the Corporation are responsible for their actions.' While talking of 'the best possible talent' for Governors, the Government decided, nonetheless, to reduce their salaries.[6]

Meanwhile, Haley had reorganised the internal structure of the BBC on his own lines, not those of Mann, creating in 1947 a small Board of Management consisting of himself and five Directors. He had told Inman that he intended to do this, and Inman

[1] Note on an Interview with the Prime Minister, 25 May 1947.
[2] Simon, op.cit., p.61
[3] See below, p.155–6.   [4] See below, pp.93–4.
[5] Beveridge Committee, *Verbatim Evidence*, 34th Meeting, 18 May 1950.
[6] Cmd 6852 (1946), *Broadcasting Policy*, para. 23. The White Paper also announced that on the dissolution of the Ministry of Information on 31 March 1946 the powers under the Licence reverted to the Postmaster-General (para. 22).

had suggested that he should wait until he as Chairman had 'got to know the BBC better'. On the news of Inman's resignation, however, Haley presented his proposals direct to the Governors. In them he put considerable emphasis on the question of the succession. 'The Director-General is very much tied to his desk in Broadcasting House. Should anything happen to him the Governors would not find anyone trained whom they could even consider as his successor.'[1] Other matters raised by him were 'co-ordination' and the establishment of a new key post, Director of the Spoken Word. Yet there was to be no Television Director on the Board of Management, a historic omission which was to be a matter of argument with the Beveridge Committee and a factor in the eventual break-up of the BBC's monopoly.[2]

Before Simon took over as Chairman, even before the White Paper was published, the first salvos had been sounded against the BBC in a letter to *The Times* by the ex-Director-General, Sir Frederick Ogilvie. 'What is at stake is not a matter of politics, but of freedom. Is the monopoly of broadcasting to be fastened on us for a further term?' Monopoly of broadcasting, he had gone on, 'is inevitably the negation of freedom, no matter how efficiently it is run, or how wise and kindly the boards and committees in charge of it.'[3] Ogilvie mentioned 'the boards and committees' which ran the BBC, but not his successor as Director-General. Apparently he had drafted a memorandum before he left the Corporation focusing on 'the evils of monopoly and the gallant work of a very able and delightful executive staff in trying to overcome them'. The BBC itself, 'good as it is – would gain vastly by the abolition of monopoly and the introduction of competition. So would all the millions of listeners who would still have the BBC to listen to but would have other programmes to enjoy as well.'[4]

Ogilvie's outburst in 1946 was somewhat premature. Nor was it heeded by Lord Beveridge who presided over the protracted committee of enquiry. Beveridge began his enquiry as a determined liberal critic of monopoly; during the course of it, however, he came round to the view, as did the Chairmen of all

[1] 'The Executive Control of the BBC: Note by the Director-General', 23 May 1947.
[2] The matter is dealt with at length in *Sound and Vision*.
[3] *The Times*, 26 June 1946.
[4] Quoted in W. Altman, D. Thomas and D. Sawers, *TV: From Monopoly to Competition and Back?* (1962), p.28.

other public enquiries into broadcasting in this country, that 'the achievement of broadcasting in Britain is something of which any country might be proud'. He paid a 'tribute', therefore, both to the 'efficiency of the BBC, to the sense of public spirit which animates it, and to its substantial success in maintaining impartiality and high standards of taste and culture' and to Haley as Director-General. 'We count the country fortunate in having his service.'[1]

Like his fellow-Liberal, Lady Violet Bonham Carter, he urged the BBC to become more 'controversial'. 'We do not count among the dangers to be guarded against the danger of making occasional mistakes, or the danger of shocking established ways of thought or opinion. We hope that the broadcasters of the future will take the risk of making some mistakes and of offending some listeners.'[2] This advice was to be taken by Greene with consequences that Beveridge did not foresee.

During the course of the Beveridge enquiry many questions were asked and answered about the role of the Governors. In their written evidence they had emphasised one point themselves – that appointments to the Board should be 'staggered' so as to provide adequate continuity. It was a mistake to create the situation where the Board was divided, as it had been since the war, into 'two nearly equal groups of Governors – those with considerable experience on the one hand, and those who are relatively new to the work on the other'.[3] In his final oral evidence Simon stressed that the success of the BBC as an institution depended on the 'quality and experience' of the Governors, attributes it is never easy to judge from the outside either at the time or later. 'I am a different sort of person from the Director-General,' he began, and the Director-General would outlast him. Yet his task as Chairman had been 'by far the most responsible, and by far the most interesting' of any that he had tackled.[4]

Haley had somewhat qualified this picture earlier. 'The general conception of the Corporation is that there is a body of Governors who are the Corporation, and they are responsible for all its actions. But there is the professional body, which is the

[1] Cmd 8116 (1951), *Report of the Broadcasting Committee, 1949*, para. 183, p.47.

[2] Ibid., para. 186, p.48.

[3] Cmd 8117 (1951), *Report of the Broadcasting Committee, 1949: Memoranda Submitted to the Committee*, p.223.

[4] Beveridge Committee, *Verbatim Evidence*, 45th Meeting, 13 July 1950.

working part of the Corporation which does carry out the policy of the Governors and the Governors devolve to them from day to day the general broadcasting service.'[1] When asked if the Governors could keep a 'detailed check on all the professionals', he talked of the need for them to exercise 'a broad control'. Haley felt that for them to attend Board of Management meetings would be to confuse executive and policy-making functions.[2]

In its Report the Beveridge Committee listed 'the function, method of appointment, amount of service (whole or part-time) and tenure of the Governors' as the seventh of seven 'Fundamental Questions' which it felt had to be answered. It rejected the idea of 'assimilating them' to the board of a nationalised industry, a topical as well as a fundamental issue in that there had been several large-scale examples of nationalisation under the Labour Government and that nationalisation was a major – perhaps, then, *the* major – bone of contention between the Labour and Conservative Parties. The reason given for the rejection went back to 1926, however, not to 1946. 'The fundamental difference between a broadcasting authority and the board of a nationalised industry is that the former should not have, as the latter must have, a specialised Minister able to give directions of policy and to answer policy questions in Parliament.' It was the Governors, therefore, who were 'agents of democratic control'.

At this point a new notion was introduced into the historical discussion of Governors' powers. 'The Governors in effect must themselves undertake the function of the Minister, that of bringing outside opinion to bear upon all the activities of the permanent staff, of causing change where change is necessary, of preventing broadcasting from falling in any way into the hands of a bureaucracy which is not controlled.'[3]

There were three corollaries of this statement about the 'ministerial function' of the Governors. First, the Whitley Document should be thrown into the wastepaper basket and 'anything like it' should be resisted. Second, the Governors should have 'unquestioned authority over the staff, in detail as in principle'. Beveridge and his colleagues were at pains to insist that this 'unquestioned authority' was 'collective': 'they can decide and give orders to the staff only by resolutions of the Governors as a

---

[1] Ibid., 34th Meeting, 18 May 1950.   [2] Ibid., 38th Meeting, 14 June 1950.
[3] Cmd 8116 (1951), para., 209, p.52.

whole in formal session'.[1] Third, since the Governors were not elected or subject to 'stimulation by continuous criticism in Parliament', they should have an organ of their own for keeping them in continuous contact with public opinion, 'informed and uninformed'. The Committee proposed 'a Public Representation Service', headed by a new Director, to meet this requirement: it would deal with audience research, receipt of individual and group criticisms, the commissioning of critical reports, the servicing of advisory committees, and the study of broadcasting methods and programmes in other countries. The service would at last fulfil one key task in the discarded Whitley Document concerning the responsibility of Governors: 'to judge of the general effect of the service upon the public'.[2]

The basic recommendation of the Committee was that Governors should remain part-time, but that their remuneration should be increased and their possible length of service extended. The Chairman – and the choice of Chairman was described as 'critical' – was to be expected to make broadcasting his 'first interest', and to be 'a main link with the world outside and be active in the world outside'. The Committee stressed that Governors could and should 'take a more positive part in bringing new ideas into broadcasting than they do at present': 'attention to programmes' was their 'prime responsibility'. Moreover, specialisation should be permitted if it were thought wise: 'insofar as a tradition against specialisation exists, it should be broken down'.[3] In this context Beveridge quoted his favourite poet – a bone of contention between himself and the BBC programme-makers, who had not invited him to broadcast in the programmes marking the centenary of Wordsworth's death. The Whitley Document, it appeared, had been designed to make the Governors resemble Wordsworth's cloud

'. . . that heareth not the loud winds when they call,
And moveth altogether if it move at all.'

[1] Ibid., para. 555, p.166. For reference to the Whitley Document, see paras. 54, 554, 556, 575 and Appendix E, pp.282–3.

[2] Ibid., paras. 558–64, pp.167–9, and para. 574, p.172. BBC witnesses had been pressed in giving oral evidence to explain why the BBC had abolished its Public Relations Division (Beveridge Committee, *Verbatim Evidence*, 34th Meeting, 18 May 1950).

[3] Cmd 8116 (1951), paras 577, p.173, 210, p.52, and 556, p.167. See also Chapter 21 'Safeguards Against the Dangers of Monopoly' *passim*, pp.163–84. Paras 565–73 related to 'Programme Study by Governors'.

In future, 'any individual Governor ought to feel free with the assent of his fellows to inform himself about any problem or range of problems in broadcasting in which he has special interest or where he has special knowledge.' [1]

Finally, the Committee recommended that National Governors should be appointed for Scotland, Wales and Northern Ireland and that they should become the Chairmen of five-person Broadcasting Commissions in each of these national Regions. This had been one of the major issues raised in the oral sessions with the BBC, [2] and it marked the most significant extension of the representative principle in the history of the Board.

The Beveridge Committee saw the need for devolution, but did not want to 'break British broadcasting into fragments'. [3] By making the Chairmen of the Commissions Governors there would be the right links, it believed, between the national Regions and London. In the event, one existing Governor, Lord Clydesmuir, was appointed the National Governor for Scotland, and the BBC avoided having to draw upon the services of locally elected politicians, a danger which it greatly feared. The national Regional Commissions were called National Broadcasting Councils in Scotland and Wales, and Northern Ireland continued to have an Advisory Council whose Chairman was the National Governor.

The Beveridge Report was a very long report, and it went into far more detail than any previous report on the position of the Governors – as it did about almost everything else, except the one great issue of the future, television, the controversial issue taken up by the new Conservative Government. It even included a few paragraphs on the relationship between the Chairman of the Governors and the Director-General, referring *en passant* to Reith's autobiography. The Chairman of the Governors, it suggested, should attend Board of Management meetings, until then 'a solid phalanx of officials', as pre-war Chairmen had attended meetings of the Control Board. There should not even be a trace of suspicion that the only job of the Governors was to watch 'the

[1] Ibid., para. 556, p.167. There is a veiled reference to the contention in ibid., para. 569, p.170.

[2] Beveridge Committee, *Verbatim Evidence*, 34th Meeting, 18 May 1950.

[3] Cmd 8116 (1951), para. 535, p.161.

great broadcasting wheels go round'. The Chairman would be present as 'the representative of the policy deciding Corporation'.[1]

Lord Simon, backed by over forty years' wide and varied experience of public affairs, warmly approved of most of the sections of the Beveridge Report relating to the duties of the Chairman and the Governors, although he believed that the Chairman should serve for more than five years and that preferably he should have been a Governor or Vice-Chairman for two years before becoming Chairman. He went further than Beveridge in suggesting that Governors should spend one to two days a week on their tasks, not half a day. (They then, as now, held fortnightly Board meetings.) Simon had always disliked Reith's approach to broadcasting organisation not only as set out in the Whitley Document, but as encapsulated in what he called Reith's 'unfortunate and even disastrous phrase – "the brute force of monopoly"', and he wanted the Chairman to have far more responsibilities.[2]

The kind of tasks which Reith envisaged the Chairman doing – presiding over Board meetings, dealing with correspondence and representing the Corporation formally – could be done in less than one day a week. Simon, however, devoted four days a week to the BBC. He used the rest of his BBC time first to listen to and to view programmes, second to travel round the Regions, and third to talk to staff and 'outsiders'. He was the first to spend much of his time in the Chairman's office at Broadcasting House, but he also used his Westminster flat to talk to staff and (along with his formidable wife) to try to entertain them.

The BBC from Within provides an account of his side – and his side only – of the relationship between Chairman and Director-General, which he admitted would be a difficult one if both of them were 'men with strong personalities'. If they both agreed, of course, he explained, no one could challenge them.[3] Simon dwelt, not without a touch of envy, on the vast amount of *de facto* power the Director-General had at his disposal and resented the fact that he had never been invited to Board of Management meet-

---

[1] Ibid., paras. 580, pp.173–4, and 581, p.174. The Board of Management met every Monday afternoon. On policy and major questions, recommendations were made to the Governors: on all other matters, the Board of Management took decisions. A Director-General's (finance) meeting was held every Wednesday morning.

[2] Simon, op.cit., pp.55, 50.   [3] Ibid., p.63.

ings even after the publication of the Beveridge Report.[1] He recognised that a full-time Chairman would be in danger of undermining the responsibility of the Director-General, but he was insensitive to BBC criticisms that he himself – serving almost as a full-time Chairman – was sometimes acting in parallel with the Director-General and was occasionally pressing senior (and even junior) members of BBC staff into talking more about internal organisation than they wished or thought wise.

His own judgement could be suspect, as was shown in his unilateral decision to ban the retransmission of a Val Gielgud play which he held to be against the interests of parliamentary democracy;[2] and although there was a basic truth in his statement that 'the Chairman tends to take an outside view of the Corporation and the Director-General an inside view',[3] things did not quite work out in that way. Politics cannot be left out of the picture in the years 1950–2, years of stronger contention in British politics than any since the late 1930s, with the contention centred mainly on domestic issues. Simon's position as a Labour peer influenced him in 1950 and placed him in immediate difficulties when a Conservative Government was returned following the general election of October 1951. Although he believed that Chairmen of the BBC should serve for longer terms – normally of ten years in two spells of five, following two years as Governors – he did not face up to the fact that these would be very long terms indeed in relation to the rhythms of British party politics.

In fact the new Conservative Government did allow Governors to serve for a second term.[4] On the other hand, the appointments to Governorships in 1952 were made in such a way that none of the nine Governors who were on the Board under the new Charter had served for more than two-and-a-half years, and five of them, including the Chairman Sir Alexander Cadogan (who replaced Simon in August 1952) were completely new to the job.

It was not so much Simon's views on constitutional and administrative responsibilities that caused problems as his personality and politics. Yet it should be added that he made an important point which has echoed through the history of the BBC. 'As regards criticism, my habit, developed mainly in competitive

[1] Ibid., p.58.   [2] See below, pp.206–9.   [3] Simon, op.cit., p.60.
[4] Cmd 8605 (1952), *Broadcasting* (the Fourth Charter of the BBC), para. 8(1).

industry, has been constantly to seek and welcome criticism and to try hard to use it to make my own concerns more efficient. I did not find this to be the case in the BBC.' [1]

Nonetheless the BBC – with Simon as Chairman – did not choose to appoint a Director of Public Representation following the Beveridge proposals. The Governors asked, instead, for more reports from outside experts. This was one sign of independence. Another was fierce resistance to the dying Labour Government's proposal that local authorities should nominate members of the new National Broadcasting Commissions for Scotland, Wales and Northern Ireland. [2] This was an unpopular suggestion inside and outside the BBC, [3] and no action had been taken to implement it before the Conservative victory at the general election. The new Government extended the existing Charter until 30 June 1952 and asked the old Board of Governors, including the Chairman, to carry on until that date.

The Governors had spent an enormous amount of their time over the previous two years preparing for Beveridge, meeting Beveridge and examining the Beveridge recommendations. Indeed, the existence of the Committee of Enquiry determined the pattern of their work, including its timetable, more than any personal interests or constitutional doctrines. There was a revealing exchange between Haley and Beveridge during the oral sessions after Haley had claimed that the existence of the Beveridge Committee was one of the public safeguards against abuses by the BBC. 'You do not want this Committee again for a good many years, do you?' Beveridge asked. 'We do not, if we can avoid it,' Haley replied. 'We do not think we shall be able to avoid it.' [4]

By the end of 1951 the result of the general election was proving more important to the BBC than the Beveridge proposals, and the Governors were moving again into unknown territories. They had decided in May 1950 that they did not need a formal document setting out their functions and duties, and

[1] Simon, op.cit., p.60.

[2] Cmd 8291 (1951), *Memorandum on the Report of the Broadcasting Committee 1949*, para. 20, p.7.

[3] A strong BBC protest was sent by Simon to Herbert Morrison, 2 March 1951. Another full statement was 'Observations by the Governors of the BBC on the Government's Memorandum', July 1951.

[4] Beveridge Committee, *Verbatim Evidence*, 34th Meeting, 18 May 1950.

Lord Simon of Wythenshawe and Lady Reading

when Simon recirculated an old Foot two-page note of March 1944 on the subject they responded by saying that they did not think any such note 'necessary' or 'desirable'. 'The Document,' their minute reads memorably, 'was therefore annulled,' and it is crossed out, if not totally obliterated, in the file of numbered Governors' Papers for 1950.[1] This may have been a rebuke for Simon, who had asked Governors to see it, since the Governors (with Lady Reading, John Adamson, Lord Clydesmuir, Ernest Whitfield and Professor Barbara Wootton present)[2] expressed 'their complete confidence' in the Director-General.

Before the Conservative Government worked out its own broadcasting proposals – and under persistent pressure there were sharp differences within the party about what they should be – the Governors were trying to steer their way into the unknown future while still dealing with the aftermath of Beveridge, who was never consulted by the new Government about his Report.

No new Governors were appointed between January 1951 and

[1] Board of Governors, *Minutes*, 11 May 1950: 'Note on the Position and Functions of the Governors', 21 March 1944, adopted at the Board Meeting of 30 March 1944.
[2] For brief profiles of these Governors, see below, pp.152–3, 157.

August 1952, although two had been appointed in January 1951 – Ivan Stedeford, a former member of the Beveridge Committee, who was specially interested in finance, and Francis Williams, a close associate of Attlee. In the same month Marshal of the Royal Air Force Lord Tedder, appointed a Governor a year before, became Vice-Chairman. It was a relatively experienced Board, therefore, which was confronted with the first Government White Paper to break with 'traditional' broadcasting policy in May 1952. This was the White Paper which included 'a Trojan Horse clause' [1] – 'In the expanding field of television, provision should be made to permit some element of competition when the calls on capital resources at present needed for purposes of greater national importance make this feasible.' [2]

There were links, of course, between this clause and Selwyn Lloyd's minority report which was printed as a one-man appendix to the Beveridge Report. [3] And there were links also, of course, between this clause and the first Television Act of 1954 which broke the BBC's monopoly. In retrospect there was an inevitability about the outcome – the break-up of the monopoly – which was not always apparent at the time. There was also a noisy battle both of opinions and of interests. From the sidelines, Reith believed that if the Governors had planned a 'military campaign' to protect BBC interests they would have been able to outwit a divided and vacillating Government. Instead they spent their time 'toadying to the Mother of Abominations', the House of Commons. [4] There is no evidence to support this view.

It was a serious blow to them, however, when Haley, who for some time had been contemplating a move from the BBC, resigned as Director-General in June 1952 to take over the editorship of *The Times*. The Governors were now alone. They were sharply critical of one proposal in the new White Paper which had nothing to do with commercial television at all – the proposal that in future they should not be appointed by the Crown on the advice of the Prime Minister, but that they should be selected instead by a small committee. And whether they liked it or not, they had to pay attention to Herbert Morrison's state-

[1] *Annual Register*, 1952, p.38.
[2] Cmd 8550 (1952), *Broadcasting, Memorandum on the Report of the Broadcasting Committee, 1949*, para. 7.
[3] Cmd 8116 (1951), pp.201–10.
[4] Reith, *Diary*, 25 April, 29 March 1952.

Sir Ian Jacob

ment in the parliamentary debate on the White Paper that 'they should not regard themselves as a mere advisory committee to the Director-General. They are the masters of the show. They are the captains of the ship.'[1]

Their first task, however, was to appoint a Director-General. B.E. Nicolls, a BBC veteran, who had joined the old British Broadcasting Company in 1924, was made Acting Director-General 'until such time as a permanent appointment can be made'.[2] He would have liked to become Director-General, and from the outside Reith, for one, would have approved of his selection.[3] Nicolls was then 58 years old, and his chief rival inside the BBC, George Barnes, was 47. Instead the Governors chose Sir Ian Jacob, a former soldier, close to Churchill, who in 1952 was on secondment from the BBC as Chief Staff Officer to the Ministry of Defence. Jacob was 53 years old, and took up his post on 1 December 1952.[4] *The Times* stressed the continuity. 'Sir Ian Jacob has been chosen to safeguard and to keep fresh and con-

---

[1] *Hansard*, vol. 502, col.236, 11 June 1952. For an earlier Morrison statement, see Simon, op.cit., p.49: 'The Governors *are* the BBC.'

[2] Press release issued by the Governors: *Minutes*, 17 July 1952.

[3] Reith, *Diary*, 7, 8 Oct. 1952.

[4] He was interviewed by the Governors in October and his appointment was announced then (*Minutes*, 2, 8 Oct. 1952).

temporary the tradition of British broadcasting created by Lord Reith.'[1] Reith disputed this, and Jacob himself – with a very different background from any of his predecessors – was prepared not only for new styles but for new men and new measures.[2] He remained Director-General until 1960, when he was sixty years old, so that his period of office spanned the break-up of the monopoly, the transition from sound broadcasting to television as the major medium, and the advent of fierce competition with the commercial companies.

Jacob's personal qualities fitted him for this age of transition. He was a fighter, and he had to fight. He had none of the doubts about television which had been shared by Reith and Haley – and possibly Ogilvie. And he knew many people outside the BBC. Indeed, his standing in the community derived as much from his pre-BBC activities as from his position as Director-General, and after he ceased to be Director-General he held a wide variety of posts. He was the first Director-General to emerge from Bush House rather than Broadcasting House, and he was in a strong position, therefore, to resist Government moves to cut the BBC's External Services. He was a good manager and, like his predecessors, drew individual members of his Board of Management, which still met on Mondays, into Board meetings with the Chairman's approval. The Chairman, however, did not attend Board of Management meetings. This time neither of them felt that it was either desirable or necessary. Jacob had attended Board of Management meetings himself, of course, before becoming Director-General, and at Simon's invitation had occasionally attended Board Meetings.

As Director-General Jacob never had to work with Simon, for by the time he took over, the diplomat Sir Alexander Cadogan, whom he knew from pre-BBC days, had become Chairman. Moreover, on 1 August 1952 five other new Governors were appointed at the same time as Cadogan: Lady Rhys Williams, Sir Henry Mulholland (National Governor for Northern Ireland), Lord Macdonald of Gwaenysgor (National Governor for Wales) and Sir Philip Morris (later to be Vice-Chairman in 1954). A very new team of Governors, therefore, was dealing with a very new Director-General at a crucial point in the BBC's history, although the new Chairman was assured by his prede-

[1] *The Times*, 9 Oct. 1952.   [2] Reith, *Diary*, 17 Dec. 1952

cessor that he was inheriting 'an admirable machine'.[1] Elements
of continuity were represented by Stedeford, who continued to
'specialise' in finance, Lord Tedder, who stayed until June 1954,
Lord Clydesmuir, who had been a Governor since January 1950
and now became National Governor for Scotland, and Professor
Barbara Wootton. The last three had all joined the Board at the
same time – 1 January 1950.[2]

Five Governors were present at Simon's last Board meeting on
30 July 1952, which Cadogan attended by invitation, and Clydesmuir was the only one of the five present at the next meeting on 4
September. Not surprisingly, the first item on the agenda was
future arrangements for Board meetings. It was decided to adhere to the existing arrangements of meeting on alternate Thurs-
days from 4 September onwards. 'The forthcoming establishment of National Broadcasting Councils' figured prominently on
the agenda also: they were to come into operation on 1 April
1953.[3] The Governors also had to find a new head of the Third
Programme, a programme which was already under attack.
Television was discussed only as a minor item, although the
Board approved of a proposal by Nicolls to put in an application
to Government for permission to go ahead with five low-power
stations and noted that a commercial company with which Lord
Duncannon and Norman Collins were associated had applied for
a television operating licence. 'It seemed unlikely,' they agreed,
'that the Postmaster-General would approve the application at
present.'[4] On taking up his appointment Cadogan had confessed
that he had never seen a BBC television programme and that
what he had seen of American television he had disliked.[5]

A statement of Stedeford revealed a new approach to broadcasting development which Jacob was to share. 'It was a questionable policy', Stedeford stated, 'for the BBC to delay development
of its services for financial reasons when the Corporation had
power to borrow.' It was agreed to discuss this point when ten-
year estimates were before the Board.[6] Haley had maintained
large reserves and the Governors had backed him; Jacob, who
saw that borrowing was reasonable if large increases in income

[1] D. Dilks (ed.), *The Diaries of Sir Alexander Cadogan* (1971), p.792.
[2] See below, pp. 156–7.
[3] Board of Governors, *Minutes*, 4 Sept. 1952.
[4] Ibid.
[5] Dilks, op.cit., p.792.   [6] Board of Governors, *Minutes*, 4 Sept. 1952.

Sir Alexander Cadogan

would flow into the BBC coffers from a massive expansion in the number of television licences, introduced something like corporate planning. The Board of Management had re-examined the BBC's five-year and ten-year forecasts in July 1952, and in March 1953 the Governors approved in principle a new 'Ten-Year Plan'.[1] When Government procrastinated, Jacob tried to get in the lead. 'We must be alert, and one jump ahead of events,' he told the first General Liaison meeting which he addressed in June 1953.[2]

The relationship between Jacob as Director-General and Cadogan as Chairman was close and easy. Indeed, there had been complaints in the Press that it might be too close and easy: 'Too many Brass Hats' in the BBC was one headline.[3] Cadogan appeared in his small office in Broadcasting House three days a week. It had never been his habit in any of his previous posts to 'jog the elbows of those who bore the chief responsibility', and he himself said of his relationship with the Director-General that it was 'pleasant' and that 'he seems to suffer me gladly, though it must waste a lot of his time putting me wise'.[4] Jacob for his part

[1] Ibid., 5 March 1953.
[2] General Liaison meeting, record, 16 June 1953. General Liaison meetings, introduced by Haley, were attended by senior staff from all sections of the BBC. They were not held at fixed intervals.
[3] *Reynolds News*, 7 Dec. 1952.   [4] Dilks, op.cit., p.792.

expected his Chairman not only 'to run the Board properly' but
to come to the aid of the BBC wherever there was 'some kind of
contretemps or crisis . . . between the Government and the
BBC'. Jacob found working with the enlarged Board for the most
part pleasant and effective, although he had difficulties with
Lady Rhys Williams somewhat similar to those Reith had had
with Lady Snowden. Liberal, intelligent and unbelievably in-
dustrious, Lady Rhys Williams, who *inter alia* was Chairman of
the United Europe Movement, did not appreciate the difference
between policy making and executive action. She had many
pet ideas of her own, and was reluctant to accept compromise
solutions. She seems to have been taken in hand by the other
Governors, however, when she was being exceptionally
'difficult'.[1]

While fighting what proved to be a losing battle against the
introduction of commercial television, there was ample room not
only for 'contretemps or crisis between Government and BBC'
but also for considerable differences of opinion among Governors
about the right tactics to employ.[2] At the same time the Governors were drawn into rather more discussion of individual programmes than had been the case during the Simon/Haley
regime, and several 'doubtful' programmes were discussed by the
Board before being broadcast. Jacob decided which ones to put
on the agenda, and chose in particular those which seemed to
introduce a new element into broadcasting like the series *This is
Your Life*. Cadogan confided to his diary that unless the Governors saw selected scripts in advance they could 'only pick up
bricks already dropped', which he found 'undignified and not
very effective'.[3]

The intervention of the Chairman and Director-General was
not reserved to such cases. Before the Suez crisis of 1956 in which
the BBC and Cadogan played a prominent and difficult part,[4]
there had been several controversial decisions. Thus, both Jacob

[1] BBC transcript of interview with Sir Ian Jacob, 6 Oct. 1976.

[2] The story is dealt with at length in my volume *Sound and Vision*. One argument
often employed by the opponents of commercial television was that the issue was not
whether television should be run by 'Whitehall' or by 'the people', but whether it
should be run 'by persons answerable to the representatives of what is compendiously
called "big business"' (*The Times*, 30 Oct. 1953).

[3] Dilks, op.cit., p.793.

[4] See below, pp.209–17 and Sir Ian Jacob, 'The Suez Crisis and the BBC' in *Ariel*,
Jan. 1957.

and Cadogan – independently and with no Government pressure – decided in January 1953 not to put out a critical *International Commentary* talk by a former Minister on the creation of a Central African Federation while official discussions were in progress, and their decision was endorsed by the Governors. 'They regretted, however, that the cancellation had had to be made at the last minute, and felt that the consideration which had led to it might have been evident at an earlier stage.' [1]

At the same meeting when the issue was discussed, the Governors rejected a strong Foreign Office protest against the BBC's decision to broadcast Professor Toynbee's Reith Lectures in the External Services 'as being against the national interest in the cold war'. They agreed to a reply stating that 'in the BBC's view any disadvantage to the anti-Communist cause from the broadcasting abroad of Professor Toynbee's controversial views would not be so great as the damage which would be done both to the BBC's reputation and to the cause of free speech by the deliberate suppression of lectures which were well known to be broadcast normally in the External Services'. Cadogan personally refused at a later date to submit scripts for a projected television programme on nuclear warfare to the Government on the grounds that it would be both impossible and undesirable, and likewise refused to discuss with Government a contemplated programme – eventually not completed – about the experiences of prisoners of war in enemy hands. Intimate though he was with Ministers, he refused to compromise the BBC's 'independence'. It would be 'fatal', he thought, 'to relegate us to the position of an organ of the Government.' [2]

While the Governors had some difficulties with the Government during the late 1950s, they also met the first sustained organised opposition to their policies from a significant minority section of the public. Faced with the decision in April 1957 to change the pattern of sound broadcasting – including the demise of the Third Programme as it had existed earlier and the introduction of Network Three – the Sound Broadcasting Society, formerly the Third Programme Defence Society, launched a forceful attack on Corporation policy. Its chairman, Peter Laslett, had worked inside the BBC, and he mobilised the support

[1] Board of Governors, *Minutes*, 8 Jan. 1953.
[2] Quoted Dilks, op.cit., p.794.

amongst others of T.S. Eliot, Dr Ralph Vaughan Williams and Sir Laurence Olivier.[1] A deputation which included these three outstanding public figures met the Governors in July 1957.[2] Letters were exchanged in *The Times*, with Cadogan coming off worst,[3] but despite the galaxy of talent arrayed against the BBC, Cadogan's confident statement that the plans for changes in sound broadcasting were 'a sensible, realistic and honest attempt to cater for the varying taste of the community' prevailed.

In fact, the policy for sound broadcasting was already less a matter of concern to the majority than television policy, and just as important after 1955 as relations between BBC and Government were relations between BBC and ITA. At the first meeting of the Board after the start of Independent Television, Cadogan found it necessary to explain to the members why he and Jacob had accepted an invitation to ITA's inaugural dinner at Guildhall.[4] Amid the glitter, Sir Kenneth Clark, the first Chairman of the ITA, had described the new Authority as 'an experiment in the art of government'. 'Free television, like the free Press,' he went on, 'would not be controlled by any committee but by the television companies.'[5] Jacob was impressed neither by the glitter nor the speeches, and in his review for the Governors of the first week's television programmes, he maintained that no new ideas had been apparent in them. He was followed by Lord Macdonald, who echoed a very familiar theme of the old National Television Council (opposed to commercial television) when he urged the BBC to maintain its standards and the quality of its programmes in the face of competition.[6]

At first there seemed little reason to urge any change in BBC policy. During the early months of competition the Board was concerned mostly with the problems of peaceful co-existence with the ITA: the problems of sharing the use of the Crystal Palace mast; common interests such as copyright in television,

[1] Foreign support came from Albert Camus, Jean Cocteau, Gabriel Marcel, Jacques Maritain, Lionel Trilling and others.
[2] See *Unsound Broadcasting, the Case Against the BBC's New Policy* (1957).
[3] *The Times*, 26 April, 3 May 1957.
[4] Board of Governors, *Minutes*, 29 Sept. 1955.
[5] *Daily Telegraph*, 23 Sept. 1955.
[6] Board of Governors, *Minutes*, 29 Sept. 1955. For the determination to maintain standards, see H. Grisewood, *One Thing at a Time* (1968), p.185. See also a memorandum he wrote for Jacob on the policy implications of the end of the monopoly, 29 May 1953.

labour relations, and audience research; discussions on the use of BBC coaxial lines and the televising of royal occasions when only one television camera could be accommodated. The two broadcasting organisations also shared thoughts about political broadcasting and the inhibiting 'Fourteen Day' rule, which held back political broadcasting far more than any particular governmental pressure or intervention in programming. There were discussions, too, as to whether the ITA should accept advice from the BBC's Central Religious Advisory Committee.[1]

The relationship changed as the new commercial companies acquired an increasing share of the growing television audience. Over the first three months of competition the BBC/ITV ratio was 54:46. A year later it had dropped to 38:62, and by the summer of 1957 it reached the nadir of 28:72.[2] The Governors' reactions can be traced in successive Board papers. Thus, by September 1956 the Board was focusing on 'the preoccupation of commercial television with light entertainment', adding that this was to be expected since the programme companies were 'in direct contact with the advertisers who, as they provide the funds of the programmes, are exclusively interested in the number of viewers ("viewership").' One of the two London companies, Associated Television (ATV), responsible for output on Saturdays and Sundays, had from the beginning stated its intention to gain a majority audience by 'straightforward entertainment', and this aim had never changed.

The other London company, Associated-Rediffusion (A-R), responsible for output on weekdays, had begun with programmes 'reminiscent in some ways of the BBC', but it had 'cut out most of its more intelligent programmes, or shortened them, and put them late in the evening'. As for the regional companies, despite initial claims that they would give more stress to programmes of local origin and content than did the BBC, all of them, with the exception of Granada, the weekday company at Manchester, had turned more and more to material 'of metropolitan origin

[1] The Fourteen Day rule had been operated by the BBC since 1944 and was codified in a specific regulation by the Postmaster-General, then Charles Hill, in July 1955, and reluctantly accepted at that stage by the BBC. It was not revoked until 1956 (see *BBC Handbook 1960*, p.162). On 17 August 1955 Clark and Cadogan met to consider joint action. See also Board *Minutes*, 15 Sept. 1955. The story is dealt with at length in *Sound and Vision*.
[2] Audience Research Bulletins, 1955, 1956, 1957.

and content'. The Governors quoted Howard Thomas, a former BBC producer, then in charge of ABC's Manchester weekend programme, who had remarked that its audience had shown that it did not want local material: 'it's a pity, but there it is'. [1]

Irritation about what was happening was manifest in statements made to the Governors by officials of the BBC, so that they were not reaching these verdicts on their own. Thus in May 1957, Cecil McGivern, then Deputy Director of Television, reported to the Governors that 'in this so-called competitive television situation, there are some unpleasant things. The spokesmen of ITA are not content simply to praise the output, aims and plans of ITA, which would be legitimate, but they seem unable to refrain from criticising the BBC, giving the impression that the BBC's very existence is an irritation and an upset and they would be happy only if the BBC ceased to exist.' [2]

There was an improvement in the ratios by March 1958, when the Board sent its congratulations to the staff of the Television Service 'on their success in substantially redressing the Band III audience ratio in favour of BBC programmes, noting that this had been achieved by a steady improvement in the quality of output, without lowering of standards'. [3] The ratio at the time was 42:58, but the average over that first quarter of 1958 was only 38:62, and it was not until the last quarter of 1962 that the BBC finally achieved parity with ITV. [4] Anxieties had remained during the late 1950s even when there were lulls in the 'battle of the figures', and they brought the television staff of the BBC into a rather special relationship with the Governors. 'It is simply no good telling television staff to forget the Band III figures and to get on with the job,' McGivern told the Board in April 1958, possibly with an eye on Jacob. 'The television staff is considerably concerned with the future of the BBC, some of them because of their interest in the BBC itself, many of them because of their own future.' [5]

In dealing with 'the competitor', as commercial television was

[1] Board of Governors, *Papers*, 'Commercial Television – the First Year', 20 Sept. 1956.
[2] 'Report by the Deputy Director of Television Broadcasting, 1 January–31 March 1957'.
[3] Board of Governors, *Minutes*, 27 March 1958.
[4] Audience Research Bulletins, 1958, 1962.
[5] 'Report by the Director of Television Broadcasting, 1 January–31 March 1958'.

always called inside the BBC, the Board was not acting like the board of a commercial company. It had no financial interest in what was happening and was doubtless amused when rumours circulated in 1958 that many of the commercial programme contractors were concerned that they were making too much money.[1] It was greatly concerned, however, with what the next large-scale official enquiry into British broadcasting, the Pilkington Committee, set up in 1960, was to call the 'realisation of the purposes of broadcasting as defined in the Charter'.[2] The limitations were set by the amount of revenue derived from licence fees, although this continued to rise as the television audience increased.

Before there was any talk of alternating programmes there were approaches in 1959 from the Chairman of one television company, Associated-Rediffusion, to see whether ITV and BBC might not co-operate in producing 'real alternative programmes'. Spencer Wills, the A-R Chairman, felt that the two services were watching 'each other very closely and tended to match programmes against each other so that too often the same kind of programme was going on in both services'. Interestingly enough, the approaches were made to Jacob, not to the new BBC Chairman, Sir Arthur fforde, who took over from Cadogan in December 1957 after retiring as Headmaster of Rugby School. The Board felt that the subject deserved full consideration and asked Jacob to prepare a paper. He and the Board concluded that 'cooperation could have little reality without machinery for joint planning' and that joint planning was not practicable 'except perhaps where certain world events like the Olympic Games and the World Football Cup were concerned'.[3]

Wills's approach to Jacob was based on a hint from the Postmaster-General that there was likely to be an early enquiry into the possibility of new services in Bands IV and V,[4] and from then on the Board of Governors became increasingly concerned

[1] 'Report by the Director of Television Broadcasting, April–June 1958'. He explained that they feared a tax on television. They were planning *inter alia* to distribute £10,000 a year to the arts. 'They appear to be adopting the role of patron of the Arts which, until the war, was the BBC's role, later taken over by the Arts Council.'

[2] Cmnd 1753 (1962), *Report of the Committee on Broadcasting, 1960*, para. 468, p.137.

[3] Board of Governors, *Minutes*, 16 April 1959.

[4] Board of Management, *Papers*, 'Relations with Independent Television: Note by the Director-General', 11 March 1958.

with the jockeying for position before the appointment of what was to become the Pilkington Committee. ITV's effective use of Press advertising prompted the Board to authorise a study by Colman, Prentis and Varley, the well-known advertising agents, into whether it would pay the BBC to follow suit. The Board decided against any plan of Press advertising, not because of any deficiency on the part of Colman, Prentis and Varley, but because 'by buying space in newspapers to advertise itself, its staff, and its broadcasts, the BBC would seem to be abandoning, in the most public way, that national status which it had earned from its foundation'.[1] However, elaborate plans were made for improving press and publicity work, including BBC exhibits at important trade fairs, open days at transmitting stations, new pamphlets and even a new film, *This is the BBC,* a remarkable and still enlightening documentary made by Richard Cawston.[2]

At the same time, the Governors submitted to the General Advisory Council a long and thoughtful paper on 'The Future of Television', which was essentially concerned with plans for another television network. 'The matter is currently being presented in the press and elsewhere as though the right to start an additional service is a prize for which the BBC and the ITA are in competition. This is regrettable, but it is something that the BBC must take into account in considering its case for a second programme.'[3]

There was to be no second channel until 1964, and by then the Pilkington Committee had come and gone, the BBC had a brand-new Charter, and there was a new Television Act on the statute book. The Pilkington Committee, more interested in output, perhaps, than were previous committees of enquiry, praised the BBC for providing 'good broadcasting', thereby setting 'a standard of public service'. It disposed of the 'misconceived' argument that the BBC should by-pass competition and restrict what it offered to 'the educative and educational aspects of television'.[4] It reserved its programme criticism for the commercial companies and the network they had built up between 1955 and 1960.

[1] 'Public Relations: Press Advertising – note by the Director-General', 18 Sept. 1958.   [2] Ibid.
[3] 'The Future of Television', 16 Sept. 1958.
[4] Cmnd 1753 (1962), paras. 468–9, pp.137–8.

The Governors had been told in January 1960 at the first meeting which Hugh Carleton Greene attended as Director-General that 'the announcement of the Government's intention to appoint a Committee of Enquiry could be expected in the near future'.[1] The decision was announced, in fact, in July[2] – when it was stated that the existing Charter would run until 1964 – and the membership published in September 1960. Thereafter, the Governors spent as much time discussing Pilkington as their predecessors had discussing Beveridge. They agreed at their first October meeting that Harman Grisewood, Chief Assistant to the Director-General, and Maurice Farquharson, the Secretary, should be asked to take part in all the Board's discussions on this 'standing item', and at their second with Greene's proposal to invite television producers to offer their views on the effects of the introduction of competition in television.[3] There were hints of the future in a remark that 'interest had been expressed also in the principles governing the selection of news'.[4]

It is difficult to judge from the minutes to what extent Governors were themselves involved in the presentation of the case to Pilkington, which was a highly planned operation. Yet when the Report appeared, they were quick warmly to congratulate the Director-General 'on the acceptance by the Committee of the BBC's recommendations'.[5] 'The Corporation welcomes the Report', it was stated in a Press communiqué, 'as a comprehensive survey of broadcasting and its future. It hopes to be empowered, a soon as possible, to carry out those recommendations which affect the BBC.'

None of the BBC's published evidence refers to the Governors, except the very brief paper on the constitutional position of the BBC, which is mainly concerned with the powers not of the

[1] Board of Governors, *Minutes*, 14 Jan. 1960.

[2] Cmnd 1753 (1962), para. 1, p.1. On 16 June 1960 (Board, *Minutes*) the Board was told by Greene that a Chairman had not by then been found. The BBC had submitted the name of Humphrey Mynors.

[3] Board of Governors, *Minutes*, 6, 20 Oct. 1960.

[4] Ibid., 20 Oct. 1960.

[5] Ibid., 27 June 1962. This was a special meeting. The Board had discussed how to deal with the reception of the Report at its previous meeting (*Minutes*, 21 June 1962). They agreed not to make individual statements about it and to make their initial collective statements brief. The hope was expressed that the National Broadcasting Councils would also confine themselves to brief formal statements. Later Pilkington expressed gratitude for the BBC's 'reticence on the subject of the Report' (ibid., 2 Aug. 1962).

Governors but of the Government. 'The Corporation is very conscious of the fact,' the key sentence reads, 'that the traditional freedom of the broadcasting service from Government control needs for its preservation a continuing vigilance on the part both of the Corporation itself and on the part of successive Governments. Otherwise, that freedom could easily be eroded.'[1] It was left to Sir Ian Jacob, the ex-Director-General, to state that the Charter invested the Governors 'with full responsibility, and power over the whole broadcasting operation which is thus a unity'. A Charter, he argued, conveyed much greater independence than an Act of Parliament and conveyed greater responsibility, and the preservation of the Charter 'intact in essentials' was of 'great importance'.[2]

The Pilkington Committee rejected the idea of a Broadcast Consumers' Council, which had been put forward by a member the Viewers' and Listeners' Association, on the grounds that it would reduce the status of the public corporations and raise doubts as to where responsibility lay: 'which, the public corporation or the council, would be the guardian of the public interest in broadcasting?' 'In fact, the task envisaged for it is part of what the Governors and Members [of the ITA] are themselves appointed to undertake.'[3]

The rejection did not kill the idea, which was revived – and rejected again, this time by the Government – in 1966,[4] even though it was accompanied in the Pilkington Report by statements that the Governors and Members should 'welcome, and indeed invite, criticism,' and that the Authorities' annual reports

[1] Cmnd 1819 (1962), *Report of the Committee on Broadcasting, 1960: Memoranda submitted to the Committee*, Vol. I, Appendix E, p.204.

[2] Ibid., Vol. II, Appendix E, p.1133.

[3] Cmnd 1753 (1962), para. 426, p.127. The Viewers' and Listeners' Association was founded by members of the former Third Programme Defence Society (see above pp.103–4). Peter Laslett, its energetic chairman, explained in a letter to *The Guardian*, 25 June 1965, that the VLA had no connection with Mrs Whitehouse's National Viewers' and Listeners' Association.

[4] Cmnd 3169 (1966), *Broadcasting*, para. 49, pp.10–11: 'The Government has discussed with the broadcasting authorities, and with other parties in Parliament the idea of establishing . . . a council to consider general issues of broadcasting policy. They have concluded that additional machinery of this sort would serve little useful purpose if the independence of the two public corporations is to be maintained. Since full responsibility is required of them, they must be afforded full authority to secure that their services are conducted in the general interest.'

should 'be the occasion for an explanation of policy and for a revealing examination of criticisms'.[1]

In the sections of the Report dealing with the Governors, many of the points raised about Governors in previous Reports were repeated in slightly different language, although this time they were related also to points about Members of the ITA.[2] Both groups had to consist of 'remarkable men and women' whose task it was 'hard to over-emphasise'. They had to be able to comprehend 'as ideas, as basic policies, the purposes of broadcasting' and they had to ensure that 'so far as possible, policies are translated into programming fact'. (The differences between the BBC and ITA in this last respect were not noted.) They had to 'know and care about public opinion; but, in appraising and interpreting it' they had to 'represent the public conscience'. They had to be ready, in certain circumstances, to 'stand up to the Government' and they had to resist all pressures, 'conscious or unconscious, well intentioned or not, to use broadcasting for anything less than its proper purposes'.[3]

If there were any doubts about the 'proper purposes of broadcasting' in 1962 – and there were many – the Pilkington Report ignored them in statements of this kind. It placed the stress throughout more on purpose than on organisation. Thus, while it said that it 'understood' the BBC's position that a larger Board than nine would be less efficient than the existing Board, it noted with approval that Article 7(1) of the Charter permitted the appointment of additional Governors.[4] Thus, when it dealt with remuneration – and it was the first Report on broadcasting to deal with this subject at length – it stated firmly that 'the rewards are, we believe bound to lie in the value and interest of the service those appointed are invited to give, and not in the particular remuneration', although it said also, perhaps more specifically, that 'the fees payable should not be so small as to involve personal financial sacrifice nor so big as possibly to impair a willingness to resign if necessary'. The Chairman was then receiving £4000, the

---

[1] Cmnd 1753 (1962), para. 427, p.127.

[2] E.G. Wedell, op.cit., p.114, states on the basis of a comment by A. Wolstencroft, Deputy Director General of the Post Office, who was seconded to become first Secretary of the ITA, that the new Authority proceeded on the basis that 'relationship of the Board to the Director General would be analogous to that established between their respective opposite numbers at the BBC'.

[3] Cmnd 1753 (1962), para. 410, p.123.   [4] Ibid., para. 412, p.123.

Vice-Chairman and National Governors for Scotland and Wales £1500, and other Governors £1000, and the Pilkington Report considered that these were 'of the right order', except in the case of the National Governors, who ought to receive more, and the Chairman who ought to receive £6000.[1]

If there was one distinctive element in these sections of the Report it was their emphasis on the role of the Chairman. 'By his personality and his grasp of principle the tone of the service can be set.' If there might be a temptation to appoint people near retiring age this ought to be resisted, for the Chairman should have 'vision and imagination'. 'Experience, wisdom, judgment and the ability to give the executive arm full power of action within the framework of chosen policy are of course necessary', the Report added.[2] It touched at more than one point on the relationship between Chairman and Director-General, emphasising that the latter should always have access to the former, although it had very little comment to make on management problems, which were to be the subject of great controversy inside and outside the BBC by the end of the decade.

One slightly controversial paragraph of the Report emphasised that it was always the duty of the Chairman, not of the Director-General, to give advice to Government about 'the sort of experience and qualities' which would be 'most useful' in new Governors. 'There must be no room even for the suggestion that the Director General plays a decisive part in the choice of Governors.' His position was already 'a very strong one'. It is interesting to note that even before the Governors of the BBC discussed the Report, the then Chairman, Sir Arthur fforde, stated at once that 'he was not conscious of anything done by D.G. by way of infringement of the Chairman's prerogative'.[3] His relationship with Greene, a strong Director-General, was obviously close enough for him to say this with no reserve.

Before the Governors turned in detail to the Pilkington issues, they were presented with a preparatory paper from the Board of Management.[4] A year earlier they had carefully considered their own position as Governors and had decided not to give evidence on this subject to Pilkington, and they now decided not to make

---

[1] Ibid., paras. 415, 418, pp.124–5.   [2] Ibid., para. 418, p.125.
[3] Ibid., para. 400, p.120; Board of Governors, *Minutes*, 27 June 1962.
[4] Board of Governors, *Minutes*, 5 July 1962.

any public speeches on the Report. [1] They were in obvious agreement with what Pilkington had said about their own role, which they themselves had considered quietly in terms of seven questions:

(a) Proper number of Governors
(b) Method of appointment
    (i) National
    (ii) Regional
    (iii) General?
(c) Terms of office and extension of office
(d) Should any of them be whole time?
(e) Is the rate of remuneration a bar to getting younger people?
(f) Are younger people desirable?
(g) Are these right questions?

They had invited Sir Philip Morris, who had just retired from the Board after two years as a Governor and six as Vice-Chairman, to answer the questions, and he had replied very succinctly. Everything was right as it then was in relation to (a), (b), (c), (d) and (g); on (e) he had no points; and on (f) he felt that young people should serve on Advisory Committees, not on the Board. He added, however, a long and confessedly 'drearily expressed' note on BBC structures, emphasising that 'the blurring of issues as between executive and policy aspects of problems rarely occurs'. [2]

At least one Governor, Mrs Cazalet-Keir, did not concur with all his points, but thought that there should be 'at least two or three younger (much younger) Governors on the Board', Governors who had been brought up in the age of television, that the size of the Board should be increased by two, and that the Chairman's salary should be increased. She pointed out *en passant* that one reason why the announcement of the Pilkington Committee had been favourably received was that *it* included several young members. [3] This did not mean, however, that it cut much ice with the Government.

After the publication of such a favourable Report, the most immediately important issue for the Governors was not their own

[1] Ibid., 23 Feb. 1961, 19 July 1962. They went into private session on the former occasion to consider the paper by the Chairman.

[2] 'BBC Board of Governors: Note by the Chairman', 2 Feb. 1961.

[3] 'BBC Board of Governors', Note by Mrs Cazalet-Keir, 14 Feb. 1961.

role, but the finance of the Corporation. The Report had emphasised that the Governors must be ready to convince Ministers that broadcasting 'must obtain or retain the resources it needs',[1] and this was the main issue of the years 1962 and 1963, as it was to be of many of the years in the future. In the name of 'independence', the Governors resisted all suggestions that deficiencies in Corporation finance should be met by subsidy;[2] they were successful also in challenging the £1 excise duty which had been added to the listeners' and viewers' £3 licence in 1957. They believed that the licence fee should be raised as soon as possible to £5, but they were prepared in certain circumstances to agree to £4, and this was the proposal which they put to Government. After the Chairman had seen Reginald Bevins, the Postmaster-General, and been told by him that he would not recommend the increase, the Vice-Chairman, Sir James Duff, after several months' delay, met R.A. Butler, then the Deputy Prime Minister, in October 1962.[3]

The second meeting was 'friendly', but although there had been a succinct, if cautious, clause in a Government White Paper of July 1962 that 'the Government accepts its responsibility to see that the BBC can secure sufficient income to finance adequate services',[4] nothing was done to implement this clause until the spring of 1963. A further Government White Paper of December 1962 noted that 'widely differing opinions' had been expressed in Parliament and in public on broadcasting matters, but this Paper dealt mainly with the ITA, not the BBC.[5] The Board did not believe that the implementation of the eventual settlement – an increase in licence fees to £4 from October 1963 – was dated properly in order to fulfil the Government's obligation as set out in July 1962.

In retrospect Reginald Bevins dealt with the complex issues not so much succinctly as brusquely. 'The BBC attitude is very simple. "We ask for a licence fee . . . The Government's duty is to give it to us." Between 1962 and 1964 they campaigned for this in the Press, quite indifferent to the politics of it and the effect of it

[1] Cmnd 1753 (1962), para. 409, p.123.
[2] Board of Governors, *Minutes*, 19 July 1962.   [3] Ibid., 11 Oct. 1962.
[4] Cmnd 1770 (1962), *Memorandum on the Report of the Committee on Broadcasting, 1960*, para. 59, p.8.
[5] Cmnd 1893 (1962), *Broadcasting, Further Memorandum on the Report of the Committee on Broadcasting*, para. 3, p.3.

on old people and poor people. I stubbornly refused and deliberately forced them to borrow, hoping it would make them cut out extravagance. A government has a responsibility not only to keep the BBC in funds but also to protect members of the public from an excessive licence fee.'[1] Brusque though the attitude was, it was not to disappear with Bevins.

Finance was not the only item which recurred regularly at Board meetings in 1962 and 1963. The reports of these meetings are long and detailed – important changes in minuting practice having taken place even before the retirement of Maurice Farquharson as Secretary in 1963 – and they reveal a quite different broadcasting 'universe' from that of twenty or even ten years before. There had been an argument about minuting at the very first meeting of the Board, when Mrs Snowden had objected to the Chairman not having given notice that he had designated as secretary to the Board Miss Shields, Reith's secretary;[2] and at the next meeting she stated that the first minutes were unsatisfactory. Thereafter, Governors' statements were not usually attributed to them during the Reith era of broadcasting, and Board decisions only were recorded.[3] Barbara Ward asked for fuller minutes, however, in 1946,[4] and between then and 1962 they grew in length both by creepage and by design. At the beginning of 1946 the average length was two or three pages, but by 1959 this had risen to over ten, and during the 1960s there were many meetings which demanded fifteen pages. The number of items minuted increased dramatically too – from 340 in 1946 to 485 in 1959 and 770 in 1964.

Minutes of controversial items were exceptionally full. Thus, the report of Governors' views on *That Was the Week That Was* ran to four columns in 1963.[5] *That Was the Week That Was* seemed to set the style for a whole age. It first figured on the Governors' agenda in November 1962,[6] two days before it was first broadcast, and it was subsequently discussed at almost every Board

[1] R. Bevins, *The Greasy Pole* (1965), p.119.

[2] Reith, *Diary*, 4, 11 Jan. 1927. Board of Governors, *Minutes*, 11 Jan. 1927 records the formal appointment of Miss Shields for six months but there were difficulties again later in the year (undated verbatim note, 1927).

[3] Board of Governors, *Minutes*, 8 Feb. 1928.

[4] Ibid., 19 Sept. 1946.   [5] Ibid., 5 July 1963.

[6] Board of Governors, *Minutes*, 22 Nov. 1962. Sir James Duff, the Vice-Chairman, presided over this meeting as he did over many in Sir Arthur fforde's absences through illness after October 1962.

meeting from then until July 1963, when the Governors met at Television Centre half an hour earlier than usual to assess the completed first series. The Governors welcomed the essentially serious intention of the programme and, in a phrase of Kenneth Adam, 'the potential for development which had been revealed by it', but they were restive about what some of them thought to be 'smut'. [1] At no time were they split down the middle, as some newspapers reported, although by 1963 a number of them were far less happy about the idea behind the programme and its mode of execution than they had been at the beginning. At first, it had been possible to believe that 'the cleansing draught of satire could be in the true Reith tradition': Greene himself took this line. [2] 'The young were going to poke fun at the old: at people in power, at everything shoddy and commercial and hypocritical in Macmillan's England.' [3] By November 1963, however, Greene himself had come to a conclusion which is said to have surprised

[1] Ibid., 4 July 1963. Sir Arthur fforde is said to have remarked in a phrase not picked up in the *Minutes*, 'a pity to spoil the ship for a ha'porth of dirt' (Note by K. Adam, 30 April 1963).

[2] *Sunday Telegraph*, 17 Nov. 1963, in an unsigned, percipient article 'Which was the Week?'.   [3] Ibid.

the Board – that the programme should cease at the end of the year.[1] He was wise to propose the change himself, for by then there were greater conflicts about standards of satire than there were even about the people and institutions being satirised.

It is often forgotten that *That Was the Week That Was* came and went during the first years of Greene's Director-Generalship. There were many other facets of change, some big and some small, almost all the change representing a challenge to convention, some of the change representing a challenge to authority. *Z Cars*, with its own complex history, was as much a sign of change in television programming as the dropping of the nine o'clock sound broadcast news.[2] Greene saw the 'national mood' of his own age as contributing to the new tone of broadcasting, recognising in it a split not between 'old and young or between Left and Right or between those who favoured delicacy and those who favoured candour' but between 'those who looked back to a largely imaginary golden age . . . and hated the present, and those who accepted the present and found it in many ways more attractive than the past'.[3] It is doubtful whether or not this was the division. What was important was that Greene believed that it was. He spoke with the same depth of conviction as Reith, and it was not entirely ironical that the 'age of Greene' began with a 'rapprochement' with Reith, duly reported by Greene to the Board in February 1960.[4] Reith, was present too at the fortieth anniversary celebrations of the BBC in 1962 and expressed his gratitude for the invitation. While it is not surprising that the 'rapprochement' did not persist, there were some continuing affinities. Thus Greene, like Reith before him, did not view the Governors as the arbiters of broadcasting policy. They were there to learn, to discuss and to approve; although they had the right, of course, to disagree, and ultimately to decide. The changes he wanted, however, were controversial even in the Board, and he did not get his way at once, for example, on the announcement of racecourse betting odds on which the Board was divided: it was

[1] An Interview with Frank Gillard, 19 March 1977. See also Grace Wyndham Goldie, *Facing the Nation* (1977), p.234.
[2] Board of Governors, *Minutes*, 25 Feb. 1960, when it was agreed by the Board that no public announcement of the decision in principle should be made. There was protracted controversy in the newspapers later in the year (*Minutes*, 6 Oct. 1960).
[3] Hugh Greene, *Third Floor Front* (1969), p.136.
[4] Board of Governors, *Minutes*, 25 Feb. 1960.

Hugh Greene greets Lord Reith at the BBC's Fortieth Anniversary dinner

not until February 1961, and then by a majority vote, that the decision to authorise the reporting of odds before races was eventually made.[1]

Greene enjoyed probing accepted stances and seeking to change them, but the free play of his independence of mind and spirit inevitably provoked sharp criticism from people outside, among them Bevins, who complained about 'the inability of the BBC Governors to exercise any real influence'. 'It always seemed to me', he went on, 'that they were governed by the professionals. In my time and before I am sure that the real power was wielded by the Director General, Sir Hugh Greene, and the top professionals. They knew all the answers.'[2]

In fact, during an uneasy decade when many institutions, economic, political, religious and educational, came under attack, the Governors were becoming more alert to a wider range of responsibilities than they had ever known before. They knew, too, that they would inevitably be more in the limelight, for even before existing institutions were seriously under stress there was pressure for innovation. The tone of argument was changing, and there were many highly publicised shifts in modes of behaviour, ranging from violence to 'permissiveness'. It is interesting to note, for example, that the Governors first discussed violence on television at a Board meeting in February 1960.[3]

They all took their widening responsibilities seriously, and from the very moment of their appointment asked questions and contributed to discussions. Thus, Robert Lusty asked for guidance in November 1961 on the extent to which it was thought valuable for individual Governors to visit BBC premises and departments to meet staff, and was told by Sir James Duff, speaking as Vice-Chairman, that he had been assured on first becoming a Governor that 'his interest in any matter of detail would be appreciated and that this had been fully borne out by experience'. Greene concurred, adding that the more remote the place, the more welcome the visit would be. Lusty went on to discuss programmes at the same meeting. He thought Governors

[1] Ibid., 24 March, 5 May 1960, 23 Feb. 1961. There was, in fact, little public reaction (ibid., 23 March 1961). In trying to deal with this issue Greene had been anticipated by Jacob who was surprised by the Board's reactions (Transcript of interview, 6 Oct. 1976.)

[2] Bevins, op.cit., pp.116–17.

[3] Board of Governors, *Minutes*, 25 Feb. 1960.

Sir James Duff and Sir Arthur fforde

were inclined to deal only with 'the more prominent pro-grammes'. In fact, 'less conspicuous programmes might be com-mended with advantage from time to time'.[1] The same point was to be made years later by Stephen Hearst. Listeners and viewers 'can be roused to fever heat over programmes, but are silent and almost unconcerned over policies.'[2] And Governors cannot deal with particular programmes unless they frame and interpret policies.

Lord Normanbrook, who became Chairman in 1964 at the age of 62, felt in general that Governors should not interfere in programme decisions, but should make their judgements after-wards. Yet there were notable exceptions to this policy. One retains a topical interest. In the Director-General's absence abroad, the Chairman decided not to renew an invitation to Ian Smith, the Prime Minister of Rhodesia, to appear in the tele-vision programme *Twenty-Four Hours* on 8 October 1965. There were protests from the Television Current Affairs Group, sum-marised in a memorandum from Paul Fox to Kenneth Adam, a memorandum which quoted a letter written by Greene to *The*

[1] Ibid., 9 Nov. 1961.
[2] S. Hearst, 'Right of Entry?' in *The Listener*, 26 Oct. 1978.

Lord Normanbrook

Times two years earlier under the title 'Providing a Platform: What the Public Should Know'.[1] Fox claimed that there had been a consequent 'drop in staff morale', but Normanbrook insisted then, and later, not on the correctness of his decision, but on his right to take it.[2] From the centre of the dispute, Oliver Whitley, son of the former Chairman and a man who was coming to be thought of as 'the conscience of the BBC', maintained that the cause of truth was not at stake in 1965 as it had been at Suez: 'the public was already pretty well-informed of Smith's views'. He admitted that 'it was a nasty decision to have to take' and that it might have done or might do 'more *visible* harm than good'.[3] One factor in the situation was the desire to compete for news with ITN; to its professionals the BBC had missed a scoop. The feeling that competition mattered – not only in news, but in general programming – was never stronger than during the Greene years. It was a new element in BBC life.

In the same year the Chairman was involved in another, perhaps more controversial, programme decision. *The War Game,*

[1] Memorandum by Fox to Adam, 12 Oct. 1965. Fox said that he had been associated earlier with interviews with Bidault, Kenyatta and Makarios. Greene's letter in *The Times* was printed on 7 March 1963.

[2] Note by Lord Normanbrook, 15 Oct. 1965; Normanbrook, 'The Functions of the BBC's Governors', *BBC Lunch-time Lectures, Fourth Series*, 15 Dec. 1965.

[3] O.J. Whitley to Greene, 13 Oct. 1965.

described by Normanbrook as 'an impressive documentary', had been made by Peter Watkins, then a Production Assistant on Programme Contract, and from the start it was known that it would be bound to be 'horrifying and unpopular'.[1] Indeed, it has been said that when it was shown on an internal circuit at Television Centre several secretaries fainted.[2] After Normanbrook and Greene had seen it, they both felt that 'the responsibility for its public showing was too great for the BBC to bear alone'.[3] The Director-General then left for a four-week Commonwealth Broadcasting Conference in Nigeria. The Chairman subsequently arranged a showing at which there were present five 'outsiders', including Sir Burke Trend, the Secretary of the Cabinet and representatives of the Home Office, the Ministry of Defence and the Chiefs of Staff. This action was deeply resented by the producer, many other BBC documentary producers and sections of the Press.[4] Eventually the BBC decided not to screen it indiscriminately for home viewing, but to make it available for cinema distribution. The Governors seem to have played a smaller part in this decision than the Chairman, although Lusty, who after seeing the film approved of the Chairman's decision, told him that he found himself wondering what might have been the fate of Christianity 'if our producer had shown in advance to the followers of Jesus a documentary showing the details of his inevitable crucifixion'.[5]

There were two other factors in the story. First, Lord Normanbrook himself had second thoughts. He felt that he should have had 'the courage of his convictions' when he first saw the script of *The War Game* and should have made it plain at that initial stage that the programme could never be shown on home television. 'If I had taken this line firmly at that stage,' he told the Director-General, 'the Corporation would have been spared a lot of embarrassment,' and Greene, who always got on well with Nor-

---

[1] Huw Wheldon to Adam, 31 Dec. 1964.

[2] S. Hearst, loc.cit.

[3] Reported by Adam to Television Controllers' Meeting (*Minutes*, 6 Sept. 1965).

[4] Note by Whitley, 4 Oct. 1965, beginning 'The more I think about *The War Game*, the more disinclined I am to accept that it cannot be broadcast.' This was a note to the Chairman. Most newspapers supported the BBC's decision. 'It must have been a difficult decision,' wrote the *Daily Mail*. 'The BBC have shown great courage in tackling subjects that have been taboo for years . . . Yet we also think the BBC were right to prevent *The War Game* from being indiscriminately seen.' (9 Feb. 1966.)

[5] Lusty to Normanbrook, 28 Sept. 1965.

manbrook, replied that his own thinking had led him 'to very much the same conclusions'.[1] Second, Mrs Mary Whitehouse wrote to the Prime Minister objecting to the film being shown, but was told by him that 'decisions on matters of this kind are made at the highest level in the BBC after appropriate consultations, and take full account of public policy'.[2]

Mrs Whitehouse had emerged two years earlier as a critic of the 'permissive society' and had written as a teacher to Greene in 1963 to complain about certain BBC programmes. Soon she had built up an active pressure group, the National Viewers' and Listeners' Association,[3] which submitted a petition to Parliament bearing 365,355 signatures in June 1965 and to which the Governors had to pay attention.[4] Thereafter, indeed, she frequently figured in BBC Governors' minutes, and by 1970 the notes of Lance Thirkell, Controller, Staff Training and Appointments, for his lectures to the course for new television producers began with the words 'sex, violence, four-letter words and Mrs Whitehouse'.[5] Three years later one of Mrs Whitehouse's Parliamentary supporters, Sir John Eden, was demanding 'a new type of research which accepts the power of television to affect the thinking and behaviour of people in the long term':[6] he was dissatisfied with what seemed to him 'whitewashing' surveys.

Shortly after *The War Game* decision the whole Board took the very rare step of pre-viewing a television programme. This was *Matador*, a documentary film on the emotive subject of a Spanish bullfighter. Sir Ashley Clarke, among other Governors, felt strongly that no programme involving bullfighting should be shown on BBC screens, even late at night and with adequate screen warnings beforehand.[7] The other Governors gave their

[1] Normanbrook to Greene, 28 Feb. 1966; Greene to Normanbrook, 2 March 1966.
[2] Mrs Whitehouse to Harold Wilson, 6 Sept. 1965; the Prime Minister's Private Secretary to Mrs Whitehouse, 13 Sept. 1965.
[3] See above, p.110, n.3.
[4] See Mary Whitehouse, *Cleaning Up TV* (1967) and *Who Does She Think She Is?* (1971). The 1965 petition included the words 'your petitioners pray that the BBC be asked to make a radical change of policy and produce programmes which build character instead of destroying it, which encourage and sustain faith in God and bring Him back to the heart of the British family and national life'. Among the programmes strongly criticised was *Swizzlewick* (1964).
[5] L. Thirkell, Notes for talk to Television Production Course (undated).
[6] NVLA, *Recommendations as to How Viewers and Listeners Can be Best Represented* (1973), p.22.
[7] Board of Governors, *Minutes*, 14 April 1966.

views for and against. In summing up, Normanbrook said that he would have preferred that the film had never been made, and that if the project had been referred to the Board in the first instance they would have withheld permission. But he agreed with Lady Baird's view that to suppress the film would have a bad effect both on the morale of the television production staff, and on the reputation of the BBC for courage in tackling difficult subjects.[1] In the event *Matador*, produced by Kevin Billington and with Alan Whicker as commentator, was transmitted on 29 July 1966, to an audience of eight million people. The Reaction Index of 70 showed that it had caused little offence.

Just as emotive as bullfighting was the subject of Nazi war-criminals. On 6 October 1966 at the end of his regular report as Director-General, Sir Hugh Greene passed on to the Board a message which had just been sent in to him: Baldur von Schirach, who had recently completed his Nuremberg prison sentence, had agreed to be interviewed in the television programme *Twenty-Four Hours* without a fee. Greene had earlier ruled that a payment of £500 demanded by the war criminal's agent was exorbitant. The Director-General had strong personal views on the enormities of the Nazi regime. As chief Berlin correspondent of the *Daily Telegraph* he had been expelled from Germany as a reprisal in May 1939. But he felt that it would be useful to show the depths to which apparently normal men could sink when they surrendered themselves to a political movement like National Socialism.

Greene was surprised at the vehemence the news of the proposed interview immediately engendered in a smaller than usual Board. (Lusty and Glanmor Williams, who normally supported Greene's liberal views, were both absent that day.) The Board overruled the Director-General and ordered that the interview should not take place. Greene felt closer to resignation than he ever had before, and told Normanbrook so afterwards. He recollected the Chairman's reply: 'It's your own silly fault, you should never have raised the issue.'[2]

Like sexual morality, violence, whether in bloodsports, war-games or drama, was a never exhausted issue. The same might be said of politics. Sometimes, indeed, moral and political issues

[1] Ibid..
[2] R. Lusty, *Bound to be Read* (1975), p.208.

were inextricably interrelated, since 'permissiveness' often came (wrongly) to be thought of as a left-wing manifestation rather than as an aspect of society as a whole. There were big differences in society and culture at the beginning and end of the 1960s – in education and in literature, indeed in all the arts and in politics, although there was a cynical strain running through the whole decade. Harold Wilson opposed Harold Macmillan, but he also admired him. *Private Eye* opposed both and admired neither, and though it saw the country through London spectacles, there were tensions in the provinces too.

Leaving on one side the content of broadcasting, which reflected much in the times, there were other developments which made the BBC's position difficult. Political leaders and political parties were uneasy throughout about the growing power as they saw it, of television, and of the threats to their own identity and sense of purpose. The fact that television seemed to be a special source of political power *in itself* was what alarmed them most.[1] The decade opened in March 1960 with an argument about the presentation of a Harold Macmillan broadcast,[2] and two years later there was a confrontation with the Labour Party about the tone and content of an interview between Kenneth Harris and George Brown.[3] On the first occasion peace came soon. On the second, however, Dame Anne Godwin, an early trade-unionist Governor, claimed that the row was continuing to have 'an unfortunate effect on the BBC's relations with the Labour Party'. The difficulties on the second occasion arose less on account of the BBC's style of interviewing than because of differences within the Labour Party leadership about Europe, a debilitating influence in itself. Yet the reason was less significant than the consequences.

This was shown when the next serious confrontation with a section of the Labour leadership came in 1965 and 1966 – on a quite different – and, at first sight, surprising – issue. Anthony Wedgwood Benn, Postmaster-General in the Labour Government of 1964, agreed with his Conservative predecessor that the BBC's licence could not be increased 'without upsetting people'. In his opinion, like that of many Conservatives before him, the right way to deal with the BBC's financial problems – and by

---

[1] A. Smith, *The Shadow in the Cave* (1973), Ch. 4 'Broadcasting and the Politician'.
[2] Board of Governors, *Minutes*, 10 March 1960. [3] Ibid., 11 Oct. 1962.

then it had a large deficit – was to raise some of its revenue by advertising on television and the radio Light Programme.[1] And he pushed the case, which the BBC resisted, as it had resisted similar pressure in 1939,[2] event to the point where he contemplated dismissing the Governors if they continued to resist.

When in February 1966 there was a leak of Wedgwood Benn's proposal that the Light Programme should take a moderate amount of advertising – a proposal which was about to be submitted to the Cabinet – Professor Glanmor Williams, the National Governor for Wales, was given an assurance by Greene that he had written to the Post Office making 'it clear beyond doubt that a resort to advertising revenue in any form would be quite unacceptable to the Board';[3] and this assurance was followed by further letters to the Post Office and a letter from Sir John Fulton, then Acting Chairman of the Governors, to the Prime Minister, Harold Wilson.[4] A meeting duly took place at 10 Downing Street between Fulton and Greene on the one side and Wilson, Herbert Bowden (Lord President of the Council) and Wedgwood Benn on the other.[5] R.H.S. Crossman, who tended to favour Wedgwood Benn on the issue (with qualifications) noted that thereafter it would have to be 'put under the mat until after the election'.[6]

Meanwhile, Wedgwood Benn had been enquiring formally about the exercise of the Postmaster-General's power to dismiss the Governors, which was technically possible under the Charter,[7] and when this line of action looked impracticable (if only because it touched on the independence of other Crown appointees besides the BBC's Governors) he turned to an alternative idea of setting up a new radio broadcasting corporation, financed

[1] R.H.S. Crossman, *Diaries of a Cabinet Minister*, Vol. I (1975), p.167: entry for 22 Feb. 1965. See also, ibid., p.227.

[2] See above, p.85.

[3] Board of Governors, *Minutes*, 3 Feb. 1966.

[4] Greene to Sir Ronald German, 8 Feb. 1966; Fulton to Wilson, 11 Feb. 1966.

[5] This was an important meeting historically at which Wilson raised the whole question of 'the University of the Air' and how to finance it (Note by Greene, 16 Feb. 1966).

[6] Crossman, op.cit., p.459.

[7] The previous year Wedgwood Benn had said in the House of Commons that 'the Director-General is appointed by the Board of Governors. What I have the power to do is to dismiss the Board of Governors'. (*Hansard*, vol. 712, col.511, 12 May 1965.)

by advertising and with a programme like that of the future Radio 1. This new corporation would lease its technical facilities from the BBC. This second idea was not dropped until after the general election, won by Labour with a comfortable majority, and Wedgwood Benn's promotion to the Ministry of Technology in July 1966.[1]

There were Labour Party divisions on most of these issues, however, particularly the issue of advertising, which went back to the battles against the commercial television lobby; and Crossman rightly believed, even after more than ten years of commercial television and Wilson's blessing of the ITA on its tenth anniversary, that to try to commit the Party on such issues would 'split it wide open'.[2] He pinned his faith rather on 'a severe investigation of the BBC without commitment on Government policy'.[3] Yet characteristically he told the BBC's Board of Management annual dinner in 1966 that the defeat of Wedgwood Benn's independent corporation idea would go down to history as the first time an 'all-powerful corporation' (with the support of the Musicians' Union) had successfully overturned a decision of the British Cabinet.[4]

This was not the view from Broadcasting House, and in the following year, 1967, the BBC's assessment of threats and dangers seemed to be confirmed by a dramatic sequence of events following the death in office of the Chairman of the Governors, Lord Normanbrook, in June. (He died on a day appointed for a Governors' meeting.) Normanbrook had very recently emphasised how delicate were the balances maintaining the BBC's independence;[5] and he had been concerned about suggestions made by the Prime Minister (perhaps in the light of the events of 1966) that the size of the governing body should be increased from nine to twelve 'to achieve parity' with the ITA.[6] At that time the Chairman of the ITA was Lord Hill of Luton, an experienced politician, former 'Radio Doctor' and life peer (1963), who had been in the chair since 1963. He had published

---

[1] C. Shaw to C. Curran, 'The Events of 1966', 22 March 1976.
[2] Crossman, op.cit., p.227.   [3] Ibid.
[4] Note by Curran, 8 July 1977. The Musicians' Union had refused the extra needle-time required. Wedgwood Benn's proposal, though already endorsed by a Cabinet Committee, had not formally been adopted by the Cabinet.
[5] Normanbrook, 'The Functions of the BBC's Governors', p.4. See above, p.18.
[6] Note by Lusty, 9 June 1974.

Sir Robert Lusty

Both Sides of the Hill in 1964, a prophetic title in the light of his
overnight move from ITA to BBC in 1967.

Events moved very fast on Wednesday 26 July 1967, described
by Lusty as probably 'the most shattering day' the BBC had
'endured' in its history,[1] and certainly the sequence of events on
that day was more controversial than any controversial BBC
programme. It began, it has been stated, with the Prime Minister, Wilson, telling Crossman that 'Charlie Hill has already
cleaned up ITV, and he'll do the same to BBC now I'm appointing him chairman',[2] and it ended in furore.

Greene had been expecting that Fulton would be given the
post as soon as he was available, and that Lusty, meanwhile,
would be asked to continue as Acting Chairman.[3] Lusty himself,
who had not been consulted about how best to fill the vacancy,
was amazed by the turn of events in the day. He had been
telephoned in the morning by the secretary of the Postmaster-
General, Edward Short, quietly suggesting a meeting the following day, but less than an hour later he had a second call summoning him to the Post Office that afternoon. There he was told that a

[1] Lusty, op.cit., p.248.

[2] Crossman, op.cit., Vol. II (1976), p.442.

[3] Fulton, who was close to Wilson, had resigned the Vice-Chairmanship on
becoming Chairman of a large-scale enquiry into the organisation of the Civil Service.
Fulton remained an ordinary Governor and Lusty was recalled *ad interim* as Vice-
Chairman, and thus, after Normanbrook's death, as Acting Chairman.

new Chairman would take over from him on 1 September and that his name would be announced that evening. Short added to the sense of confusion by telling him first that the new Chairman's name was Charles Smith and then having it corrected to Charles Hill. Hill, too, had been surprised when Wilson asked him to move, telling him confidentially at the same time that if he (Hill) felt after taking office that it were better that the BBC should operate under an Act of Parliament (as the ITA did) than a Royal Charter, he should say so.[1] That evening, when Hill informed the guests at a farewell dinner, arranged in honour of the retiring ITA Vice-Chairman, that he was about to move, there was a feeling that he was joking; and when Greene told the news to his colleagues in the Board of Management before they, too, went off to a dinner party, with the Chairman of the Conservative Party as their guest, they were equally incredulous.[2]

There might have been several resignations in consequence – including Lusty's and Greene's – but Oliver Whitley wisely told his colleagues, 'there should be no talk of resignations tonight. It may well be what they hope for.' In fact, there were none later, and two days after the sensational Wednesday the Privy Council formally approved Hill's appointment along with the appointment of two new Governors and the enlargement of the Board from nine to twelve. On Tuesday 25 July, Ted Castle had given the television correspondent of *The Sun* an inside tip that Hill was about to be appointed Director-General (*sic*) of the BBC. He dismissed it at the time as 'a load of nonsense' but when the news broke he apologised, and Castle is said to have told him, 'Well, it's not a major story anyway. He is only Chairman and not Director-General.'[3]

Hill was determined to be an 'active Chairman', as the Government wished him to be, and set about at once trying to mobilise an active Board, underestimating the activity of previous Boards and resenting at first the cool, in some cases hostile, reception the BBC gave him.[4] Lusty, in particular, believed that it was the end of the BBC as he knew it 'and the end of Hugh Greene too'.[5] Yet the first Board meeting Hill attended was a

[1] Lord Hill television interview with Robin Day, 31 July 1975.
[2] Lord Hill, *Behind the Screen* (1974), Ch. 8; Lusty, op.cit., pp.248–9.
[3] Philip Phillips, Telephone Conversation with Leonard Miall, 3 Nov. 1976.
[4] Hill, op.cit., pp.73 ff.
[5] Lusty, op.cit., p.250.

"And here's the four letter word that caused the biggest shock of all — H-I-L-L!"

quiet one, characterised by the resolution in minute 394 that he be appointed a Trustee for the Corporation of the BBC New Pension Scheme in place of Lord Normanbrook deceased.[1] Hill welcomed two new Governors – Lord Dunleath and Sir Ralph Murray – but no one welcomed him. Greene's story was to be far more complex than Lusty had forecast. He resigned as Director-General at the end of March 1969, but returned in July 1969 as a Governor, the first Director-General in the BBC's history to do so – although Reith had tried hard, after a long interval, to do the same. It was a move which carried with it many problems.

There was an awkward squabble between Hill and Greene in the autumn of 1969. After Hill had proposed that all Governors should be placed in the same position as himself and the Vice-Chairman and should receive copies of the minutes of some of the BBC's internal meetings, including those of the Board of Management, Greene received some support in the Board for his objection that such a change might undermine the authority of the Director-General. And when the issue was put to the vote, five voted for seeing sample minutes at the next meeting and five against. Hill, who had suggested this proposal as a compromise, voted in favour of his own suggestion, of course, but between then and the next meeting felt bound to 'withdraw the item until another day'. 'How the senior staff resent the Governors showing

[1] Board of Governors, *Minutes*, 21 Sept. 1967.

the slightest signs of governing,' he recorded in his diary after the casting vote,[1] and it was not until January 1972 that he felt that he had a Board willing to govern.[2] By then, only one Governor survived who had preceded Hill to the Board Room – Professor Glanmor Williams, the National Governor for Wales. The Director-Generalship had gone to Charles Curran in April 1969. Curran was then 47 years old and Hill 65.

Hill felt that he had got 'a little wiser in handling matters' by 1972.[3] He had certainly broken with one convention of the Board by supporting the idea of voting. When votes had taken place under fforde on the pre-race broadcasting of odds, fforde is said to have remarked from the Chair that when two Governors were against a proposal 'two is too many', and that when the two dropped to one 'one is too few'. There was one vote taken, too, when Lusty was Acting Chairman.[4] Hill liked votes, and in his early days as Chairman there were many of them. He also introduced more BBC executives into Board meetings. Thus, in December 1972 at his last meeting, eleven executives were in attendance for particular items; at his first there had only been two.[5] However, he abolished the regular reports by Directors on their work.

These were only two of many signs of change. Organisational change was much in the air during the late 1960s inside and outside the BBC, and much of the recommended change was funnelled through management consultancy firms, such as McKinsey and Company, who were called in by Hill to advise the BBC. The underlying theme was 'rationalising the networks', and it was a theme which 'chilled' many people inside the Corporation. The three heads of Radio, Television and External Services now became known as Managing Directors, and sound broadcasts were now segregated by content through Radios 1, 2, 3 and 4. This was the end of large-scale Regional broadcasting in sound and the beginning of local radio.

A BBC working party considered the many problems of *Broadcasting in the Seventies*, the title of a controversial document published in July 1969 with a foreword by Hill. There was little in the pamphlet, however, about overall control; it concentrated

[1] Hill, op.cit., p.144.   [2] Ibid., p.215.   [3] Ibid., p.216.
[4] Lusty, op.cit., p.262.
[5] Board of Governors, *Minutes*, 14 Dec. 1972, 21 Sept. 1967.

rather on setting out details for discussion – and the discussion at times was bitter – of 'a pattern which we believe would be more logical, more attractive and solvent'.[1] Television, which Hill believed was on 'its high road', received little attention: the main focus was upon sound. Above all the need to plan was stressed, and when the Director-General gave an address on *Broadcasting in the Seventies* he called it 'Planning and Consent: The Technocrat's Dilemma'.[2] The leaders of the 'Campaign for Better Broadcasting' questioned the whole approach, however, and described the 'slim, white pamphlet' as 'a masterpiece of devious and subtle generalisation, as elusive of attack as a cloud of feathers'.[3]

The House of Commons spent five hours debating *Broadcasting in the Seventies* in July 1969, and Conservative spokesmen, taking up the opposite stance to the campaign leaders, stated that when they returned to power they would reserve the right to adjust the BBC's Charter and introduce their own plans for commercial radio. The Minister responsible for broadcasting was by then John Stonehouse, Minister of Posts and Telecommunications, a new office set up that year following changes in the constitution of the Post Office. He argued that in the past there had been 'flabby' and inefficient organisation in parts of the BBC, but he believed this was now being put right, and he described Conservative plans for local commercial stations as likely to provide 'a great deal of mush'. The Governors followed the debate with great interest and were pleased that some speakers, including Patrick Gordon Walker, said the House of Commons itself must bear part of the blame for the BBC's financial problems. It alone could increase the licence fee.[4]

Lively though the debate was, the volume of correspondence received by the Corporation about the proposals, the Governors were told, was smaller than had been expected. Hill said that this was true of his own correspondence also. Most of it related to such programming policy items, important to listeners and to national cultural policy, as the disbanding of orchestras and the move of Radio 3 to VHF only.[5] There was one other main theme in the continuing argument, however – opposition to the proposal

[1] *Broadcasting in the Seventies* (July 1969), p.13.
[2] Curran, Lecture to the Royal Town Planning Institute, Feb. 1974.
[3] J. Donat, *Crisis in Broadcasting* (1969), p.1.
[4] *Hansard*, vol. 787, cols.1523–1624, 22 July 1969.
[5] Board of Governors, *Minutes*, 17 July 1969.

to abolish the established English regional radio structure. Whatever the outside reactions – and they did not fade out in July 1969 – there was 'alarm and dismay and disaffection right through the ranks' in the BBC about what was happening or what might happen.[1] This was an 'unhappy period' in broadcasting history, still too near to see in full perspective, which left its mark, more on the staff of the BBC than on the Governors. Already at the overall level of control Hill had appointed two special Committees of the Board in 1968 – the first, headed by Sir Robert Bellinger, to deal with finance, the second, headed by Paul Wilson, to deal with staff policy – and despite serious BBC worries about the former topic, the second topic was more disturbing inside the Corporation. The remit of the Wilson group was 'to consider and report to the Board on proposals falling within the scope of the Board which relate to policy on appointments, pay and conditions of service and relations with the unions', and by 1970 there were great difficulties with both the Musicians' Union and Equity. This range of issues was to dominate much of the discussion about policy during the 1970s. The Committees subsequently 'fell into desuetude' because those members of the Board who were not included in them felt 'left out'.[2]

The Board was already intimately connected with finance, for in the summer of *Broadcasting in the Seventies* the Government rejected proposals for an increase in television licence fees – after Stonehouse had strongly supported them. The financial straitjacket restricted the range of policy options open to the BBC and posed a direct threat to its staff. Indeed, it was the trade union leader, Sir Tom O'Brien, General Secretary of the National Association of Theatrical, Television and Kine Employees, who described the interconnection most acutely in a letter to *The Times*. Demanding an increase in licence fees, he stated bluntly, 'I immensely dislike negotiating with a bankrupt: I prefer to use militancy with a millionaire.'[3] *The Times* itself had put the matter less colourfully on the day O'Brien wrote his letter. 'A thriving broadcasting system cannot be main-

---

[1] Frank Gillard, Statement made in March 1978. Cf. Burns, op.cit., p.160, where he refers to a sense of 'trauma' among some members of staff.

[2] Sir Charles Curran, 'Notes on the White Paper Proposals', 1978.

[3] *The Times*, 22 July 1969.

*"The way you say 'Tck! 'Tck!' as
though we've ever paid the five quid."*

tained on a static revenue base in an era of increasing costs.'[1]

Politics was just as difficult as finance or administration during the last two years of Hill's Chairmanship, and his autobiography has several chapters with titles which speak for themselves – 'shock at the BBC', 'candidates for top posts', 'clashes with management', 'responsibility or censorship?'. There are two chapters also which refer to episodes discussed more fully in Chapter IV of this essay – *Yesterday's Men* (1971) and *The Question of Ulster* (1972). The fact that three other chapters are entitled 'Mr Wilson's suspicions', 'another clash with Mr Wilson' and 'sensitive politicians' reveals also, however, that whatever the circumstances of his appointment, Hill struggled hard to preserve the BBC's independence vis-à-vis Government – for this is how he saw it – in far from easy years.

He was Chairman at the time of the surprise election result of 1970, when the Wilson Government fell, to be replaced by that of Heath, and he was Chairman when the Irish question suddenly burst out again as a major issue in British politics, raising issues of order and security for the first time since 1945. It is with this experience in mind that the arguments centred on *Yesterday's Men* and *The Question of Ulster* should be assessed. Yet these were merely two of the most dramatic out of a series of many political entanglements. It was after he retired at the end of December 1972 – to be succeeded by Sir Michael Swann, Chairman in an

[1] Ibid., 19 July 1969.

equally difficult period – that he stated eloquently in the House
of Lords how deeply he believed 'that the independence of the
BBC is not only a great source of its strength but is something
which the rest of the world would wish us to retain'.[1] At his last
meeting of the Board, when he announced the appointment of
Swann, he was warmly thanked by the Governors, one of whom
said that he had been 'taught much' by the Chairman.[2]

By then, in theory at least, the Governors had access to a
greater body of systematised information about the Corporation
than they ever had before, and they were devoting more of their
time than ever before trying to ensure that the BBC was living
within its 'prospective income'. In fact, however, they were also
devoting a larger and larger part of their time than ever before to
public reactions (including Parliamentary reactions) both to the
organisation of the BBC and to its programme policies. This last
preoccupation led to the setting-up in October 1971 of a Programmes Complaints Commission which issued its first Report in
May 1972. Lord Parker was its first chairman, and the other two
members were Lord Maybray-King and Sir Edmund Compton.[3] The work of the Commission did not immediately reduce

[1] *House of Lords Official Record*, vol. 348 No. 35, col.1500, 23 Jan. 1974.
[2] Board of Governors, *Minutes*, 14 Dec. 1972.
[3] *BBC Programmes Complaints Commission, Annual Report 1972–73*. Lord Parker died in
September 1972 when Compton took his place as chairman and Sir Henry Fisher, a
retired judge of the High Court, joined the Commission. There were only three
adjudications in 1972–3 and two in 1973–4.

the burden on the Governors, however, for complaints were only one form of criticism. Meanwhile, they were being forced to look increasingly into the more distant future: to the likely impact of new technologies, a subject which was unfamiliar to most of them; to relations with the IBA, which were affected both by BBC finance and by economic factors influencing the fortunes of the commercial companies; and to their own constitutional arrangements, which were taken for granted less than they had ever been.

Just before Hill left the Corporation, a number of important internal papers were prepared on 'The BBC and the Future'. The Governors had taken the initiative in asking for a 'fundamental examination of future purposes', setting April 1973 as a target date for the end of the exercise, and the papers were wide ranging.[1] One of the first of them was produced by the Director-General and while it left out any detailed discussion of 'constitutional' questions – 'the function and composition of the Board of Governors' and 'the nature of the BBC's relationships with the public' – it asked three important questions: 'Should the responsibilities of the various Advisory bodies be changed? Should more of such bodies be formed? Are there means which might be devised for changing the present system of public accountability?'[2]

The Board decided to ask the BBC's Secretary, Colin Shaw, who was to move to the Independent Broadcasting Authority in 1977, to prepare the drafts of future papers, including one on the role of the Governors and one on public service broadcasting.[3] The other drafts included 'Financing the BBC', still a major issue in the BBC's relationship with the Government; 'News and Current Affairs: the Philosophy', a major issue in the BBC's relationships with the public;[4] and 'The Control of Broadcasting'.[5]

Paper IV on 'the Control of Broadcasting' rejected as 'un-

[1] George Howard, Paper I, 3 Aug. 1972.
[2] Charles Curran, Paper II, 3 Aug. 1972.
[3] Board of Governors, *Minutes*, 10 Aug. 1972.
[4] Paper VI, 26 Oct. 1972. The News and Current Affairs draft never became a Board Paper.
[5] Paper IV, 28 Sept. 1972. It stated that 'we have come to recognise that, in broadcasting's claim to mirror society, the selective nature of its reflection is all-important, and that not only the process of selection, but the selectors themselves, will no longer be taken on trust'.

palatable' the idea of an overall regulatory body for the whole of broadcasting,[1] an idea which was still being canvassed both by Mrs Whitehouse and by sections of the Labour Party, while admitting that 'the continued appeal of a Broadcasting Council, such as it is, reflects a failure in projecting in ways capturing public imagination how [the] trusteeship [of the Board of Governors] is discharged.' It also rejected, with the support of the Board of Management, the idea of including within the existing constitution a 'professional element' consisting of BBC executives on the Board.

In retrospect, one of the most interesting points made in the paper was that there might be 'working Governors', for example 'a Governor appointed by the Crown to run the Television Service and sit upon the Board'. At the time, however, a more relevant sentence was 'Governors are much more aware of "the product" and public reaction to the "product" than are, say, the non-working directors of a manufacturing company . . . They could not hope to be aware of everything that is broadcast, but almost anything that is broadcast is capable of provoking someone in the audience to complain. A Governor who hoped for a quiet life would rapidly be disabused.'

This paper was produced at a time when it could be stated that 'no Hanoverian mother prompted her son to be king more urgently than some voices now prompt the Governors to govern.'[2] Yet such urgent prompting was placed in longer perspective. Was it wise to continue the present system under which 'essentially amateur men and women exercise control over professional broadcasters'? The system produced 'frustrations for both groups of people: for the former because they suspect the professionals of trying to blind them with expertise and even occasionally of succeeding; for the latter because they feel their problems are not properly understood.' This way of putting it, to become so familiar in other contexts during the 1970s, tended to leave out the listeners and viewers as such, though they figured in the sentence that 'the Board is under much greater pressure than previous Boards to respond not in terms of some overall public interest, but in terms of some minority interest which, however worthy, cannot often be satisfied except at the expense of other minority interests.'[3]

[1] Ibid.   [2] Ibid.   [3] Ibid.

Paper VI, which took a cautious view on borrowing, rejected advertising even in part, because any part would be 'the thin end of a very big wedge'; and it also rejected both grant-in-aid proposals and a suggestion made by E.G. Wedell that part of future revenue should come from a common fund created from the levy on the commercial television companies. This, it argued, would offer no guarantee. 'The propensity of governments to retain money is well illustrated by the £100,000,000 of licence money retained over the years.' There was one new note. 'To say that the BBC would not welcome the taxpayer's money to finance all its domestic services is not necessarily to rule out the possibility of accepting it for some.'[1]

These and other themes were being fully and critically discussed inside the BBC before they were widely discussed outside. Yet there was a new turn of events in 1974. Five years earlier, when Hill was still Chairman and Harold Wilson was Prime Minister, the Minister of Posts and Telecommunications, John Stonehouse, had announced the terms of reference of a Committee of Enquiry into Broadcasting to be set up under the chairmanship of Lord Annan. The new Conservative Government had dropped the idea of such a committee before the names of its members were announced, but the idea was revived in April 1974 after Labour returned to power. Indeed, very quickly after the return, with remarkable speed, the new Home Secretary, Roy Jenkins, who had now been made responsible for the oversight of broadcasting policy, reappointed Annan to the chairmanship he had never taken up.

The names of the other members of his Committee were announced in July 1974. Two of them, Antony Jay and Phillip Whitehead, had been television producers inside the BBC, and the latter had gone on to become a Labour Member of Parliament. There was also a Conservative ex-Member of Parliament, Sir Marcus Worsley, who had worked inside the BBC as a Programme Assistant in the European Service during the early 1950s. The presence of politicians with broadcasting experience gave the new Committee a different composition from that of Beveridge and Pilkington. But this was not the only – or the biggest – change. The Committee noted from the outset what it

---

[1] Paper VI, 26 Oct. 1972. On borrowing the paper said that the BBC had 'always regarded its borrowing powers as its last reserve'.

called a change in the 'climate of opinion' since the earlier enquiries, a change not only in Britain but throughout the West.

It is doubtful whether those in charge of British broadcasting were 'taken by surprise' by what was happening quite as much as Lord Annan suggested. Yet he was right to insist that 'for years British broadcasting had been able successfully to create, without alienating Government or the public, interesting and exciting popular network programmes from the world of reality as well as the world of fantasy. . . . These now began to stir up resentment and hostility, and protests against their political and social overtones.'[1] Running through the Annan Report when it finally appeared – as through the BBC's internal papers of 1972 – is a perception of the increasing sensitivity of Government to the media and an increasing articulation of grievance and pressure not so much of the public as a whole as of a variety of different 'publics', some of them in confrontation with each other.

Swann was Chairman of the BBC throughout the whole of the Annan enquiry and Curran was Director-General, and both were aware of all these aspects of change, as an important BBC lecture on 'The Responsibility of the Governors', delivered by the Chairman in 1974, reveals. It is in line with similar statements by some of his predecessors, but it has a sense of a new context.

Swann, like Hill before him, began by claiming that Normanbrook's basic argument still stood. The argument, indeed, had by then acquired the same kind of standing that the Whitley Document had for many years. What had changed, Swann said – in line with what Annan was to say – was the social context. No Government, 'even the most liberal', was prepared to leave the mass media 'solely in the hands of the broadcasters'. When Government appointed the Governors, it was settling for 'remote control', an easier form of control than trying to deal directly with broadcasting. For the first time a BBC Chairman produced a military analogy about the whole organisation; Jacob had talked of 'campaigns' and Haley of 'orders of the day', but Swann went further and painted a picture of broadcasting as 'a service situation, with its clear network of people, all doing their jobs in a tightly controlled way'. It is a picture which contrasted sharply with that of the BBC as an arena where all the conflicts and uncertainties of society are exposed.

[1] Cmnd 6753 (1977), paras 2.26, 2.27, pp.14–15.

Perhaps the Board of Governors had to be more in the public eye, Swann went on, although he doubted if the Governors wanted to be. They had to concern themselves with routine administrative decisions at their fortnightly meetings, but they also had to take upon themselves four highly responsible tasks – to choose senior staff, 'the most important way in which Governors influence the BBC' (and they were to choose a new Director-General, Ian Trethowan, in 1977); to supervise the broad patterns of expenditure and the policies associated with them; to watch programme output – through 'the upward referral system' and through exchange of information and ideas with the Managing Directors (who attended Board meetings to deal with their own business); and 'to help create a climate of opinion in broad matters of programme policy'. 'The Board, if you like, has something of the function of management consultants, a body of people standing outside the everyday rush and bustle, thinking about the organisation on behalf of the public, and from a variety of experiences.' [1]

Swann laid emphasis on 'fair dealing' on the part of the BBC with all sections of the public – admitting conflicts and occasional failures – while at the same time protecting broadcasters against undue 'pressure from politicians and governments'. He admitted that 'few senior staff [of the BBC] know more than a very little of what the Governors do in their defence, or of the validity of the decisions, criticisms or comments they make'. [2] Efforts were made to rectify this after 1974.

The Governors' evidence to the Annan Committee dismissed the idea of their having a 'detailed executive role', but claimed that 'over the years the Board has increased its influence'. It was now meeting more often than ever before with members of senior management as well as the Director-General. Evidence on these and other points followed closely the lines of the Chairman's statement, although the submission responded more precisely to three complaints made against the Board – first (and least well founded) that of inadequate financial control; second, that of 'undue interference, direct or indirect, with the prerogative of the

---

[1] Sir Michael Swann, 'The Responsibility of the Governors', *BBC Lunch-time Lectures, Ninth Series*, 29 Oct. 1974. For Trethowan's approach, see 'Broadcasting – into the Eighties', a Speech to the Annual Conference of the Radio Electrical and Television Retailers' Association, 11 April 1978.

[2] Swann, 'The Responsibility of the Governors'.

programme-makers' (a charge which was flatly rebutted); and
third (and in contradiction with the second) that of exerting too
little influence 'in the politically sensitive areas of sex, violence
and taste and standards generally'.[1]

The latter – taste and standards generally – had always been a
sensitive area, although the sensitivities had varied strikingly
from generation to generation and there were always tendencies
and counter-tendencies to take into account. The former – sex
and violence – was the new area where there was less agreement
about values than ever before and for Mrs Whitehouse, who met
Swann in January 1974, sex was a more disturbing issue even
than violence.[2] It was in the light of public comment, often
minority comment, that the Board was to take outside advice
itself. It praised, for instance, the BBC's Consultative Group on
the Social Effects of Television for its contribution to the new
guidelines on the portrayal of violence. These guidelines were
revised following the report of senior BBC programme-makers
under the chairmanship of Monica Sims, Head of Children's
Television programmes before becoming Controller of Radio 4.[3]

Not surprisingly, the Board in its evidence to Annan rejected
the idea of a Broadcasting Council, as it had done in 1972. It also
rejected as it had done then the idea of a Board with a different
composition, including members of the Board of Management.
The size of the Board, some but not all Governors thought, might
well be reduced, and the timing of appointments to the Board
was rightly thought by all of them to need more careful attention:
there had been too 'cavalier' an attitude towards appointment
and renewal. There was agreement also that 'the unwritten
convention which provides for a Trade Unionist, a diplomatist
(to take a particular interest in External Broadcasting), a financial expert and an educationist to be members of the Board
should be continued'. 'Beyond that', they concluded, 'we see no
real need for particular interests to be represented, other than

[1] BBC Memorandum to the Committee on the Future of Broadcasting, 'The
Structure of the Board of Governors', June 1975.

[2] 'The Chairman's Meeting with Mrs Whitehouse', 9 Jan. 1974. Normanbrook had
refused to meet Mrs Whitehouse, but Hill, who had already met her at ITA
headquarters in 1965, received her at the BBC. She met BBC Television people 'on
their own ground' for the first time in 1967. For a recent account of the origins of her
activities, see the report of her interview with Paul Callan in the *Daily Mirror*, 27 Oct.
1978, 'The Caped Crusader'.

[3] BBC Press Release, 8 March 1979.

those of the National Governors.' [1] On the National Governors a whole monograph could be written. If changes of social and cultural context were the most striking changes between Beveridge and Pilkington, no political context had changed more between Pilkington and Annan than that of Scotland, Wales and Northern Ireland.

After the publication of the Annan Report in March 1977, the debate continued, and it still continues, with Cmnd 7294 as the latest official statement. The constitutional problem remains inextricably interlinked with the financial problem – whether the BBC's income derived from licence fees will be adequate to enable the Governors to act independently in relation to all kinds of programming and in face of strong competition from ITV. During the autumn of 1978 there were sharp arguments involving popular programmes, including sport, between BBC executives and the executives of the commercial companies, just when the Governors were involved on many other fronts, and never did the BBC look more vulnerable. The Governors were less involved in trade-union issues than management which reports to them, but the importance of such issues – and their effects on broadcasting operations – has greatly increased.

They are being forced to concentrate on their relationship with Government while at the same time watching the attitudes of the public who pay the licence fees; and to lobby discreetly but actively, separating contingency from crisis in an uncertain political situation, where there are declared differences in the approach to broadcasting policy between the parties and where a general election would totally alter the situation. They are expected to strengthen the processes of internal enquiry into complaints while at the same time resisting imposition; to improve the communication of the Board's views and wishes 'down the line' while at the same time maintaining morale; to make occasional public pronouncements about programme matters, even when opinions are divided, and recognising that to lay down 'codes' might be to lose a great deal of flexibility. In these difficult circumstances the performance of the Governors continues to depend less on their formal powers – and these remain immense on paper – than on the qualities of experience, under-

[1] BBC Memorandum to the Committee on the Future of Broadcasting, 'The Structure of the Board of Governors', June 1975.

standing, imagination and vision which singly and together they can bring to broadcasting. This is not just a public relations task: it involves an understanding of the essential character of public broadcasting and the forces that sustain, erode or destroy it.

CHAPTER II

WHO ARE – AND WERE – THE GOVERNORS?

Why commercial companies choose particular people to sit on their boards is largely a matter of private interest. It has been possible, indeed, for major changes to take place after fierce internal argument, without even shareholders being drawn in.[1] There has been general discussion from time to time, of course, about the size, composition and role of boards, to what extent they should include 'executive Directors', and the range of their responsibilities.

The British Broadcasting Company had a not untypical commercial board with an 'executive', J.C.W. Reith, who attended board meetings. The nine members, 'paid £200 a year tax free', all 'represented' members of the original consortium; in other words, they had separate as well as corporate interests.[2] One member was outstanding, Godfrey Isaacs of the Marconi Company – the only one to die during the history of the Company. He was so outstanding, indeed – as was his company – that he had to be 'counter-balanced' in the board. The Chairman of the BBC, Lord Gainford, was a former Postmaster-General, as was Isaacs's replacement, F.W. Kellaway, the Postmaster-General who had summoned the consortium, and who had subsequently become a Director of Marconi's. He is said to have been the first choice of General Manager of the BBC – before Reith. Another Post Office man (later to be prominently associated with Rediffusion) was the engineer, Sir William Noble, a Director of General Electric. The Vice-Chairman was Sir William Bull, MP, a politician and businessman, for whom Reith had worked for a time as honorary secretary. One member of the

[1] This was the case, for example, when the Reed Paper Group replaced Lord Cornwallis by Cecil King in 1963. 'A fundamental change has taken place in the boardroom of the second largest paper-making company in the country,' *The Times* commented after the July annual meeting which followed, 'and the stockholders' reticence on this occasion is baffling. Only a little less baffling is that the Chairman also failed to refer to this matter, and the short proceedings ended as they began as if nothing whatsoever had changed.' (25 July 1963.)

[2] See obituaries of Basil Binyon, the Managing Director of the Radio Communications Company and a member of the committee of the BBC Board which appointed Reith, in *The Times* and *Daily Telegraph*. He did not approve of the 1927 change. (*The Times*, 9 April 1977, *Daily Telegraph*, 7 April 1977.)

Board was American – H.M. Pease of Western Electric.[1]

The Governors of the new Corporation, who held their first Board meeting on 4 January 1927 at Savoy Hill, were paid substantially more than the Directors of the Company. The Chairman, the sixth Earl of Clarendon, received £3000. Clarendon, the owner of Kenilworth Castle, was then 49. He had been for the past two years Undersecretary of State for Dominion Affairs, and before that Chief Government Whip in the House of Lords. A cold and insensitive man, he had difficulty from the outset in establishing a relationship of mutual respect with the experienced, though only 37-year-old, Sir John Reith.

Lord Gainford, 66, the new Vice-Chairman, received £1000. He had been Chairman of the British Broadcasting Company and a former Postmaster-General, and he was Reith's first choice for Chairman of the public corporation. But for the Baldwin Administration, which had recommended to the King-in-Council – in the year of the General Strike – the nominations to the first Board, Gainford had two disadvantages. He was both a Liberal and a coal owner. Unlike Clarendon, Gainford had had plenty of experience in sitting on boards. So had Sir Gordon Nairne, formerly Comptroller of the Bank of England. He was then 65, a year older than Dr Montague Rendall, an ex-Headmaster of Winchester. Sir William Mitchell-Thomson, the Postmaster-General who recommended him, was a former pupil. Rendall composed both the BBC's English motto 'Nation shall speak peace unto Nation' and the Latin inscription which adorns the reception hall at Broadcasting House. All three men were old enough to be Reith's father, and it was frequently to them that he looked for consolation and support in his difficulties with the Chairman and with the fifth Governor.

Baldwin must have had in mind (though there is no surviving evidence to this effect) the desirability of having at least one Governor with Labour sympathies or affiliations. But Mitchell-Thomson's failure to consult the Labour leader, Ramsay MacDonald, before nominating Mrs Philip Snowden, was bitterly resented. Ethel Snowden, then 45, 'the would-be Sarah Bernhardt of the party, small, buxom and fearsome when

---

[1] The other members were W.W. Burnham of the small electrical firm of Burndept, John Gray, prepresenting the British Thomson-Houston Company, and Archibald McKinstry of Metropolitan Vickers.

crossed, with an unerring knack of squeezing the last drop of drama out of the most trivial incident',[1] was the wife of the former Labour Chancellor of the Exchequer. At stirring up unnecessary trouble she had few equals, and she was not the most popular member of the Labour Party.

The first Board was an uneasy team, which stayed together until May 1930, when MacDonald, to Reith's relief, appointed Clarendon Governor-General of South Africa. He was replaced by the Rt Hon. J.H. Whitley, Speaker of the House of Commons from 1921 to 1928. The next to go was Sir Gordon Nairne at the end of 1931, on the expiry of his five-year term of office. The remaining three, Gainford, Rendall and (by then) Viscountess Snowden, all received a one-year extension, and retired in December 1932.

Although five years had been specified as the term of office, and she had had six, Lady Snowden felt that she had been 'axed' and made statements to this effect in the Press.[2] There had been an official declaration in the House of Commons in 1926 that at 'the end of five years, those who wish to continue in office may be reappointed'.[3] The use of the word 'may' was characteristic of the first Charter, but the *Sunday Times* pointed rightly to the need for 'a wise policy which provides for reasonable variety of control'. There was certainly nothing 'sinister' about her non-reappointment after the one-year extension.[4]

It was doubtless in the light of Lady Snowden's protests that the Ullswater Committee recommended three years later that there should be no eligibility for reappointment. The post-Ullswater Charter, however, did not go quite so far. A retiring Governor was to be ineligible 'unless Our Postmaster-General shall certify to Us that it is in the public interest that he should be

[1] Lord Shinwell, quoted in Andrew Boyle, *Only the Wind Will Listen* (1972), pp.215–16.

[2] *The Times*, 17 Dec. 1932.

[3] *Hansard*, vol. 199, col.1569, 15 Nov. 1926.

[4] *Sunday Times*, 18 Dec. 1932. Cf. *The Times*, 17 Dec. 1932 and *Truth*, 21 Dec. 1932: 'It is difficult to see where Lady Snowden's grievance against the Postmaster-General lies.' Her protests made 'good copy' (*Spectator*, 23 Dec. 1932), particularly since there had been (obviously untrue) rumours in some sections of the Press that she might replace Clarendon as Chairman (*Popular Wireless*, 29 March 1930). Lady Snowden's protests were certainly naive. Commenting on the letter of termination of appointment which she had received from Sir Kingsley Wood, the Postmaster-General, she said, 'If we are deserving of all this praise, why have they retired us?' (*Birmingham Gazette*, 13 Dec. 1932).

Viscount and Viscountess Bridgeman

reappointed'.[1] By then, Whitley and his successor, the seventy-year-old Viscount Bridgeman, a former First Lord of the Admiralty, Home Secretary and President of the MCC,[2] had died and R.C. Norman, aged 61, the brother of the Governor of the Bank of England, an old-Etonian and for one year Chairman of the LCC, had taken over the Chairmanship (in October 1935).[3] H.G. Brown, a lawyer, was Vice-Chairman from October 1935 to December 1936. Lady Snowden's successor had been another 'Labour woman', a friend of Ramsay MacDonald – although she did not follow him during the crisis of 1931 – Mrs Mary Agnes Hamilton, former MP for Philip Snowden's old seat. The *New Statesman* described her as the first BBC Governor with a first-hand knowledge of broadcasting.[4]

    H.A.L. Fisher, Warden of New College and a former Liberal President of the Board of Education, and Lady Bridgeman, the

[1] Cmd 5091 (1936), *Report of the Broadcasting Committee, 1935*, para. 13; Cmd 5329 (1936), *Broadcasting, Draft of Royal Charter*, Clause 10(iii).

[2] *Daily Mail*, 2 April 1935, 'No one is more English than he'. Cf. Herbert Morrison's comment, quoted in the *Manchester Guardian*, 5 April 1935: it would be unfortunate if the Chairmanship of the BBC came to be regarded as 'a suitable remunerative resting place for elderly Tory politicians'.

[3] The *Daily Mirror*, 20 Aug. 1935, complained of his age in an article headed 'Another "Over 60" Chief for BBC: "Give Youth a Chance" Demand by Listeners: "Age is Curbing Us" – One of the Staff'.

[4] *New Statesman*, 24 Dec. 1932.

Viscount's widow, were appointed to the Board on the recommendation of the National Government before the Ullswater Committee reported. By then there had been twelve Governors in the ten years of the BBC's history, most of them 'respectable rather than distinguished figures'.[1] Their average age on appointment was 59. 'Persons who accept high public office can legitimately be criticised as public characters', O'Brien wrote at the time, 'and it is no reflection on the private capacities of the twelve Governors . . . to say that few of them could have been described at the time of their appointment as widely-known and respected public figures.' They were 'little but names to the great body of the public'. Their occupations and social status 'represented a strictly limited range of the universal callings and conditions of the public which broadcasting serves'.[2]

Alternative names were certainly being considered seriously. Thus, Tom Jones wrote in his Diary in 1937: '[R.H., later Lord] Brand has been offered the post of Vice-Chairman of the BBC and asked me what I should do. I advised against, saying that he would be better employed writing his views on international finance, a subject few understood, whereas many could fill the BBC post.' Jones added – and it might have been added on many later occasions – that 'he had not been told who was to be Chairman'.[3] The same procedures persist, and they involve protracted discussions behind the scenes. As a later Governor, Sir Robert Lusty, put it in 1975, 'The choice of a BBC Chairman is entirely a matter for the Government of the day. It is not a matter for consultation with the BBC at any level. Various names are bandied about in the Press and from a variety of quarters come suggestions that a strong Chairman is what the Government has in mind.'[4]

Among the names being 'bandied about in the Press' during the early and mid-1930s were those of Dick Sheppard, pacifist clergyman and pioneer of religious broadcasting, J.C. Squire, the literary critic, C.B. Cochran, showbusiness leader, Colonel J.T.C. Moore-Brabazon, R.H.S. Crossman – not yet thirty, and

[1] *News Chronicle*, 16 Dec. 1932.
[2] T.H. O'Brien, *British Experiments in Public Ownership and Control* (1937), pp.120–2. See above, p.63.
[3] Thomas Jones, *A Diary with Letters, 1931–1950* (1954), pp.327–8, entry for 16 April 1937.
[4] Robert Lusty, *Bound to be Read* (1975), p.247.

Dr J.J. Mallon and Lady Violet Bonham Carter

the blind Sir Ian Fraser, who had served as a member of the
Crawford Committee.[1] It was often suggested, too, that such
better-known names could be associated on the Board with
specific aspects of broadcasting – e.g. C.B. Cochran with 'the
lighter side' and Fraser with Empire broadcasting. O'Brien referred more generally to 'sections of the public which clamour,
and are likely to continue to do so, for a Welshman, . . . a
professional musician, or some other direct representative to be
chosen by a geographical or occupational group for service on the
Board'.[2]

Fraser was, in fact, the only one of the group of names most
often mentioned whom the Government recommended for appointment. As early as 1930 the case for his inclusion had been
described as 'unanswerable', but it was not until January 1937
that he joined the Board, resigning from his seat in Parliament to
do so.[3] He was then thirty-nine years old. The other Governors
appointed under the pre-war National Government were Dr J.J.
Mallon, Warden of Toynbee Hall (then aged 61), who was said
to have a more profound knowledge of how 'the other half' lived

[1] *Popular Wireless*, 6 Dec. 1930. For Crossman, see *Star*, 21 July 1936, where it was
pointed out first that he had acted as Warden of New College in Fisher's absence and,
second, that he held the record for the largest amount of mail after his first broadcast.
For Press comments, see also below, Chapter III, *passim*.

[2] O'Brien, op.cit., p.122.

[3] *Popular Wireless*, 6 Dec. 1930.

Harold Nicolson and A.H. Mann

than any previous Governor, and who joined at the same time as Fraser; C.H.G. Millis (aged 43), a banker with a gallant wartime record who joined in June 1937; Miss Margery Fry (aged 63), former Principal of Somerville College, Oxford, who joined in January 1938 (in place of Mary Agnes Hamilton); and Sir Allan Powell, who became Chairman in April 1939 (at the age of 63) in place of R.C. Norman.

Powell, who had served as Clerk to the Metropolitan Asylums Board, was well known to Neville Chamberlain, the Prime Minister, although he was to survive Chamberlain and to serve as Chairman mainly under Churchill. He stayed on until December 1946. Millis, his Vice-Chairman, remained in his post for nine years.

'These new Governors . . . are an infernal nuisance', Reith had written in his *Diary* in 1937.[1] He was not counting Powell, of course, whom he did not meet until he had become Minister of Information in 1940. He never got on well with Fraser, and he had little regard for Mallon who believed Governors should 'departmentalise'.[2] He would have been shocked had he known that soon after his appointment Mallon had written to Sir Stephen Tallents, one of the most important senior officials in the BBC, that 'the present Governors are absurd'.[3]

[1] Reith, *Diary*, 20 Jan. 1937. [2] Ibid., 10 Feb. 1937.
[3] Letter from J.J. Mallon to Sir Stephen Tallents, 28 Oct. 1937.

Barbara Ward

No one could have called the new wartime Governors absurd.
A.H. Mann, a former editor of the *Yorkshire Post* (until 1939) and
a forceful critic of appeasement, was joined by Lady Violet
Bonham Carter, Asquith's daughter, in April 1941 in her first
major public post outside the Liberal Party, and Harold Nicolson, then aged 54, joined them in July 1941. He had been
Parliamentary Secretary to the Ministry of Information, and had
produced his first BBC script ten years before. He had also
appeared on pre-war television.

Some of the members of the post-war team were equally
striking, including two women who had much to offer the BBC.
Barbara Ward, appointed under the Labour Government in
April 1946, was described at the time as an 'economic night-
ingale' and 'Britain's Dorothy Thompson'.[1] She was a Roman
Catholic, but also a 'modern girl', aged 31, who was actually
known to listeners as a lively and polished broadcaster: she did
not bother over labels, but she was 'more Left . . . than Right,
passionately earnest over the rights of people'.[2] The Dowager
Marchioness of Reading, appointed a few days later, was the
founder of the Women's Voluntary Service, and it was natural
that she should become Vice-Chairman of the BBC in January

[1] *John Bull*, 15 June 1946; *News Review*, 21 Oct. 1948.
[2] *Catholic Herald*, 12 April 1946.

1947. She had been a young member of the Ullswater Committee, and in 1946 was 52. One writer called her 'the most remarkable woman alive', and this was not just flattery.[1]

Powell's successor as Chairman, Lord Inman, was a Governor for only a few months from 1 January 1947 to 22 April 1947. Churchill asked Attlee in the House of Commons for the party affiliations of both Inman and, rather surprisingly, Lady Reading, and was told that Inman was a Labour peer and that he was not sure what Lady Reading's were.[2] This was a period when the Labour Party was in office, for the first time with a large majority, and there were more questions about the political affiliations of Governors than at any other time in the BBC's history. Dr Ernest Whitfield (later Lord Kenswood), the blind Governor who succeeded Fraser in July 1946, was a member of the Labour Party also, as was Lord Simon of Wythenshawe who took Inman's place in June 1947. Geoffrey Lloyd, who had been appointed in April 1946, was attacked by some Labour members of Parliament because he was an ex-Conservative Minister of Information in the Caretaker Government of 1945 who had been defeated at the general election.[3] (He returned to Parliament in 1950 and stayed in the Commons for 24 years.)

The two other members of the post-war Board had no party affiliations, however. Air Marshal Sir Richard Peck, who served as a Governor from April 1946 to 31 December 1949, had been Air Spokesman during the Second World War and was President of the RAF Association in 1949, while John Adamson, who was a Governor from January 1947 to July 1952, was President of the Scottish Chartered Accountants in London. He had served as a Governor of Charing Cross Hospital under Inman's powerful Chairmanship, and he took the place of Millis as the Governor most interested in finance.

Philip Inman, who had revealed great financial flair at Charing Cross Hospital, was not a popular choice with Haley or with the other chief officials inside the BBC. He had strong views about programme content (particularly 'dubious' jokes in Variety), and in a widely reported speech a month before

---

[1] *Everybody's*, 11 Dec. 1948.   [2] *The Times*, 12 Dec. 1946.

[3] See, for example, a letter to *The Tribune*, 2 April 1946: 'I have just read of the appointment of a sworn enemy of Socialism, Mr Geoffrey Lloyd, to a directorship of the BBC.'

Lord Inman

he became Chairman he had stressed that 'the Governors of the BBC . . . are public servants' and must be 'very careful about public opinion'.[1] His Labour views were less relevant, perhaps, than the fact that he had originally intended to be a Wesleyan Minister and that he was Chairman of the Central Board of Finance of the Church Assembly. Powell had always described himself as 'an ordinary listener', but Inman, like Simon after him, was something more. Indeed, both he and Lady Reading had done a great deal of listening before taking up their duties.[2] While at the BBC Inman's slogan was 'Listeners First', adapted from 'Patients First' which he had coined when he went to Charing Cross.[3] The reason why he left the Chairmanship was that he became Lord Privy Seal, a surprise choice, in Attlee's Government.

Simon was more interested in the staff of the BBC than he was in the listeners. Indeed in 1948, 1949 and 1950 he was attacked by the small but vociferous right-wing Listeners' Association, founded two years earlier, for bringing politics into broadcasting.[4] This was perhaps the first outside group to try to put pressure on the Governors as a body. One of its founders had been

[1] *Yorkshire Post*, 12 Dec. 1946; *Star*, 12 Dec. 1946.
[2] *Evening Standard*, 12 Dec. 1946.   [3] *Everybody's*, 3 May 1947.
[4] For the founding of the Association, see *Evening Standard*, 16 Oct. 1947.

taking notes on BBC broadcasts since 1935 in an effort to identify 'pro-Communist bias', and the considered view of the Association was that the Corporation had 'pursued a consistent policy of advocating and advertising Communism and of trying to disrupt the life of the country, spread discontent, and discredit our British institutions'. The Association was irritated with Simon for refusing to 'dismiss all Communists from the BBC', and in 1949 obtained 3656 signatures to a petition that the BBC should broadcast 'regular and frequent talks' on 'the dangers and real meaning of Communism'. The Prime Minister refused to accept the petition while the Beveridge Committee was holding its hearings, and in its evidence to that Committee the Association recommended the break-up of the monopoly.[1] The extreme views it expressed on programme content roused George Wigg to found a rival Social Democratic Listeners' Association.

Simon's socialism did not easily fit into the categories of the Listeners' Association. He was after all a businessman, who believed in 'efficiency',[2] and a 1947 peer, who must have been impressed by one of the indictments in the Association's evidence to Beveridge that among the 'objectionable' BBC programmes was a broadcast of Somerset Maugham's *The Title*, 'a lampoon on the system of hereditary titles which should not have been broadcast at the height of the controversy about the House of Lords early in 1949'.[3]

Simon had known Haley in Manchester, where they were fellow directors of the *Manchester Guardian*. A revealing insight into their relationship, for long a favourite legend in Broadcasting House,[4] has recently been confirmed by Haley:

One morning in the summer of 1948 I found Lord Simon in a state of great pleasurable excitement. He had heard we were both going to be on holiday at the Saunton Sands Hotel at the same time. We must make full use of the happy accident. He proposed we should meet every afternoon for an hour and a half of concentrated discussion on a subject we had agreed upon the previous day, and had had time to think about.

We did. It was a great nuisance. My wife and our children had to be

[1] Cmd 8117 (1951), *Report of the Broadcasting Committee, 1949, Appendix H, Memoranda submitted to the Committee*, p.303.
[2] See his book on housing, *Rebuilding Britain, A Twenty Year Plan* (1945).
[3] Cmd 8117 (1951), p.305.
[4] See Oliver Whitley, 'The BBC's Ladder', *The Listener*, 1 Feb. 1979.

B.B.C. BOOGEY

L to R: Lord Simon of Wythenshawe (Chairman), Ernest Whitfield, Lady Reading (Vice-Chairman), Barbara Ward, Sir Richard Peek, Geoffrey Lloyd, John Adamson

left on their own each day from 4.30 to 6 p.m. . . . We solemnly engaged in ninety minutes of earnest talk on all kinds of subjects, only a few relevant to the BBC. The exercise was of no practical value, except to keep happy a man who had a disinterested devotion to the public good.

Lord Simon and I had many battles of will and intellect. Not one of them lessened the respect each had for the other's motives.[1]

Haley was 47 at the time, and Simon 68. The Chairman was 72 when he retired, so that there was also a sizeable age gap between himself and most of the other Governors. He was more articulate about broadcasting policy than any of his predecessors – on becoming Chairman he had to resign from the 17-strong Royal Commission on the Press – and he is the only Chairman to have left a substantial private archive.

Four other Governors were appointed before the fall of the Labour Government in 1951. Lord Tedder, who joined the Board in January 1950 and became Vice-Chairman a year later, was the best known to the public. He had been Chief of the Air Staff during the two years immediately before his appointment and had written a book on *Air Power in War* in 1948. 'I know

---

[1] Letter from Haley to Leonard Miall, 9 March 1979.

nothing at all about broadcasting, but I can learn,' he said on being appointed. One of his favourite sayings was 'specialisation is one of the most dangerous tendencies. It has given us experts, not wise men.'[1] This was a fitting text for a Governor. Tedder's promotion to the Vice-Chairmanship was unusual in that he had been absent from the BBC during his first year as Governor while he was serving as Chairman of the British Joint Services Mission in Washington.[2]

The other Governors appointed at the same time included one able and energetic Labour sympathiser, Barbara Wootton (created Baroness Wootton of Abinger in 1958), Professor of Social Studies at the University of London and in later life a distinguished Labour peer and for a time Deputy Speaker of the House of Lords, and one ex-Governor of Bombay, Lord Clydesmuir, former Conservative Secretary of State for Scotland, who became National Governor for Scotland when National Governorships were introduced in 1952. He died in office two years later.

Professor Wootton, who had often broadcast, had published *Freedom Under Planning*, in 1945, and in the year that she became a Governor, *Testament for Social Science*. She brought to the Board experience and opinions which had hitherto not been represented on it, and her interesting autobiography throws light on her attitudes both to public service in general and to governing the BBC. She felt that the difference between the income she received for attending the fortnightly meetings of the Board and for working (only for expenses) for two days a week on Royal Commissions was 'irrational'. But she found her BBC work 'rewarding': 'of all the worlds in which I have moved, including the academic and political, in none have I met and made friends with so many congenial people as in the BBC in the nineteen-fifties'.[3] She admired Haley and quoted a pertinent conversation with him about the role of the Governors. 'I look on them,' Haley had said, 'as a reserve of wisdom.' To which she replied, 'Like the gold reserve of the Bank of England, I suppose – not to be drawn upon.'[4] She believed in a small, not a large Board; assessed its

---

[1] *Daily Graphic*, 10 Dec. 1949.

[2] For the discussion in the Board about his leave of absence, see above, p.23. Tedder became Chancellor of the University of Cambridge in 1950, and on leaving the BBC was appointed Chairman of Standard Cars.

[3] B. Wootton, *In a World I Never Made* (1967), p.259.   [4] Ibid., p.263.

activities modestly (we cannot be said to 'have initiated any major developments of policy'); noted Normanbrook's action in not renewing the invitation to Ian Smith as being 'personal' not 'collective', like Simon's actions in relation to *Party Manners*; and welcomed 'trade unionism' inside the BBC, while criticising too much stress on 'professionalism'.[1]

Barbara Wootton was soon joined on the Board by another Socialist. Francis Williams, close to Attlee – he had been his Adviser on Public Relations for two years from 1945 to 1947 – was at first sight a straight Labour appointment, a nominee of Herbert Morrison. Yet as a journalist he was keenly interested in the media and wrote more than one book on the subject. He said when he was appointed that he was particularly interested in 'the development of television educational programmes and talks'. Francis Williams was not very happy as a Governor, however, and was not sorry when his term ended in July 1952.[2] He became a Labour life peer in 1962 – of Abinger, like Barbara Wootton.

Ivan Stedeford, the last of the Labour Government appointments (in January 1951) had no Labour sympathies, but he had exceptional qualifications. He had been a member of the Beveridge Committee set up in 1949 and he was also a member of the Television Advisory Committee from 1949 to 1950. At the time of his appointment as a Governor he was serving also on the Advisory Council of the Department of Scientific and Industrial Research. It was not so much for his technical knowledge, however, as for his knowledge of finance that Stedeford became best known as a Governor of the BBC. He was Chairman and Managing Director of Tube Investments, and he was quickly put to work inside the Board on questions relating to licence fees, borrowing powers and capital funds for the development of television. He was the most specialised of the Governors in 1951, and he stayed on the Board for over four years.

It is interesting to consider the extent to which Governors were offered the opportunity of feeling that they belonged to the same team for a long enough period of time to give the Board some kind of corporate identity. Sir Alexander Cadogan, Chairman from August 1952 to the end of November 1957, worked throughout

---

[1] Ibid., pp.260 ff. See also her article on 'The BBC's Duty to Society' in *The Listener*, 22 July 1965.

[2] See F. Williams, *Nothing So Strange* (1970), Ch.15.

most of his period of office with four Governors appointed at the same time – Lady Rhys Williams, who retired one year before him, Sir Henry Mulholland (National Governor for Northern Ireland), Sir Philip Morris and Lord Macdonald of Gwaenysgor (National Governor for Wales). In his last year in office, he welcomed another batch of three at one time – the Earl of Balfour (National Governor for Scotland), Mrs Thelma Cazalet-Keir and Dame Florence Hancock. There had been only three Governors between – Lord Rochdale, President of the National Union of Manufacturers, the 73-year-old Thomas Johnston, former Labour Secretary of State for Scotland, who was Lord Clydesmuir's successor as National Governor for Scotland but stayed only eighteen months[1] (to be replaced by the Earl of Balfour), and Sir Edward Benthall, who replaced Sir Ivan Stedeford as finance Governor. His background was the Indian Civil Service and he had been leader of the House in the Indian Assembly of 1946.

Lady Rhys Williams was the most vociferous and determined of what a Belfast newspaper once called an 'august group'[2] – although she was little known to the public. Her friends said that she had 'the best brain of any woman in Britain',[3] while her biographers noted that she was the daughter of the novelist Elinor Glyn. Lord Macdonald had just relinquished the presidency of the National Band of Hope Union, and Lord Rochdale, the youngest of the group (48) when he was appointed a Governor, was a frequent speaker in the House of Lords on the textile industry.

Lady Rhys Williams undoubtedly had ideas of her own both about how best to fight the campaign against commercial television and how to develop the BBC. 'I want them to take a real interest in colour television,' she told an interviewer just after her first Board meeting, 'instead of just saying it would cost a lot of money.'[4] Her successor, Mrs Thelma Cazalet-Keir, had different political views: she had been a Conservative Member of Parliament from 1931 to 1945. Yet, like Lady Rhys Williams, she was a forceful advocate and often took an independent line on the

[1] The *Evening News* in Glasgow (22 Dec. 1954) described his appointment as 'one of the most sagacious moves in the history of broadcasting'. This was a great exaggeration.

[2] *Belfast Telegraph*, 14 April 1956.   [3] *The Recorder*, 28 Oct. 1953.

[4] *Everybody's*, 9 Oct. 1954.

Board. She was joined by a second woman, Dame Florence Hancock, in July 1956, the first trade-unionist to be appointed and Chairman of the TUC from 1947 to 1948. Mrs Cazalet-Keir was 57 when she joined the Board and Dame Florence 63, and the former at least believed that a few younger members of the Board would have been an advantage. [1]

It was Sir Philip Morris, however, who became the 'elder statesman' of the group. Vice-Chancellor of the University of Bristol for twenty years from 1946 to 1966 and a former Director-General of Army Education, he had already served as Chairman of the BBC's West Regional Advisory Council for five years before becoming a Governor. He was the only Governor, indeed, to have had that particular experience. And after leaving the Vice-Chairmanship of the Board, which he held from July 1954 to June 1960, he continued to be consulted by the Board about broadcasting problems. [2] The BBC has often been said to be afraid of criticism; [3] Cadogan, indeed, once said so quite explicitly. 'It is wrong that the officials of the BBC should think they are above all criticism. It is this attitude which is going to bring us trouble.' [4] By contrast, Morris went on to the offensive, complaining of 'the impregnable ignorance' of critics who said BBC programmes were unbalanced. [5]

Unlike Cadogan, Sir Arthur fforde, who had just retired as Headmaster of Rugby, inherited a Board when he was appointed Chairman by Harold Macmillan. He was the only person to join it in December 1957, and, as Robert Lusty put it, 'no less obvious or more inspired choice' could have been made. By the time fforde left, however, in January 1964, he was very much senior Governor. A quiet and unobtrusive Chairman, he saw the BBC through the Pilkington enquiry, trying at every point to draw the best out of all his colleagues. He was thanked both by the Postmaster-General and by the Prime Minister when he decided that he had to resign for health reasons in January 1964. [6] Characteristically he in turn thanked Greene and the Board of Management for 'six years and more of informative, educational, entertaining, and, therefore, wholly enjoyable experience'. [7]

[1] See above, p.113.   [2] Ibid.   [3] See above, pp.94-5.
[4] Quoted in D. Dilks (ed.), *The Diaries of Sir Alexander Cadogan* (1971), p.793.
[5] *Bristol Evening News*, 4 June 1954.
[6] *The Times*, 30 Jan. 1964. The letters were printed in *Ariel*, Feb. 1964.
[7] Letter from fforde to Greene, 29 Jan. 1964.

Sir Arthur fforde

The first Governor to join fforde was a new Northern Ireland
National Governor, J. Ritchie McKee, who replaced Mul-
holland. The second, Sir James Duff, who had just retired as
Vice-Chancellor of the University of Durham, has an in-
dependent claim to fame as a Governor. He was twice Vice-
Chairman; and during a critical period in 1964, after fforde's
departure, he proved a shrewd and successful Chairman. His
views, expressed with great clarity, always commanded respect.
Yet he preferred Durham to London, and had no desire to act as
Chairman for any longer period than was strictly necessary.

Among the new Governors the Earl of Halsbury, a former
President of the Institution of Production Engineers, lasted for
only two years, but all the other Governors appointed to serve
under fforde had long records of service. Two new National
Governors appointed in 1960 — Mrs Rachel Jones (for Wales),
much criticised on her appointment because she did not speak
Welsh,[1] and Sir David Milne (for Scotland), a former Permanent
Under-Secretary of State at the Scottish Office[2] — served out
their full five-year terms, and Lusty, Chairman and Managing

[1] *South Wales Echo and Evening Express*, 1 July 1960; *Daily Telegraph*, 23 June 1960.
Mrs Jones, who was wife of the Dean of Brecon, stood up firmly to the criticism. See
below, pp. 170–1.
[2] Milne took the place of the Earl of Balfour, who resigned eight months before his
period of office was due to end.

Director of the Hutchinson Publishing Group and former Chairman of the National Book League, also appointed in 1960, followed in the footsteps of Duff and had two periods as Vice-Chairman with a period as Acting Chairman in between. Apart from Simon, Hill and Greene, he has written more about his experiences in broadcasting than any other Governor.[1]

Lord Normanbrook, who had been selected by Sir Alec Douglas-Home after consultation with Harold Wilson, took over from Duff in May 1964. Before that time four other Governors had been appointed: Gerald Coke, Chairman of Rio Tinto, who was also Chairman of the Glyndebourne Arts Trust; Sir Richard Pim, a former Inspector-General of the Royal Ulster Constabulary, who became National Governor for Northern Ireland; Dame Anne Godwin, the Chairman of the TUC, who replaced Dame Florence Hancock; and Sir Ashley Clarke, who joined the Board in 1962. He had just retired as Ambassador to Italy and was as much interested in music as Coke. Clarke was the first to occupy what by convention became the Foreign Office seat on the Board. The last three of these appointments were originally only made to July 1964, when the BBC's Fourth Charter expired, but all the new Governors, 'a refreshingly mixed bag',[2] served full five-year terms, and Dame Anne was given a one-year extension. Dame Anne's favourite programme was said to be *The Rag Trade*, and she had the right qualifications to serve on a Board to which Greene was reporting as Director-General. She was opposed to censorship of all kinds, wanted to see 'full and proper expressions of all points of view' and liked 'experimental plays'. 'I would like to see a writer come forward in television,' she added, 'who could accurately depict the working classes.'[3]

Lord Normanbrook's three-year Chairmanship ended in June 1967 with his death in office. As former Secretary to the Cabinet (for fifteen years, first of Labour, then of Conservative rule) and as Head of the Home Civil Service, he was familiar with all the corridors of power. He had also been for one year a Director of Tube Investments. Several newspapers described him as 'the ideal choice for the job of Chairman of the Governors'. He was said to be more 'unflappable than Macmillan', and it was re-

---

[1] See above, pp.128–30. There is a good profile of him in *Smith's Trade News*, 13 July 1963.
[2] *Daily Express*, 7 June 1962.   [3] *Daily Mail*, 8 June 1962.

called that Churchill had made him a Privy Councillor while he was still Secretary to the Cabinet. Normanbrook not only knew from experience the difference between 'executive action' and policy making, but he also carried 'immense authority'.[1] At the same time, he was said to be unlikely to prove 'the strong man' to carry out 'a political policy within the BBC for whom some Tories have been asking'.[2] There had been rumours in the Press that the Government was seeking to 'curb' Greene by giving much of his powers to a new Chairman of Governors,[3] but Normanbrook soon made it clear himself that he did not envisage his role in this way. Very soon, of course, he was dealing, after the general election of October 1964, not with a Conservative but with a Labour Government.

Like fforde before him, Normanbrook inherited his Board complete. Indeed, it was more than a year before any new Governor joined him. The first was Professor Glanmor Williams, an intelligent and forceful Professor of History at the University College of Swansea and National Governor for Wales. He was only 45 when he joined the Board, and he was to stay on it beyond Normanbrook and through into the last year of the Hill regime. Sir John (later Lord) Fulton, who had been Principal at Swansea before becoming Vice-Chancellor of the new University of Sussex, was the second. He joined the Board one month after Williams and was to have two spells as Vice-Chairman – one immediately on appointment. The other was after he had served as Chairman of a Royal Commission on the reform of the Civil Service (during which time he dropped to being an ordinary Governor) in the difficult months following the appointment of Hill as Chairman from February 1968 to September 1970. Fulton, energetic and conscientious, was, in fact, the main link between the Normanbrook and Hill regimes; he also had the ear of Harold Wilson. The third Governor was Lady Baird, who became National Governor for Scotland in November 1965. She and Williams were said to be 'a formidably vocal pair and great fighters for their national interests at meetings'.[4]

Learning the news of Lord Hill's controversial appointment in

[1] Obituary notice in *The Times*, 16 June 1967.
[2] *Sunday Telegraph*, 29 March 1964.
[3] *Daily Herald*, 9 March 1964. See below, pp.177–8.
[4] *The Guardian*, 29 May 1969.

September 1967 was described by Lusty as being rather like receiving news during the Second World War that Rommel had been made Commander-in-Chief of the Eighth Army.[1] And this time it was a Labour Prime Minister who was looking for a 'strong man' in the BBC. Wilson did not inform Edward Heath, the Leader of the Opposition, about the appointment, which might have gone to Herbert Bowden, later Lord Aylestone and Chairman of the Independent Television Authority.

The story of the Board during the Hill period has been described in earlier chapters: it has also been described in detail and the work of the Board criticised in detail by Hill himself.[2] It is interesting to add, however, that by December 1972, when Hill retired, he was working with an almost entirely new team. Only Lord Dunleath and Sir Ralph Murray survived. J.H. Trower, a Director of Proctor and Gamble, had joined the Board before Hill – in November 1966 – but he died in January 1968. Two new Governors were present at Hill's first meeting – Murray, recently British Ambassador in Athens and the first Governor to have worked on the staff of the BBC (from 1934 to 1939), and Dunleath, an Ulster landowner and a keen territorial army officer, who was National Governor for Northern Ireland, the youngest Governor (34) since Barbara Ward. It is Murray, the diplomat, then an observer, who is said to have introduced Hill to the members of the Board at their first meeting, when the old members of the Board still felt 'numbed and shocked'. Edward Short, the Postmaster-General, is said to have wanted 'a much closer liaison' between BBC and ITA, and the first item at Hill's first meeting, introduced by him, was, appropriately enough, 'Top Salaries in the BBC' and comparability with those in the ITA.[3]

The other members of Hill's Board – 'with the fate of radio in its hand'[4] – were Tom Jackson (February 1968 to February 1973), Secretary of the Union of Post Office Workers; Sir Robert Bellinger (February 1968 to June 1971), recently Lord Mayor of London and President of Kinloch's, the provision merchants, as well as a Director of Arsenal Football Club; Paul Wilson (Feb-

[1] Lusty, op.cit., p.253. See above, p.129.
[2] See above, pp.43–4, 129–31, and Hill, *Behind the Screen* (1974), *passim*.
[3] Lusty, op.cit., p.262; Board of Governors, *Minutes*, 21 Sept. 1967.
[4] *The Guardian*, 29 May 1969.

ruary 1968 to February 1972), civil engineer and industrial archaeologist; Sir Learie Constantine (July 1968 to July 1971), cricketer and former High Commissioner for Trinidad and Tobago, the first black member of the Board; Dame Mary Green (July 1968 to July 1973), Headmistress of Kidbrooke Comprehensive School and a member of the Donovan Commission on Trade Unions; Lady Plowden (November 1970 to February 1975), who like Sir John Fulton before her, was made Vice-Chairman on her appointment; Lady Avonside (May 1971 to April 1976), a former lecturer in Social Studies, who was National Governor for Scotland; Robert Allan (July 1971 to June 1976), company director and former Conservative Member of Parliament; Dr Glyn Tegai Hughes (appointed November 1971 and still a Governor), National Governor for Wales; Tony Morgan (January 1972 to December 1976), who had made a million pounds before he was 30 and was a former Yachtsman of the Year (1965); the poet Roy Fuller (appointed in January 1972); and George Howard (appointed in February 1972), who had just served for three years as President of the Country Landowners' Association.

There was a fifteenth man to complete the list of members of a team which often changed – Sir Hugh Greene, who having been Director-General served as a Governor from July 1969 to August 1971. The shift was bound to cause complications. It was not only Greene's presence, however, that made for differences of outlook on the Board during this period. Hill's appointment guaranteed that there would be differences, for as Lusty told Short, it was 'hardly realistic to expect that the appointment of the Chairman of the ITA to the chair of the BBC should be at once welcomed by the Corporation. It was only natural for the staff, the higher executives and the Board of Governors to feel disconcerted.' [1]

The phase passed, but Hill's desire to introduce voting on policy issues sometimes accentuated the differences. He was looking for ideas not for consensus. Indeed, a journalist, who believed that by 1969 Hill had produced a consensus, described him as a 'voice collector', going round the table inviting Governors to express their views. The same journalist remarked that if one added up all the committees, from the Board for Mining Qualifications to the Scottish Milk Committee that the Gover-

[1] See Lusty, op.cit., pp.258–9, also above, p.129.

nors had sat on, it would make up some sort of world record.[1]

Between the time of Sir Michael Swann's appointment as Chairman in January 1973 and the fiftieth anniversary of the British Broadcasting Corporation in January 1977, when all living Governors past and present were invited to a celebration lunch in Broadcasting House, eight new Governors had joined the Board. Victor Feather, General Secretary of the TUC, served on it from May 1973 to July 1976, not the least of the trade unionists who had been regularly invited since 1956: he died in office and was replaced by Lord Allen of Fallowfield. Bill O'Hara became National Governor for Northern Ireland in October 1973: he was a hotel owner, one of the few Roman Catholics to join the Ulster Unionist Party, and the first Northern Irish Catholic to be appointed (on William Whitelaw's recommendation) to the Board. Professor Alan E. Thompson, a former Labour Member of Parliament and the Professor of the Economics of Government at Heriot-Watt University, became National Governor for Scotland in May 1976. Philip Chappell, a banker, replaced Robert Allan, by then Lord Allan of Kilmahew, in June 1976. Diplomacy was represented after November 1973 by Sir Denis Greenhill (later Lord Greenhill of Harrow), who had been Head of the Diplomatic Service from 1969 to 1973, while Mrs Stella Clarke, aged 41, joined the Board in February 1974, and in June 1975 the Hon. Mark Bonham Carter became the first son of a Governor to serve on the Board. He was appointed from the start as Vice-Chairman and has played a major role in BBC policy making.

One move from the Board made history if not quite as dramatically as Hill's move from the ITA to BBC in 1967. Lady Plowden, Vice-Chairman of the Board, became Chairman of the Independent Broadcasting Authority in February 1975. Her comment was straightforward. 'If you have two great broadcasting organisations it is sensible that from time to time people should be moved from one to the other. Previously I have been extremely loyal to the BBC. I am now a different person and must look at things from a new point of view.'[2]

---

[1] *The Guardian*, 29 May 1969.   [2] *Daily Telegraph*, 7 Feb. 1975.

CHAPTER III

THE PUBLIC EYE

In an article of September 1963 the *Spectator* described the Board of Governors as 'that shadowy background body', and while discerning 'much activity' on the part of the Board it suggested that the members of the Board had generally been thought of as 'damp clay in the hands of a resourceful Director-General'.[1] The fact that the writer was wrong in his description of the activity of the Board does not rob the statement of its interest. The Board of the time was an active one – *pace* Lord Hill – and it showed a genuine and searching interest in the kind of broadcasting revolution which Greene was attempting to carry out.

Such comment revealed a degree of public interest in the Governors – if very much a minority interest – which has not always been apparent in the history of the Board. When they have been discussed, it has often been taken for granted that they were not really 'governing'. Thus, in 1946, after the composition of the Board had changed substantially, *Truth* wrote characteristically that 'little public interest' had been shown in the appointment of the latest set of BBC Governors. 'This may be because of the general belief that they do not "govern" the BBC,' the leader suggested, 'but merely approve the decrees of the Director-General.'[2] And a year later the same periodical, noting Haley's list of names for his new Board of Management added that 'it is obvious that in practice the Board of Management will run the show and the Governors amuse themselves at their fortnightly meetings with general matters.' 'The BBC', it added, 'is the perfect example that proves how much more important are personalities than the most perfect paper constitutions.'[3]

Sixteen years earlier a different point had been made. 'The Board,' it was said in the *Star*, a newspaper which always devoted much space to broadcasting issues, was 'beyond the reach of our slings and arrows' since they sat in 'a castle of monopoly with the throne jealously guarded'.[4]

[1] *Spectator*, 20 Sept. 1963. It suggested that the Governors 'resolved to do rather more governing', were restive about some of Greene's policies: 'If the mask of Auntie were merely replaced by that of Anti, and many programmes increasingly informed by a flippant, destructive bias, what then would justify the BBC's special position?'
[2] *Truth*, 12 April 1946.   [3] Ibid., 5 Dec. 1947.   [4] *Star*, 13 Feb. 1930.

The very first Governors had been in the public eye, and Mrs Snowden, in particular, did her best to ensure that they would stay there. Comment could often be highly unfavourable, particularly in the specialised radio press. 'The spread of undue caution, the slowing down of the machine, the entanglement of red tape and the increasing frequency of "amateur" decisions,' the editor of *Popular Wireless* maintained in 1930, 'all these are symptoms of executive intervention by the Governors.' Yet he did not blame them. They were 'merely trying to carry out the clearly expressed intention of the Parliament which appointed them'.[1]

As a preface to this article the editor quoted from a speech in the House of Commons by Sir William Mitchell-Thomson, Postmaster-General at the time the Corporation was established, to the effect that the Governors would be 'persons of wide and varied interest and with a broad knowledge of affairs'.[2] Already much of the comment then – as since – focused (usually at the time when they were appointed) on whether or how they lived up to this specification.

The *Daily News*, in an immediate comment on the names of the first Board, described the Governors as 'distinguished representatives of the various branches of public life, but they are all, to say the least of it, middle-aged. Broadcasting is still an infant industry,' it continued, 'it needs the spirit of youth and the missionary driving force and elasticity of mind that accompany it.'[3] The communist *Sunday Worker* had a different complaint. 'The board', it wrote, 'consists of capitalists, landowners, tories and empire touts – with the sugar of a "Labour" representative well calculated to make the Workers vomit.'[4]

The first Governors spent considerable time, as did their successors, in discussing complaints from the listening public. Lord Clarendon speaking at a broadcasting dinner half a year after the Corporation had been established, noted that an elderly woman had bitterly complained that the announcer, closing down the service, had failed to say 'Good Night' twice, and that a man who had bought a wireless set at a price 'including royalty' – the

[1] *Popular Wireless*, 6 Dec. 1930.
[2] See above, p.63.
[3] *Daily News*, 23 Oct. 1926.
[4] *Sunday Worker*, 31 Oct. 1926.

original system of collecting royalties on radio apparatus sold – had written to say how disgusted he was that, although he had had the set for months, not one member of the Royal Family had been heard.[1]

Mrs Snowden took the same occasion to draw attention to the motto she had promoted, 'Nation Shall Speak Peace Unto Nation', and Hilda Matheson, the first Director of Talks, mentioned the case of a woman who wanted an SOS message broadcast because her escort for a grand ball had fallen ill and she needed 'someone to take his place'.[2]

All committees of enquiry were to stress in their different ways what 'remarkable men and women' Governors had to be – 'remarkable in their understanding of their responsibilities,' the Pilkington Report put it, 'and able to defend . . . independence against the challenges it is bound to meet'.[3] It is perhaps significant, however, that following the publication of the Annan Report there was virtually no discussion in the Press of the role of the Governors nor even any straight reporting of what the Annan Committee had said about them. Only the specialist periodical *Broadcast* dealt with the subject in an article entitled 'Responsibility and Accountability: where does ultimate power lie?'; and this article, mainly straight reporting, concluded with the simple sentence from the Report that 'the chain of accountability is adequate'.[4]

Of course, there were more 'dramatic' themes to consider after the Annan Report – notably its recommendations that there should be a new Open Broadcasting Authority to take care of the fourth television channel, and that local radio, public service and commercial, should also pass under new direction. Yet *Broadcast* was alone in touching on one of the two topics concerning the Governors which have been dealt with more than any other over the years – but then only intermittently – the social composition of the Board. It referred to Annan's 'wonder' that so few members of the Authorities 'had their roots in the working class', and his quip that 'from the list sometimes referred to as the "Great and the Good", the Prime Minister and the Home Secretary' might

---

[1] *Evening Standard*, 14 June 1927.
[2] Ibid.
[3] Cmnd 1753 (1962), *Report of the Committee on Broadcasting*, para. 396, p.119.
[4] *Broadcast*, 28 March 1977.

often 'choose some of the "Lesser and the Better"'.[1] The demand
for 'working-class' Governors or 'ordinary people' was at least as
old as the Ullswater Report, and had been urged then by one
future Prime Minister, Clement Attlee, although he did little to
implement his own ideas when he was Prime Minister.[2] So, too,
was the demand for trade-union Governors before the first of
these was appointed in 1956.[3]

The article on 'Governing the BBC' which appeared in *Truth*
in 1946 mentioned a second point about the composition of the
Board which has been made on other occasions too – that Governors tend to conform to a type. 'While they may – and do –
formally represent the main parties,' and this greatly exaggerated the extent to which party loyalties counted even with
Prime Ministers, 'the particular selection of each one from within
a party suggests a common denominator to which all conform. If
a student of such matters were to be asked to bet as to who would
be selected as between certain candidates he would never go
wrong.'[4] *Truth* was right.

A third point concerning national representation was often
raised, too, before the first appointment of National Governors.
'It is disappointing not to find a Scot among the new Governors',
The Scotsman complained in 1946. 'If memory serves aright there
has never been a Scottish Governor of the BBC.'[5] It did not add
that there had been a Scottish Director-General. The Liberal
leader Clement Davies took up the question in the Commons, in
relation to both Scotland and Wales, and there were Welsh
protests even after there were National Governors for Wales that

---

[1] Ibid. Marghanita Laski, a member of the Committee, took up the social
composition theme in an interesting article 'A voice in radio: must it always be middle-
aged and middle-class?' (*The Times*, 29 March 1977); yet she was referring to the
structure of local radio not of the BBC Board. She was right in that context to draw a
distinction between '*real* ordinary people' and token representatives.

[2] See above, p.63. The *Daily Worker* remarked on 4 April 1946 that the names of
the new Governors 'hardly correspond with Mr Attlee's suggestion that the Governors
should include a greater proportion of ordinary people'. Cf. the comment of the Soviet
magazine *New Times* on the composition of the 1949 Board. 'Five of the seven members
are connected with the financial oligarchy, the sixth is a representative of reactionary
military circles, and the seventh a member of the bourgeois intelligentsia' (Quoted
Daily Telegraph, 19 Aug. 1949).

[3] *Financial Times*, 9 June 1947; TUC evidence to the Beveridge Committee 1949;
Railway Review, 8 Oct. 1954, quoting a letter from the General Council of the TUC to
the Postmaster-General, Earl De La Warr. By then a trade unionist had been
appointed to the Board of the Independent Television Authority (*The Times*, 25 Sept.
1954).   [4] *Truth*, 12 April 1946.   [5] *The Scotsman*, 4 April 1946.

non-Welsh-speaking Governors should not be appointed.[1] The subject was raised in the House of Commons on 19 July 1960 by James Griffiths, the Grand Old Man of the Labour Party. He sought to censure the Government for appointing as National Governor for Wales 'a person [Mrs Rachel Jones] who does not fulfil the requirements of the British Broadcasting Corporation's Charter.'[2] He mustered 171 votes for his motion. The Noes, in a division on fairly strict party lines, were 240.

When the Commons discussed the Annan Report it was less strictly on party lines, and as Merlyn Rees, the Home Secretary, said in winding up the debate, this was 'perhaps appropriate for such an important matter as broadcasting.'[3] Clement Freud, the Liberal Party's spokesman on broadcasting, referred to the general assumption that BBC Governors were 'anonymous geriatric fuddy-duddies', but commented 'if we want the BBC to work better we are lucky that we have people prepared to work as hard as the Governors work, often for a couple of days a week to do the job properly.' He noted that for 17 years the Governors had been paid the same amount – £1000 per annum – and urged the Home Secretary to 'think again about these most under-rewarded people'.[4] Michael McNair-Wilson, Conservative, revived the cry for a Broadcasting Council, after complaining that replies he had received from Lord Hill, Sir Charles Curran and Sir Michael Swann had 'ranged from the arrogant to the anodyne, but never to the apologetic'.[5]

David Crouch, also Conservative, praised the Annan Committee for saying that producers should be caught by the elbow rather than twisted by the arm. He wanted the broadcasting authorities to be directly accountable to the public by going out to meet them, and above all to maintain their independence.[6]

There were, of course, several, but not many, references in the 1977 Press comment on the Annan Report to the fact that the Committee had rejected the idea of a permanent Broadcasting Council dealing with both BBC and IBA and that it had sug-

---

[1] *South Wales Evening Post*, 5 July 1960; *Denbighshire Free Press*, 9 July 1960; *The Guardian*, 20 July 1960. Six members of the Broadcasting Council of Wales protested against the appointment of Mrs Rachel Jones. There was even a threat to kidnap her (*Western Mail*, 20 July 1960). See also above, p.161.

[2] *Hansard*, vol. 627, col.339, 19 July 1960.

[3] Ibid., vol. 932, col. 1149, 23 May 1977.

[4] Ibid., col. 1093.   [5] Ibid., col. 1112.   [6] Ibid., col. 1134.

gested instead 'an untidy jumble' of new bodies.[1] It was noted, too, that the members of the Committee had been divided in their approach to structural reforms.[2] Again, however, it was only *Broadcast* which took up the interesting specific point in the Annan Report that 'paradoxically the power of the Minister [dealing with broadcasting] to veto the transmission of a [particular] programme gave the broadcasters greater security from undue pressure'.[3]

A very different point about the relationship of Governors to Government was taken up frequently after the spotlight turned in 1978 on 'the March of the Quangos' – quasi-autonomous national governmental organisations.[4] It had first been raised, however, during the 1920s when it was noted widely in the Press that after 1929 Clarendon had two office jobs – Chairman of the BBC and Director of a new Communications Company. Churchill defended the arrangement in Parliament against Labour opposition. 'Is Lord Clarendon one of those supermen capable of discharging the onerous BBC job, and leaving adequate energies for the Communications Company work?', the *Daily Herald* asked, answering 'True he once performed . . . the duties of Chief Conservative Whip in the House of Lords.'[5]

Chairmen were vulnerable before the BBC as an institution became vulnerable. Lord Simon was strongly criticised, for instance, as 'a complete and utter loss' by a staunch supporter of competitive television. Nor did his Board escape. 'The only thing that the board of directors direct is a control of moral turpitude or political rectitude.'[6]

'Control' was for long felt by the Press to be mainly control of 'programming', but so long as Reith was Director-General Press complaints were usually directed at him rather than at the Board. W.A. Robson complained in 1937 that the BBC had 'only the vaguest and most remote contact with the world of listeners', but

---

[1] *The Economist*, 26 March 1977.

[2] See the revealing article by Phillip Whitehead, 'Inside the Annan Committee' in the *New Statesman*, 25 March 1977.

[3] Cmnd 6573 (1977), *Report of the Committee on the Future of Broadcasting*, para. 5.15, p.45: 'If that responsibility is taken from the Government it must be transferred to the Broadcasting Authorities: and how much easier it will be for a Minister to paint a picture of the devastating consequences, and how much more difficult for the Authority to stand out against his judgement.'

[4] *Daily Telegraph*, 14 Sept. 1978.   [5] *Daily Herald*, 30 Jan. 1929.

[6] C.O. Stanley quoted in the *Evening Standard*, 31 Oct. 1950.

by the BBC he meant its executives as much as its Governors.[1]
The *Daily Mirror* probably only had the executives in mind when
it selected a corps of critics 'representative of all shades of opinion' and offered as 'last words to the BBC' two words only: 'Look
Out!'[2]

By the end of the war, when the pattern of pre-1939 broadcasting had been completely changed, there were demands for a new
approach. But the greater freedom to manoeuvre produced more
rather than less vociferous complaints. Programming was
Inman's *forte* in 1946,[3] and in that year the *New Statesman*, which
had never liked Reith and claimed that he had a grudge against
its editor, Kingsley Martin, said somewhat threateningly that 'if
the spur of competitive commercial broadcasting is not to be
applied to the BBC' then there was 'an irresistible case' for
including among the Governors 'both people who will insist upon
a high standard in the entertainment and cultural spheres, and
men and women in touch with the mass of listeners and sym-
pathetic to the progressive purposes of democratic government'.[4]
At the same time the popular press was asking for 'a showman'.[5]

Once competitive commercial broadcasting began in 1955,
the Governors had to take special account of programming,
although they appear to have left the major initiative to the
Board of Management, as they had done in the pre-war shift from
local to regional broadcasting during the 1920s,[6] and in the
development of Home, Light and Third Programmes in 1946.
They made many forceful statements, however, in favour of the
Third Programme,[7] and just after the launching of commercial
television in 1955 Sir Alexander Cadogan chose the occasion of a
meeting of the Governors in Aberdeen – the first time they had
travelled there for one of their meetings – to make programmes
the main theme of his press conference. 'However good commercial programmes might be at the outset, it was unlikely that
there would be a steady improvement in the raising of standards.
The long-term difficulty was that competition for one big audi-

---

[1] W.A. Robson, *Public Enterprise* (1937), p.100.
[2] *Daily Mirror*, 20 July 1937.   [3] *Yorkshire Post*, 12 Dec. 1946.
[4] *New Statesman*, 13 April 1946.   [5] *Evening News*, 9 Jan. 1946.
[6] It has been suggested that the old Board of the Company was not very happy
about the shift from local to regional broadcasting (L. Gordon, *The Public Corporation in
Great Britain* (1938), pp.162–3).
[7] This theme is dealt with at length in *Sound and Vision*.

ence might squeeze out a great deal of good material and eventually lead to a dead level of popular programmes. The BBC would continue to serve the best interests of the whole public.'[1] Tom Johnston, who was beside him on the platform, had been welcomed as a Governor in Scotland because it was believed he would give the recently created Scottish Broadcasting Council 'an accession of vigour and pushfulness'.[2]

It was Normanbrook who had to deal with the 'Women of Britain Clean Up TV Campaign', led by Mrs Mary Whitehouse, who was to play such a prominent part thereafter in broadcasting politics.[3] In June 1964 he refused to receive a deputation from this body which was flatly opposed to the programming ideas of Greene, and he was still repeating his refusal a year later, when the campaign was supported by several Members of Parliament.[4] The *Yorkshire Post* supported his kind of chairmanship, which involved the Board taking full responsibility, while recognising that 'a large measure of discretion should inevitably be left to individual producers'.[5] BBC Governors, he had said in December 1965, should be 'people of equable temper and cool judgment, neither hopefully "with it" nor hopelessly past it'.[6] The Press in the provinces and London noted his opinion, never before referred to at length, that control by the Governors was bound to be 'retrospective' given 'the enormous volume of programme output handled by the BBC'.

Normanbrook's Lunch-time Lecture on the role of the Governors was given very wide publicity. For Leonard Marsland Gander, the doyen of broadcasting critics, the most significant thing about the lecture was that he had given it at all. 'Practically all his predecessors in office have been content to appear as mere figureheads and for forty years little or nothing has been known about the activities of the Governors, whose appointment has been regarded as a comfortable patronage.'[7] Marsland Gander was well informed about Normanbrook's 'emergence from the badger's sett', and he noted, too, that Normanbrook had copied Lord Hill at the Independent Television Authority, and invited

[1] *Glasgow Herald*, 16 Sept. 1955.   [2] *Edinburgh Evening Mail*, 12 June 1954.
[3] *Birmingham Evening Mail*, 12 June 1964.
[4] *Wolverhampton Express and Star*, 6 Nov. 1965.
[5] *Daily Mail*, 16 Dec. 1965.
[6] *Yorkshire Post*, 16 Dec. 1965; *Daily Telegraph*, 16 Dec. 1965.
[7] *Daily Telegraph*, 20 Dec. 1965.

'knowledgeable guests' to lunches and talked to many people ·
outside who were interested in broadcasting policy.

It was clear from this account that, whatever the record of the
past, a change was now actively taking place. This was a change
recommended by Lincoln Gordon in the distant 1930s. 'A
stronger Board,' Gordon had then urged, 'would permit reduced
concentration within the organisation. Governors would bring to
the BBC an attitude differing from that of the permanent professionals.'[1] And Gordon had added a further extremely per-
ceptive note: 'They would be on guard against the inarticulate
major premises of the staff, and would concern themselves to see
that censorship was strictly impartial and reduced to a minimum.
By accepting public responsibility for questionable decisions,
they would destroy the tendency to devitalise the service by
refusal to take risks. Finally, and in the long run perhaps most
important, they could openly resist a Government's attempt to
bring pressure to bear upon the Corporation in any manner
whatever. Their public and responsible position would allow
independence of action impossible to permanent employees.'[2]

Once he had moved to the BBC, Hill pushed it much further.
Among other things, he actually received a deputation from Mrs
Whitehouse, while refusing to confer any 'special advisory status'
on her organisation.[3] In his autobiography he referred to this
change in the same chapter as he wrote about finding a new office
and choosing his own secretary. He was less concerned with the
kind of criticism he sometimes received in *The Times* which
continued to claim that there were 'elements in the Reithian
tradition that are worthy of support today'.[4] He was described as
'jaunty and relaxed' when he was attacked personally inside and
outside the BBC for *Broadcasting in the Seventies*.[5] And he had to
face up to a different current of criticism after *Yesterday's Men*,
when sections of the Press suggested that the report of the BBC
Governors on the controversial television documentary was regarded by Harold Wilson and colleagues as even more offensive
than the programme itself.[6]

[1] Gordon, op.cit., p.243.
[2] Ibid.
[3] Lord Hill, *Behind the Screen* (1974), pp.79–80 and Ch.8 *passim*.
[4] *The Times*, 30 May 1969. This article dealt with the reorganisation of the BBC.
[5] *Sunday Times*, 7 Dec. 1969.
[6] *The Observer*, 11 July 1971.

" — And   furthermore,   Lord
Hill . . . "

The role of Chairman, like the role of Prime Minister and of
Leader of the Opposition, had obviously become more important, at least in the public eye. Chairmen had, in fact, often made
policy statements. Powell, for example had predicted in April
1943 that television would be in every home after the war,[1] and
Simon had made similar predictions each month. It was just after
Inman had ceased to be Chairman, however, that the cry was
raised that the Chairman of the BBC should have an increasing
responsibility in future. This was a post, wrote the *News Chronicle*,
'of growing importance and influence. The Chairman must be of
sufficient calibre to resist the slightest encroachment of Parliament on the independence of Broadcasting House. He must also
loyally protect the day-to-day executive authority of the
Director-General.'[2] When Simon took over the Chairmanship
was described as 'no easy position'. 'He has to strike a razor-edge
balance between the BBC's middle-line policy and the warring
political factions constantly demanding listener-time.'[3] It did
not help when Simon (like Cadogan after him) said that he
started 'from scratch, knowing nothing and having everything to
learn'.[4]

[1] *City and East London Observer*, 2 April 1943.
[2] *News Chronicle*, 19 April 1947. Much Press comment in 1946 and later was on the
remuneration of Governors (e.g. *Evening Standard*, 4 Dec. 1946, which chose as its
headline 'BBC Governors Get Pay Cut of £400 a Year').
[3] *News Review*, 19 June 1947.
[4] Letter to *Birmingham Weekly Post*, 13 July 1947.

On fforde's resignation in 1964, the Press made more noise than ever before about the Government's wish to find 'a Chairman of stature', 'a strong personality, who was to play a leading role in deciding the policy, programme contents and quality of all BBC services'.[1] But *The Economist*, querying the motives behind such a quest, also argued that 'the notion that there is something called administration, and another thing called policy, which can be separated neatly within such an organisation as the BBC is a fine example of the obscurantist ignorance which so many politicians evinced when talking about mass communications.'[2]

The Economist had always been forthright and challenging in its views on broadcasting,[3] and it stated firmly on this occasion that 'if there are hopes that the BBC may get better, it is not because of any simple policy decision at the top, but because of a series of bright appointments of individuals to top posts by Sir Hugh [Greene] . . . the Governors are indeed custodians of the BBC's Charter, but they are there to support and protect their Managing Director, not to hamstring him.'[4] One local newspaper was equally forthright. The Chairman should not be a politician. 'The politician is not necessarily the highest form of human life and should not be found at the top of this particular tree.'[5]

There was ample evidence in the spring of 1964 to suggest that the Postmaster-General, Reginald Bevins, and his Assistant, Ray Mawby, were deliberately intending to curb Sir Hugh Greene's power, but Lord Blakenham, Chancellor of the Duchy of Lancaster and Chairman of the Conservative Party, took the trouble to reassure Greene personally at the time that this move did not have the support of the Cabinet;[6] and it is significant, perhaps, that from the Opposition side Anthony Greenwood said that while he thought Greene 'a first-class Director-General', 'in principle it is always good to have a permanent official answerable to

[1] *Daily Telegraph*, 9 March 1964; *Sunday Times*, 8 March 1964; *The Economist*, 14 March 1964. When asked about possible 'men of stature', Lord Boothby suggested Lord Franks or Sir John Wolfenden; Edward Martell recommended Enoch Powell or Lord Salisbury; and John Betjeman proposed Lord Rosse, Tom Driberg or Harold Wilson (*Daily Mail*, 10 March 1964).
[2] *The Economist*, 14 March 1964, 'Free as Air'.
[3] See the important wartime articles 'A Plan for Broadcasting', 28 Oct., 4, 11, 18 Nov. 1944.
[4] Ibid., 14 March 1964.
[5] *Swindon Evening Advertizer*, 10 March 1964. [6] H. Greene to L. Miall, 5 March 1979.

a really strong and influential Board of Governors'.[1] Donald McLachlan, who knew much about both politics and broadcasting, was a public voice on his own when he urged in a brilliant article that what the BBC needed was not a strong man but a wise man, one wise enough to resolve 'the constant conflict of duties'. 'He has to weave into a management pattern the ideas and feelings of eight Governors, selected for their diversity of views and experience.' McLachlan referred also to BBC traditions, which he thought would be powerful enough to make the present Governors resign in a body if a professional politician was appointed Chairman. Noting that the Government, for all its great formal powers, had not interfered with the BBC for thirty years, he suggested that there was 'a constitutional mystery here worthy of Bagehot's eye and pen. To say that a strong Chairman is the secret of it all is like saying that the Speaker of the House of Commons should be at least six feet tall and weigh over 12 stone. The requirement is irrelevant.'[2]

Brilliant analyses do not always command political assent, and the day after McLachlan's article appeared a *Daily Express* headline read 'BBC's "Strong Man" Hunt Goes On'.[3] Wilson, then Leader of the Opposition, stated at once, however, that if the new Chairman of the BBC appeared to be what he called 'a political appointment' a future Labour Government might not feel bound by it. This was a dangerous doctrine, and reference back was made to it on more than one occasion after Wilson became Prime Minister and proved himself at least as keen as his Conservative predecessor to keep the BBC 'in order'.[4] There were certainly serious arguments behind the scenes in 1965 between Normanbrook and the Postmaster-General, Wedgwood Benn, after a group of Labour backbenchers, prompted by a belief that the BBC was moving to the right, had begun to take an increasing

---

[1] *Sunday Times*, 15 March 1964. See above, p.163.

[2] 'Top Man's Task at BBC' in the *Sunday Telegraph*, 15 March 1964.

[3] *Daily Express*, 16 March 1964.

[4] See also *The Times* editorial, 3 April 1964, on the idea of having a 'strong' political Chairman or two political Governors: 'Above the parties' interests there is the public interest. It is solely in the public interest the Governors must make their decisions, and make them as a Board. Unfortunately when half-baked ideas are only scotched, they have a nasty habit of rising again. Mr Wilson could kill this one stone dead by making it clear that at no time, either in power or opposition, would he be a party to it.' This is one of only four newspaper editorials which I have been able to trace in the BBC's history with the title 'The BBC Governors'.

interest in the internal affairs of the BBC.[1] 'I have no mandate to curb the Director-General,' Normanbrook insisted before the argument was extended to cover finance and administration.[2]

It was after the appointment of Hill as a 'strong' Chairman that the concerns both of Governors and of BBC executives began to be dealt with at length in the Press; and a key point in the story was Benn's open criticism in October 1968 of the BBC's 'enormous accumulation of power'.[3] Benn was then Minister of Technology, but he revealed in his speech that he had not lost any of his interest in broadcasting policy. As well as dealing with structures, he referred to programming, complaining of triviality, superficiality and sensationalism. The indictment, therefore, was of the widest kind. 'Broadcasting is really too important to be left to the broadcasters,' he said. 'The BBC is used to dealing with subtle pressures from politicians of all kinds – some of them, as at the time of Suez, not particularly subtle,' wrote the *Daily Telegraph*. 'But this kind of frontal assault by a Minister is something new.'[4]

Press comment was widespread. *The Times* noted Benn's interest in ideas which were to become generally current during the next ten years, not all of them relating exclusively to broadcasting. The idea of the BBC or some other broadcasting authority as a 'publisher' was one. 'Access' was another, and participation a third. 'As Mr Wedgwood Benn is aware, a politician who pitches into the BBC,' wrote *The Times*, 'is liable to be suspected either of harbouring a grudge or hankering after censorship. His own tirade . . . is interesting and thoughtful enough to win him the benefit of doubt on that score.'[5] The same might have been said also of R.H.S. Crossman's Granada Lecture on communications in the same month. This was certainly not a tirade, but it incorporated many of the same views.[6]

Not surprisingly, party considerations immediately entered the heated but very limited debate. 'The new BBC hunters,' Paul

---

[1] *Sunday Times*, 11 July 1965.
[2] *The Times*, 2 April 1964.   [3] Ibid., 19 Oct. 1968.
[4] *Daily Telegraph*, 19 Oct. 1968.
[5] *The Times*, 19 Oct. 1968. George Scott in the *Sunday Times*, 20 Oct. 1968, described Benn's views as 'alarming'. *The Observer*, 20 Oct. 1968, said on a major point of substance, 'it is easier to point out why television and newspapers [note the and] over-dramatise and trivialise them to suggest a remedy which is not worse than the disease.'
[6] R.H.S. Crossman, 'The Politics of Television', *Granada Guildhall Lecture* (1968).

Bryan, the Conservative shadow Postmaster-General, is reported as saying, 'are the very men who were against setting up the ITV and in favour of extending the monopoly of the BBC. Now we see why.' If Wilson had been suspicious of Conservative intentions in relation to broadcasting, now it was the turn of Conservatives to be suspicious about Wilson's 'sinister plans to run the BBC'. [1]

It is interesting to note that by the late 1960s there was no longer – if there ever had been – one 'public eye' watching the BBC. The political parties were divided between themselves and inside themselves, and there were bitter cleavages of public opinion concerning the kind of arguments advanced by Mrs Whitehouse. They brought into the debate backbench MPs who had previously not taken much interest in broadcasting, such as Major James Dance, Conservative member for Bromsgrove, who was an active supporter of Mrs Whitehouse and a few Labour MPs such as Robert Edwards, member for Bilston, and James Dempsey, member for Coatbridge and Airdrie.

When the Festival of Light submitted a memorandum to the BBC in December 1971, the Festival's delegation was received by the Chairman, the Vice-Chairman and the Director-General; and the BBC's Secretary minuted the view that 'the organisers of the Festival of Light have articulated an element of undoubted public concern'. He added, however, that 'evidence of popular support for the demonstrations . . . ought not to be taken uncritically as an endorsement of the particular solutions advanced by the Festival to some of the moral problems of the 1970s.' [2]

The paper went on to say that there were generational differences in public attitudes towards the BBC. 'The Corporation's role thirty years ago built up expectations which cannot be fulfilled in the 1970s. In earlier years, the BBC spoke to and, to some extent, for a society whose divisions were much less apparent. Whatever influence it had then stemmed mainly from the fact that it spoke in terms and about things of which large numbers of people could approve. The moral and political uncertainties which now confront the country had not then broken through a surface of unity.' [3]

[1] *Sunday Times*, 20 Oct. 1968.
[2] 'Memorandum from the Festival of Light: Draft Reply from the BBC', 16 March 1972.
[3] Ibid.

There was a further difference between the 1920s and 1930s and the 1960s and 1970s. It was not only society that had changed but the study of society. During the 1920s, 1930s and 1940s there had been few sociologists and no academic specialists in 'communications'. What was said by academics about broadcasting – its structure and its influence on society – tended to be said, therefore, by historians and political scientists. They and the editors of technical wireless journals had a monopoly. One of the most active of the historians and political scientists who turned to broadcasting – and he was thought to be too 'liberal' for the Ullswater Committee – was Sir Ernest Barker. [1] Another political scientist – too 'Fabian socialist' to influence action in the years of 'national government' – was Professor William Robson, who directed attention to 'the moral calibre, intellectual equipment, political opinions, social assumptions and general capacity of the Governors'. He expected them in 1935 not only to 'act as a buffer between the executive work of the BBC and public opinion outside but also [to] be able to hold the balance between contending forces or influences inside the organisation'. [2] It would have been interesting to have had the considered views of Barker and Robson and of men in the same tradition, on both the political and administrative issues in the broadcasting history of the 1960s and 1970s, including the decision in 1974 – little commented upon in the Press – to make the Home Office rather than the Post Office 'responsible' for broadcasting. BBC Governors and Prison Governors were now to fall within the same orbit.

A small number of academics remained interested in 'structures of broadcasting', the title of a symposium organised by Professor E.G. Wedell in 1968 and attended by people inside and outside the BBC; [3] and Wedell himself, a former Secretary of the ITA, wrote an important book on *Broadcasting and Public Policy* in 1968, which discussed 'consumer groups' in broadcasting under four headings – the official advisory bodies, general and specialised, central and regional; unofficial groups, among which Mrs

---

[1] See, for example, his article 'This Age of Broadcasting' in the *Fortnightly Review*, vol. 138. (1935), pp.417–29. Barker contributed to Haley's post-war *BBC Quarterly* which belonged to the same tradition.

[2] See his article in the *Political Quarterly*, No.6 (1935), 'The BBC as an Institution'. The *Political Quarterly* devoted almost as much attention to broadcasting as *The Economist*.

[3] E.G. Wedell (ed.), *Structures of Broadcasting* (1970).

Whitehouse's National Viewers' and Listeners' Association was pre-eminent; audience research; and the Press critics of broadcasting, who 'may or may not regard their task as including the provision of a link between producer and consumer'.[1] Indeed, at the symposium the critic Philip Purser was at pains to insist that 'it is a diminution of the function of any critic – in any field – to regard him merely as a tipster or a consumer's guide'.[2]

Not all critics would have agreed, for sociology began to influence criticism as well as studies of administrative structures. An interesting example of converging new approaches was Raymond Williams's Penguin on *Communications* (1962), and six years later he suggested a producer-orientated model of broadcasting without 'the intervention of an appointed and self-defining authority'. 'The ping-pong of public corporation (BBC, monopoly) and independent corporation (advertising, private capital) has gone on until most of us are mesmerised . . . but the break to freedom that is necessary means getting beyond the established assumptions.'[3]

In general, research into 'communications' during the 1960s and 1970s, a greatly expanded field, though never as active as that in the United States, passed mainly into the hands of sociologists of different kinds; and many of these, while supporting 'public broadcasting', were in broad sympathy with the ideas expressed by Benn. They wrote little either for the popular Press or for the 'quality' newspapers, but their views, which seldom included any discussion of the role of the Governors, were fashionable in university circles and were set out, often formidably, in university theses. They were augmented by voices from within broadcasting itself, notably the voices of Stuart Hood and Anthony Smith, both of whom had been prominent in the BBC, and there was sensitive listening-in to what was going on inside the Corporation by Tom Burns, who did not fit easily into any school of sociology.[4] More recently Elihu Katz surveyed the

[1] E.G. Wedell, *Broadcasting and Public Policy* (1968), p.212. See also C. Curran, 'The BBC's Advisory Bodies', in the *EBU Review*, Jan. 1966.

[2] *Structures of Broadcasting*, p.86.

[3] Raymond Williams, *The Listener*, 11 July 1968.

[4] See *inter alia*, S. Hood, *A Survey of Television* (1967), *The Mass Media* (1972); A. Smith, *The Shadow in the Cave* (1973); R. Hoggart, 'The Nature and Quality of Mass Communication' (*Harvey Memorial Lecture* 1959); T. Burns, *The BBC, Public Institution and Private World* (1977). Hoggart was a prominent member of the Pilkington Committee.

whole field at the BBC's invitation and produced a published report.[1]

Academics concerned with 'communications studies' were members of the Annan Committee, key witnesses before it, or critics of the Committee's conclusions; and the Committee itself found it necessary to state rather defensively that 'we could not try to emulate the authors of the many theoretical books and articles written in recent years on the nature and role of broadcasting, the typology of broadcasting institutions here and in other countries, and the theories of mass culture and modern society which so often are used to explain broadcasting and to evoke remedies for its condition'.[2]

Between the first appointment of Lord Annan in 1970 and the setting-up of his Committee in 1974 attention had passed back again from 'the experts' to the public – or rather to sections of the public. Sir Michael Swann's appointment as Chairman was widely reported. 'He brings to his delicate task an impressive record, intellectually and administratively, and a strong determination,' *The Times* remarked. 'He deserves a favourable wind outside and inside the Corporation.'[3] 'Mr Heath is, perhaps, giving the BBC a last chance to prove that the old system works', wrote *The Economist*.[4] When an American correspondent asked at 10 Downing Street why Swann had been Heath's choice, he was told – 'to re-establish the position of the Director-General'.[5]

At his own Press Conference, Swann said that he wanted to be 'in the front seat, alongside the Director-General who will be doing the driving'.[6] It was not 'his style', he went on, to take a back seat. Yet he brought the Governors into his first Press statement also. 'I and the Board of Governors will be doing the map reading – deciding where we are going.'

To complete the picture, Oliver Whitley brought in the staff. 'The Governors, with the disadvantage of being part-time and short-time, are trustees of the national interest only in so far as they can carry the staff of the BBC with them or in so far as the

[1] E. Katz, *Social Research on Broadcasting Proposals for Further Development* (1977).
[2] Cmnd 6753 (1977), para. 1.12, p.6.
[3] *The Times*, 15 Dec. 1972.
[4] *The Economist*, 16 Dec. 1972.
[5] L. Miall to C. Curran, 15 Dec. 1972.
[6] *Financial Times*, 15 Dec. 1972.

latter acts in the national interest of its own volition. This may, in practice, mean that the national interest is remarkably well served.'[1]

This was not and could not be the last word. 'Swann's Way' as the *Daily Telegraph* had called it in 1972, was to lead through just as difficult and hazardous territory as 'Both Sides of the Hill'. The publication of the Annan Committee Report generated much new Press discussion, little of it, however, about the role of the Governors; and the appointment of a new Director-General, Ian Trethowan, in October 1977 did the same, although less attention was paid to the fact that he had for a time worked with 'the competitor' than to the fact that he was then working for the BBC.

There was little Press notice either for the substantial re-organisation in management, less radical perhaps than that of 1947, both of jobs and of people inside the BBC. Some losses to commercial television were serious, and these sometimes hit the headlines, but little attention was paid outside the headlines, for example, to the appointment of Michael Bett from GEC as Director of Personnel, following Maurice Tinniswood, who had also come from outside the BBC – in his case from the Post Office. The post of Director of News and Current Affairs, with a seat on the Board of Management, which had been held briefly in the late 1950s by Hugh Carleton Greene, was re-created after sharp internal discussions, some of which made their way into the Press. Bryan Cowgill was the original selection for this post. After his surprise departure to Thames Television, Ian Trethowan, the Director-General designate, announced that Richard Francis, the Controller Northern Ireland, had been appointed. Francis took office in October 1977 as did David Webster, Controller of Information Services for only 18 months, who was promoted to become Director of Public Affairs. Trethowan himself created a Director-General's Quarterly Liaison Meeting consisting of some sixty heads of establishment throughout the BBC. There was a new Secretary, too, John Wilkinson.

Both structures and styles were changing, therefore, before and after the Annan Report, and a large measure of decentralisation had already been carried out before Annan drew attention to the need for it. It is far too early either to plot or to assess the range

[1] *The Listener*, 29 Sept. 1977.

and impact of such changes. Some of the changes, however, were strongly criticised, and associated as they were in the case of sound broadcasting with a radical revision of wavelengths, they did not always help the image of the BBC. They tended, however, to be overshadowed by the financial problems hanging over the Corporation and by the publication of the Government's long awaited White Paper on Broadcasting in July 1978. [1]

Before turning to the somewhat surprising and much criticised proposals made about the future of the Governors in the White Paper, it is necessary to examine in more detail a number of 'cases' which seemed to involve difficulties either with Government or the public, sometimes, indeed, with both. It is not necessarily true that the 'cases' provide the basis for Government attitudes, for Prime Ministers come and go and Governments have a far shorter life than the Corporation. Yet cases figure prominently in the folk memory of the BBC, and an analysis of them is more enlightening than any set of formulae.

When Swann stated in November 1978 that 'the BBC is not indestructible', and that 'there must come a point where politicians can do it much harm, either by continuous suspicious tinkering with it, or by plain uncaring financial meanness', he had in mind not only his years as Chairman but the whole story described in this essay. Over the last thirty years the BBC 'has been investigated by committees great and small no less than 20 times'. If the passion to investigate was not restrained then 'the plant will one day die from having had its roots dug up so often to see how they are getting on, and then left to dry out in chilly winds for so long before being replanted'. [2]

It was a biologist's metaphor, but whatever metaphor a historian might have chosen its purport would not have been different. And a historian, like a biologist, would have had grounds for suspecting that there were people interested in the BBC who did not much care whether or not the plant died.

[1] Cmnd 7294 (1978), *Broadcasting*.
[2] Swann, 'On Disliking the Media', Lecture at University of Salford, 7 Nov. 1978.

CHAPTER IV
A SELECTION OF ISSUES

Given the difficulties of generalising about the powers and performance of the Governors and even about their personal characteristics, it is necessary to explore in detail how they have handled particular situations. The case study approach is increasingly fashionable in communications studies, though it has its limitations. It encourages a detailed examination of how individuals and institutions actually work, and it enables general hypotheses to be tested – like Professor Burns's statement that 'the Governors of the BBC are trapped in an impossibly contradictory situation' and have for the most part accepted 'the compliant, consultative role the Director-General *and* the Corporation generally needs of them and – Clarendon, Simon and Hill notwithstanding – has fitted them into'.[1]

Burns dwelt rightly on the 'situation' rather than on the details of individual cases, although these by themselves suggest the outline of a history. As Howard Thomas, who had experience both of the BBC and of commercial television, put it in 1962, 'the whole fascinating history of the BBC could be chaptered around the Directors-General and their respective terms of office. The relationship between Chairman and Director-General provides the real key to the running of the BBC, and one day someone inside the BBC should put on record the fluctuations of power at the top.'[2] Yet the triangular relationship between Director-General, Chairman and Board needs to be taken into the reckoning also: so, too, do fluctuations in patterns of production at the bottom. 'Cases' require to be studied from different angles rather than from one single vantage point.

A wide range of case studies is available, and some cases, which might have been considered separately – like the decision not to allow Ian Smith to broadcast in 1965 or to restrict the showing of *The War Game* to cinema audiences in 1966 – have already been dealt with, often briefly, in the course of Chapter I.[3] The nine that have been chosen represent a selection covering a wide span

---

[1] T. Burns, *The BBC, Public Institution and Private World* (1977), p.33.

[2] H. Thomas, *The Truth About Television* (1962), p.144.

[3] See above, pp.120–3.

of time during which there were changes not only in 'mood' but in social and political attitudes and relationships. In retrospect, the element of farce in the slander case *Lambert v. Levita* is associated intricately with the culture of the 1930s. The 'talking' mongoose acquires an almost symbolic significance.[1] *Yesterday's Men*, the subject of an independent analysis,[2] is irrevocably associated with a particular moment in politics, and the programme looks different every time it is seen in retrospect. It is also freely discussed by people who have never seen it. It continues to rankle, and few Governors, even former Cabinet Ministers, would write today, as H.A.L. Fisher wrote in 1936 – 'I hope that the D.G. is not too much perturbed by the impertinent and random objurgations of the few Labour politicians in the House of Commons.'[3]

Previous accounts of most of these cases have not been based on archival material in the BBC, and it is that material – supplemented by evidence collected from other sources, including oral evidence – which is of basic importance if myth is to be separated from fact. The myths, however, are not without their importance. It was on the basis of *Lambert v. Levita* that Lambert himself wrote one of the first 'nasty' books about the BBC, and this carried the bold, not uninfluential, but fundamentally misconceived thesis that 'today the BBC holds – in the field of art, intellect and politics – the power once held by the Court. It has become the main indirect organ of Government, all the more potent because its influence is indirect.'[4] Lambert's book had the sub-title *An Impression of the BBC from Within*, and it is largely through the experience of the cases selected in this chapter that it is possible to relate internal to external pressures in broadcasting.

Of the nine selected cases, several concern pressure on the Governors to modify or cancel BBC programme plans. Government pressure to stop Captain Ernst Hashagen, Sir Oswald Mosley and Mr Harry Pollitt from broadcasting was privately applied in ways which effectively forestalled public comment

[1] For the mongoose itself, see R.S. Lambert and H. Price, *The Haunting of Cashen's Gap* (1936).
[2] M. Tracey, 'Yesterday's Men – a Case Study in Political Communication' in J. Curran, M. Gurevitch and J. Woollacott, *Mass Communication and Society* (1977).
[3] H.A.L. Fisher to R.C. Norman, 6 May 1936.
[4] R.S. Lambert, *Ariel and All His Quality* (1940), pp.316–17.

at the time, and the full evidence has only recently become available under the 30-year rule. Important pieces of evidence relating to several of the nine cases are still missing.

The cases can be regarded as climacterics in broadcasting history. Vernon Bartlett's talk on Germany leaving the League of Nations was strongly criticised in Parliament on purely party political lines, and in the opinion of John Coatman led to the rise not only of 'interest in broadcasting on the side of Parliament and the Parties but also of a kind of ingrained suspicion of the BBC'. [1]

In 1936 the 'Talking Mongoose Case' loomed starkly over Parliament's discussion of the Ullswater Report, and led to radical changes in BBC staff administration. By the time of the next Broadcasting Inquiry, Lord Beveridge himself harked back to the significance of Vernon Bartlett's role nearly two decades earlier, [2] and the Beveridge Report referred to *Party Manners* in relation to Lord Simon of Wythenshawe's action in giving the House of Lords a personal explanation of his decision to cancel its second performance. The Report noted that 'he did so only after the Lord Chancellor and the Leader of the House, Viscount Addison, had laid it down expressly that it was undesirable for peers who were Governors of the BBC to take part in debates in the House of Lords on broadcasting questions'. [3]

The Pilkington Report largely eschewed discussion of particular programmes or incidents, preferring to deal with principles, prominent among which it mentioned the independence of the BBC and the ITV in the day-to-day management of their affairs, including programme content. Yet it referred explicitly to Suez: 'One test of the principle is the performance of the broadcasting organisations. We are satisfied that their programmes show no sign of deference to the Government's views. We recall in particular the programmes of the BBC at the time of the Suez campaign of 1956.' [4]

That Was the Week That Was, sharply criticised though it had been, received praise from the Annan Committee as 'something which at the time was entirely new, new in style and new in

[1] J. Coatman, 'The BBC, Government and Politics', *Public Opinion Quarterly*, summer 1951.

[2] G.R. Parsons to M. Farquharson, 2 Oct. 1950; Farquharson to Reith, 9 Oct. 1950.

[3] Cmd 8116 (1951), *Report of the Broadcasting Committee, 1949*, para. 586, pp.175–6.

[4] Cmnd 1753 (1962), *Report of the Committee on Broadcasting, 1960*, paras. 390–1, p.117.

boldness'.[1] The Committee also noted the reference-upwards procedure involved in *The Question of Ulster* in its generally favourable comments on the coverage of Northern Ireland, both by BBC and by ITV.[2] However, the Report concluded that in the last analysis 'the Government alone can judge and decide whether a programme (such as *The Question of Ulster*) constitutes a threat to national security' and went on to recommend that the Government's power of veto should be retained.[3]

The Annan Committee noted that the appointments of Lord Hill to the Chairmanship of the BBC, and Lord Aylestone to the ITA in his place, had been widely interpreted 'as a sign that Government was firing a shot across the bows of the broadcasters to warn them that . . . they were off course'.[4] And it went on to comment, 'When Lord Hill and the Governors decided again to assert the editorial independence of broadcasters by refusing to ban *Yesterday's Men* (a programme in 1971 which gave great offence and led to charges of bad faith on the part of the broadcasters by the former Labour Government Front Bench), politicians may have wondered whether they had appointed an admiral who habitually turned a blind eye when the Admiralty made a signal.'[5]

One of the reasons why there have not been even more 'cases' is that there are elaborate procedures inside the BBC which prevent them from arising. Anthony Smith, while approving of the 'enormous individual leeway' allowed to producers within the British broadcasting system (unlike most other systems), has identified 'a system of referrals upwards of difficult decisions (those quite simply are decisions which are likely to produce a public row) and there is a system of meetings at various levels at which judgements are formed and shared. There is seldom any doubt about what the man above you thinks on any important issue. You can therefore avoid referring upwards by deciding them in a way which you know he would approve of; only if the decision is worth arguing do you refer.'[6] Likewise, Sir Michael Swann has stressed in comparing the role of BBC and IBA – a

---

[1] Cmnd 6753 (1977), *Report of the Committee on the Future of Broadcasting*, para. 16.48, p.264.

[2] Ibid., para. 17.11, p.269.   [3] Ibid., para. 5.15, p.45.

[4] Ibid., para. 2.28, p.15.   [5] Ibid.

[6] A. Smith, 'Internal Pressures in Broadcasting', in *New Outlook* (1972), No.4, pp.4–5.

comparison which the Annan Committee suggested might be more useful in practice than it is [1] – that 'the constitutional make-up of the BBC, and the realities of management, make it impossible to have a separate bureaucracy in the BBC devoted to monitoring and censorship. This function has, therefore, been built into the managerial structure, from top to bottom, with the Board of Governors at the top, laying down strategy, selecting senior staff, and maintaining a general scrutiny of programme policy.' [2]

It would be revealing to consider fully a number of 'cases' – and they would be the vast majority – where there have been no 'rows'. The cases which follow, however, have been chosen not for their drama, but for their intrinsic interest. They reveal both the vulnerability of the BBC to external pressures and the system of defences which it has been able to construct, even when mistakes have been made. Each study could be a monograph in itself, and the case studies of situations after 1955 will have to figure prominently in any future history of the BBC.

1 The Hashagen Case 1932

On 6 July 1932 the Minister of Labour, Sir Henry Betterton, drew the attention of the Cabinet, as a matter of urgency, to a question due for answer the next day in the House of Commons. He was being asked to prevent Captain Ernst Hashagen from being allowed to land in the UK to broadcast 'his experiences of sinking British and allied merchant shipping during the last war while in command of a German U-boat'.

The Cabinet felt strongly that the U-boat commander must not be allowed to broadcast. A broadcast would cause pain and resentment to those who had lost relatives in the war. Yet the Cabinet did not wish to use its statutory powers of prohibition 'as this would be represented as the exercise by the Government of censorship powers, which should be definitely reserved for use in cases of great national emergency'. In consequence, Stanley Baldwin, the Lord President of the Council, undertook to brief the Postmaster-General, Sir Kingsley Wood, so that he could com-

---

[1] Cmnd 6753 (1977), para. 9.66: 'The Governors would do well to keep the IBA in mind'.

[2] 'BBC and IBA: a Note by Sir Michael Swann', 20 Feb. 1978.

municate to Reith the unanimous view of the Cabinet that the talk must be cancelled. [1]

The Postmaster-General telephoned Reith, who had 'quite an argument with him' adding he thought it was 'all monstrous, and that he would be doing us a very good turn by declining to interfere'. Reith refused to cancel the broadcast without consulting his Chairman, J.H. Whitley. Meanwhile, General Jack Seely [2] arrived at Broadcasting House saying that he was the bearer of a message from the Cabinet and demanding that the decision to cancel the Hashagen talk be taken there and then; otherwise he would go to Buckingham Palace and ask the King to cancel the first royal visit to the newly opened Broadcasting House, due to take place the next day. [3]

The next day the Chairman and the Director-General together with the Vice-Chairman, Lord Gainford, called on Sir Kingsley Wood at the Post Office and the Chairman agreed to cancel Hashagen's talk. [4]

The reply which Kingsley Wood made on behalf of the Minister of Labour that afternoon was drafted by the BBC. [5] He said: 'I understand from the British Broadcasting Corporation that the talk was planned as a serious contribution towards the elimination of this method of warfare, and would have been so expressed. In view, however, of international discussions now proceeding at Geneva, I have been informed that it has been decided not to proceed with the talk. The question of a permit does not therefore arise.' [6]

Whitley protested to the Cabinet in measured terms, with a covering letter to Sir Maurice Hankey, the Secretary, asking that copies should be sent to each member of the Cabinet who had been present. After explaining the real purpose of the invitation to the U-boat commander, he discussed the constitutional question:

[1] Cabinet *Minutes*, 6 July 1932 (Public Record Office).

[2] Major-General J.E.B. Seely, former Liberal MP and created Baron Mottistone in 1933.

[3] J.C.W. Reith, *Diary*, 6, 7 July 1932.

[4] Ibid.

[5] Memorandum by Sir Kingsley Wood to the Cabinet, 'The British Broadcasting Corporation and Captain Ernst Hashagen', 2 Aug. 1932 (Public Record Office).

[6] *Hansard*, vol. 268, col. 596, 7 July 1932.

The impugnment of the Corporation's considered judgment in the matter of a particular talk is regretted; but the real issue is a constitutional one. The Corporation was established by Royal Charter, and the Governors appointed by the Crown. In the early stages of its existence one of the greatest obstacles to overcome was the impression that the Broadcasting Company had become a Government Department. This unfortunate idea is by no means eradicated today. There have been occasions on which, without justification, Government suggestion or Government domination has been alleged by critics. The Corporation is a new and important experiment in the management and control of a public utility service. Its progress is watched with closest attention, not only in this country but in most foreign countries. Its detachment from the Government of the day has been a cardinal element in its international prestige.

The autonomy of the Corporation has repeatedly been affirmed by successive Postmasters-General in Parliament. That a detail of its work should have been discussed and the matter settled without any attempt to ascertain the views of the Corporation would have been incredible had it not happened.

According to the Licence which accompanies the Royal Charter, the Postmaster-General is given plenary powers, but the Corporation was informed by the Postmaster General of the day (1927) that they would not be exercised except in time of national emergency; nor hitherto have they ever been used. Although on some occasions pressure from a Government Department had to be resisted in the interests of impartiality, the Corporation has spared no pains in its endeavours to co-operate with Government Departments, both in their routine work and on special occasions.

In the interests of this great public service for which it is responsible the Corporation feels that an incident so contrary to the spirit and intention of the Royal Charter should not pass without protest. The Governors venture to assume that it will not form a precedent. [1]

In his note to the Cabinet commenting on the constitutional aspect of the issue, Kingsley Wood referred to the BBC's Licence, which, together with the Royal Charter, gave the Postmaster-General 'complete power to prohibit any broadcast'. He added that he had 'no knowledge of any statement made by the Postmaster-General in 1927 that this power would not be used

---

[1] J.H. Whitley to Sir Maurice Hankey, 28 July 1932 (Public Record Office).

"except in time of national emergency" and there was no such limitation in the Licence'.[1]

Kingsley Wood, who was always mistrusted by Reith,[2] concluded by saying, 'It is certainly not my desire to invoke, nor have I invoked, this power of prohibition which if generally exercised would make me a Censor of the programmes of the Corporation. The matter was I understand regarded by the Cabinet as quite exceptional and if desired I will again explain the matter to the Corporation.'[3]

2 The Vernon Bartlett Row 1933

Vernon Bartlett was attached to the BBC's supplementary staff on 15 October 1932 to undertake liaison work abroad. He had no formal title but was usually described as 'Foreign Correspondent'. It was to be a two-year, short-term contract. Bartlett, an experienced journalist, had then virtually completed ten years as the Director of the League of Nations London office. He had previously worked for the *Daily Mail*, Reuters (for whom he covered the Paris Peace Conference), the *Daily Herald* and *The Times*. He first broadcast on 18 January 1924 on the work of the League of Nations and from 1928 onwards he regularly analysed developments in foreign affairs in broadcast talks.

Bartlett's duties on the supplementary staff were partly to travel in Europe, establishing personal liaison with European broadcasting organisations and recruiting stringers in foreign capitals (one such found by him was Ralph Murray), partly to act as a diplomatic correspondent. He was also given the task of broadcasting weekly fifteen-minute talks on foreign affairs and talks for schools.

[1] Memorandum by Sir Kingsley Wood to the Cabinet, 2 Aug. 1932 (Public Record Office).

[2] In 1935 Reith found himself at odds with Wood over the renewal of the BBC's Charter and noted in his *Diary* that it was 'utterly damnable that the BBC should be made a political catspaw by a little bounder like K.W.' (C. Stuart (ed.), *The Reith Diaries* (1975), p.110). Reith recorded that MacDonald had told him Wood should never have been in the Cabinet as Postmaster-General (*Diary*, 17 Sept. 1935), and at other times referred to him as 'the little cad' (28 April 1936) and 'the little swine' (27 June 1939). On 30 April 1935 Viscount Bridgeman, Chairman of the BBC, and Reith went to see Wood to discuss the use of broadcasting in war. Reith recorded: 'We had a thoroughly unpleasant twenty minutes with for the first time a definitely and openly hostile attitude on both sides.' (Stuart, op.cit., p.121.)

[3] Memorandum by Wood to the Cabinet, 2 Aug. 1932.

Vernon Bartlett

On 14 October 1933 Nazi Germany left the Disarmament Conference at the League of Nations. The six o'clock news that night reported the event and also included an extract from the speech of the Foreign Secretary, Sir John Simon, in Geneva that morning, a recording of Hitler speaking in Berlin and then a comment from Vernon Bartlett who said, *inter alia*, 'I believe the British would have acted in much the same way as Germany has acted if they had been in the same position'.[1]

This broadcast caused an immediate controversy. Bartlett subsequently admitted that he felt passionately on the subject and that he was acting more as a political commentator than as an impartial BBC staff diplomatic correspondent. He also said that he was strongly encouraged to take this line by his producer, Lionel Fielden,[2] who has written much of interest about the problems of broadcasting.[3] Many people felt, in the words of a London editorial: 'If we are to broadcast contentious views in an hour of crisis unmatched since 1914, they should be expressed by responsible members of the Government and not by the talented attachés of the BBC.'[4]

The Prime Minister, Ramsay MacDonald, took this view.

[1] *Daily Herald*, 16 Oct. 1933.
[2] Telephone conversation, Bartlett to Miall, Aug. 1978.
[3] L. Fielden, *The Natural Bent* (1960).   [4] *Evening Standard*, 16 Oct. 1933.

Indeed, he wrote the same day to the Chairman, J.H. Whitley: 'On Saturday there was broadcast by Vernon Bartlett an estimate of the situation which was simply absurd in its ignorance of the latest phases and its one-sidedness as a report of what had taken place before. One statement which he made – that if we had been in the same position as Germany we would have done likewise – would be repudiated by everyone of us who know the position and the true nature of Hitlerite claims. Last night I am told,' the Prime Minister went on, 'the comments when the news was broadcast were even worse in tone and in spirit, and today I am hearing all round of the effect of the two broadcasts.' MacDonald concluded by saying that at critical moments the BBC should be particularly careful 'and should ask for some advice before it puts its foot into it, as you did Saturday and Sunday'. [1]

Reith dictated a strong reply for the Chairman to send; indeed, he described it in his diary as 'rather snotty for a P.M.' [2] Whitley refused to accept the Prime Minister's strictures. He explained there had been no 'talk' on the Sunday night at all, the bulletin consisting merely of the Press Agencies' summaries of foreign opinion, and as for consultation 'before putting one's foot in it' he noted that Reith had telephoned 10 Downing Street and the Prime Minister's Principal Secretary's home but could get no reply from either. [3]

Whitley and Reith were then invited to go to 10 Downing Street where they found the PM 'in a grey suit with brown shoes' with Stanley Baldwin and Sir John Simon. They agreed to broadcast a talk by Simon that night and Reith arranged for a portable radio to be sent to the Garrick Club where MacDonald was dining so that he might listen. [4]

Meanwhile, the row over Bartlett's talk continued. The *Daily Telegraph* described it in an editorial as 'a grave indiscretion' and said that the BBC was not 'given official control of the ether' in order 'that one of its regular "talkers" should tendentiously weaken a national case, nationally presented on a critical occasion'. [5] And Brigadier E.L. Spears, MP, bombarded the BBC with letters complaining of Bartlett's strongly 'pro-German

[1] Ramsay MacDonald to J.H. Whitley, 16 Oct. 1933.
[2] Reith, *Diary*, 17 Oct. 1933.   [3] Whitley to MacDonald, 17 Oct. 1933.
[4] Reith, *Diary*, 17 Oct. 1933.   [5] *Daily Telegraph*, 17 Oct. 1933.

bias'. [1] Spears was to raise the matter again in a debate on disarmament in the House of Commons on 6 February 1934. [2]

Bartlett himself resolved to resign from the BBC unless he got a favourable response in the mail to his broadcast. He wrote in his autobiography, 'I have forgotten how many thousands there were, but well over 90 per cent of them supported the talk. But it was clear that my broadcasting days were over. Having once expressed so strong an opinion, everything else that I said in subsequent talks was subjected to the closest examination, not so much by BBC officials themselves as by officious members of parliament, to test my neutrality. It was agreed at Broadcasting House that it would be easier for me to continue my talks if I were no longer a member of the regular staff. I therefore took a job on a newspaper, after fully consulting the BBC about it, and, having done so, was almost at once told that, since I *was* on a newspaper, I could obviously not continue to broadcast.' [3]

On 13 December 1933 the termination of Vernon Bartlett's contract from the end of the year 'on his own initiative' was reported to the Board, but on 17 January 1934 the Board resolved 'that Mr Vernon Bartlett be not employed for regular weekly talks after 31 March 1934'. [4] Bartlett's popularity as a political observer was not diminished by the termination of his contract, and in 1938 he won a remarkable victory as an independent parliamentary candidate at Bridgwater.

In his old age Bartlett reflected in tranquillity, 'I think that, in view of public opinion at the time the sacking was more or less inevitable since there were questions in the House and strong articles, against me but also for me, in the newspapers. What I *did* resent was the cowardly way in which it was done. I was assured that I should be on a panel of broadcasters on foreign affairs and it was suggested that the politics of any newspaper I joined might affect the frequency with which I was asked to do other talks. I rejected a terrific offer from the *Daily Herald* to go to the more moderate *News Chronicle*, but I was not asked to talk again for several years.' [5]

[1] Brigadier Spears to Reith, 18, 20 Oct., 14 Nov. 1933.

[2] *Hansard*, vol. 285, cols. 1024–34, 6 Feb. 1934.

[3] V. Bartlett, *This is My Life* (1937), p.192.

[4] Board of Governors, *Minutes*, 13 Dec. 1933, 17 Jan. 1934.

[5] Bartlett to Miall, 18 Aug. 1978.

3 The Citizen and His Government 1935–6

In 1935 the BBC's Adult Education Advisory Committee had recommended that there should be a balanced series of 12 education talks designed for planned discussion groups under the title *The Citizen and His Government*. The first seven were to be expository, the speakers being Captain Harold Balfour, MP, and Miss Agnes Headlam-Morley. These were to be followed by five talks given by representatives of widely divergent political opinions: Sir Oswald Mosley (Fascist), Harry Pollitt (Communist), Isaac Foot, MP (Liberal), Herbert Morrison (Labour) and Kenneth Pickthorn, MP (Conservative).[1]

The project was submitted in detail to the Board of Governors who gave their formal approval.[2] Colonel Alan Dawnay, Controller of Programmes, then communicated the outline of the scheme to the Foreign Office, which objected to the Pollitt broadcast because of a speech which Pollitt had just made at a meeting of the Third International in Moscow. On 13 September 1935 Rex Leeper of the Foreign Office telephoned Dawnay urging the BBC to drop the Pollitt talk. Subsequently Sir Robert Vansittart, the Permanent Under-Secretary, spoke to Reith in the same sense and said that because of the international situation (the Italian attack on Abyssinia) a talk by Sir Oswald Mosley would be unfortunate.[3]

The Board gave careful consideration to Vansittart's views, but decided to adhere to the published plans. They 'agreed that the Foreign Office be informed that the Corporation wished to proceed with this series, undertaking that the talk on Fascism made no reference to the Italian Abyssinian war.'[4] Reith's notes on the meeting added: 'Governors felt very strongly that Pollitt should be allowed to give the talk on Communism . . . and that if it was to be stopped they [the Foreign Office] would need to get the Postmaster-General to exercise his right of veto.'

However, the Foreign Office remained obdurate, and Vansittart said he would take the matter to the Secretary of State, then

[1] S. D. Spicer to Mr Chapman, Miss Sprott, 14 Sept. 1935.

[2] Board of Governors, *Minutes*, 10 July 1935.

[3] Statement by BBC handed to Sir Robert Vansittart on 15 Oct. 1935.

[4] Board of Governors, *Minutes*, 9 Oct. 1935.

Anthony Eden.[1] The imminent general election gave an excuse for postponing the five controversial talks in the series which by then had started. The Adult Education Advisory Committee were vexed at the postponement and pressed hard for the inclusion of the talks in the April-June 1936 Quarter.[2] The Foreign Office was told in a letter from Captain Cecil Graves, who had just succeeded Dawnay as Controller of Programmes, to the Earl Stanhope, Under Secretary of State, that the Board had again carefully considered the matter and decided that the remaining five talks 'could be cancelled, providing the Corporation could state that it was taking this course because the Government was anxious that the talks should not be given'.[3]

Lord Stanhope's reply had an ominous ring: 'I imagine that the Board has considered the effect that may be produced in Parliament by a public announcement, shortly before the new Charter comes up for discussion, that the Government have felt impelled in the public interest to stop a series of talks. It seems to me that it may strengthen the case for those who demand more Parliamentary control of the BBC.'[4]

Graves consulted Reith, saying, 'I am not inclined to alter our decision',[5] but Reith's equivocating reply indicated the effect Stanhope's letter had made on the Board: 'About Stanhope, Mrs Hamilton had already gone North so I could not speak to her today. Mr Harold Brown is in the same indefinite position as the Chairman and I, and I think you. Do please make it clear to Mrs Hamilton that there is no cold feet about any of us. I hope you understand this yourself now. Nor is there any question of not having the courage to stick to our point. It is just a matter of expediency and also to a certain extent of decency. Stanhope's advice is that we should be making a mistake and this advice is based on his knowledge of opinion in Parliament.'[6]

Meanwhile the Foreign Secretary had brought the matter to the Cabinet, which discussed it on 12 February.[7] The Ministers'

[1] Cecil Graves, 'Record of Interview at Foreign Office with Sir Robert Vansittart', 16 Oct. 1935.

[2] Graves's Record of Interview with Lord Stanhope at the Foreign Office, 26 Jan. 1936.

[3] Graves to Stanhope, 31 Jan. 1936.   [4] Stanhope to Graves, 5 Feb. 1936.

[5] Graves to Reith, 6 Feb. 1936.   [6] Reith to Graves, 7 Feb. 1936.

[7] Memorandum by Anthony Eden to the Cabinet 'Proposed Broadcasts by the British Broadcasting Corporation of a series of Talks on Fascism and Communism', 7 Feb. 1936 (Public Record Office).

main concern was the attribution of responsibility for stopping the already publicised talks. The Governors had offered to cancel them only 'if they were authorised to state that "they had been given to understand that the broadcasting of these talks would be an embarrassment to the Government" or something similar'. Eden said he saw no hope of inducing the BBC not to mention the Government's intervention but hoped to substitute the words 'would not be in the national interest' for 'would be an embarrassment to the Government'. The Cabinet agreed that the Prime Minister, Stanley Baldwin, should see the new Postmaster-General, Major G. C. Tryon, and urge him to take up the matter with the Chairman and Directors (sic) of the BBC to try to induce the withdrawal of the Mosley and Pollitt broadcasts, adding 'the Postmaster-General, however, should be authorised, if necessary, to make quite clear that the Government would not permit these broadcasts'.[1]

A week later the Prime Minister was able to report that R. C. Norman, the Chairman, had agreed to withdraw the Mosley and Pollitt talks 'and no public reference would be made to Government intervention'. The Cabinet formally recorded its congratulations.[2]

Reith confided to his diary, 'Long confab with Norman about *The Citizen and His Government* series. He was very worried lest I thought I could have done better than he with the PMG. I said I thought I would have asked to see the PM.'[3]

The Adult Education Advisory Committee was dismayed by the Board's action. At its meeting on 14 February 1936 it asked Graves, the BBC representative, to withdraw from the room. It then passed a resolution viewing 'with grave concern the decision of the Board of Governors to cancel the series'; and hoping that it did not represent any change of policy 'in narrowing the field over which balanced controversy may be permitted'.[4]

Sir Francis Acland, one of its members, was even brave enough to ask Graves whether the BBC was motivated in this decision by the imminent publication of the Ullswater Report, and Graves admitted that 'naturally we were not anxious at the present

[1] Cabinet *Minutes*, 12 Feb. 1936 (Public Record Office).
[2] Ibid., 19 Feb. 1936.   [3] Reith, *Diary*, 18 Feb. 1936.
[4] Adult Education Advisory Committee Resolutions, reported by Graves to Reith, 17 Feb. 1936.

juncture that a matter of this kind should reach a stage where a great deal of public attention would be focused upon it'.[1]

An acrimonious correspondence followed between the Chairman of the Adult Education Advisory Committee, Principal J. H. Nicholson of University College Hull, and Graves, and the matter was taken up by the General Advisory Council. Norman consulted the Postmaster-General again, and the issue was neatly swept under the carpet with the following formula: 'They agreed that it should be explained to the Council, confidentially and not in writing, that the BBC do constantly keep in touch with the Government and had been in touch with the Foreign Office about these talks at an early stage, when no objection was raised; but that they were subsequently informed by the Government that these talks if given would be likely to exacerbate the international position, which had become more acute; and that therefore the BBC decided that the talks should not be given.'[2]

By the time of its June Meeting, the General Advisory Council was in fact much more concerned with the newly published Ullswater Report. Despite the misgivings of the Board, the Adult Education Advisory Committee and the General Advisory Council, the Government of the day had succeeded in forcing a cancellation of publicised broadcasts, and in keeping the fact quiet.

4 Lambert v. Levita 1936

R.S. Lambert, the first Editor of *The Listener*, decided in February 1936 to demand an unqualified apology from Sir Cecil Levita for statements he had made about his suitability to be a Governor of the British Film Institute.

Lambert joined the BBC in 1927 as head of the Adult Education Section. Previously he had been a classical scholar at Wadham College, a pacifist during World War I, a journalist on *The Economist* and a teacher at the universities of Sheffield and London. A fellow member of the British Film Institute once described him to a BBC Governor as 'a high-principled, hot-tempered, impetuous fellow, rather quixotic and quite capable of

[1] Graves to Reith, 14 Feb. 1936.
[2] Letter from Sir Donald Banks, Director-General, GPO, to Sir Stephen Tallents, Controller, Public Relations, 24 June 1936.

sacrificing his plainest material interests if he thought a point of principle was involved'.[1]

In 1928 Lambert was appointed to edit the BBC's new magazine *The Listener*. He engaged Harry Price, of the Society for Psychical Research, to contribute a series of articles over three months.[2] These contained Price's accounts of his experiences with supernatural phenomena, under the title of 'Confessions of a Ghost Hunter'. Lambert also arranged a demonstration of a so-called fire-walking test in September 1935, at which an Indian made three rapid walks along a blazing charcoal trench without apparent damage to his feet.[3] The spectators were all personally invited either by Price or by Lambert.

Among the latter were Sir Cecil and Lady Levita. Sir Cecil had been Chairman of the LCC, 1928–9, and was an adviser on matters of film censorship to the Home Office. Lady Levita was a Governor of the British Film Institute, where she was a colleague of Lambert, who had been nominated a Governor not by the BBC but by the British Institute of Adult Education. Lambert had to obtain BBC permission to accept the appointment, which involved work for the Film Institute during office hours.

Shortly before the Indian fire-walking feat, Lambert and Price had been to investigate strange happenings in a lonely farmhouse in the Isle of Man named Cashen's Gap. The farmer, Irving, and his family claimed that their house was haunted by a mongoose, and that Irving had taught it to speak. Lambert and Price published their findings in a book entitled *The Haunting of Cashen's Gap*. Lambert subsequently wrote, 'In that book, while indicating fully our reasons for refusing to give credit to the Irvings' tale, we refrained as far as possible either from unnecessarily hurting their feelings – as they had entertained us hospitably – or from saying anything that could be interpreted as libellous.'[4] In other words they hedged their bets. As Andrew Boyle put it: they showed 'a nice blend of belief and repudiation.'[5] Lambert twice recounted his experiences at Cashen's Gap to Lady Levita.

On 7 February 1936 Sir Cecil Levita gave lunch to Major

[1] W.W. Vaughan to H.A.L. Fisher, quoted in Fisher's letter to R.C. Norman, 29 May 1936 (Bodleian Library).

[2] For Price's credentials, see Trevor H. Hall, *Search for Harry Price* (1978).

[3] Lambert, op.cit., p.226.   [4] Ibid., p.231.

[5] A. Boyle, *Only the Wind Will Listen* (1972), p.279.

W.E. Gladstone Murray, who had previously been Lambert's immediate superior in the BBC, but was no longer. Murray, a convivial Canadian, who was to leave the BBC before the end of the year, [1] was on friendly terms with Lambert and provided him with a note recording his conversation with Levita. One sentence read: 'Mr Lambert's belief in the occult, taken in conjunction with his inconsistencies and manifestations of hysteria, more than establish a case for his disqualification as a Governor of the Film Institute. But the trouble is that he is a Governor for life, and the only way to get him off is to induce the BBC to withdraw him.' [2] When Lambert read the note, and heard that Murray was planning to show it to Sir Stephen Tallents, Lambert's new chief, he thought his position in the BBC might be jeopardised. He demanded an apology and withdrawal from Levita, later following with the threat of a legal action.

Levita attempted to persuade the Chairman, R.C. Norman (an ex-colleague from the LCC), and the Vice-Chairman, H.G. Brown, to intervene with Lambert on his behalf to get the legal action called off, but when the Chairman saw Lambert, there was no meeting of minds.

After a Sunday broadcast by King Edward viii from Broadcasting House, the Chairman, Vice-Chairman and Reith discussed the matter further. The Chairman said he was not concerned to protect Levita from the consequences of his own actions, but was concerned about the possible repercussions on the BBC if the case came to court. [3] The three of them then instructed Tallents to give Lambert what Reith called 'a stern warning' that though his position in the BBC was so far undamaged, if he persisted with his legal action he might make the BBC doubt his judgement. [4] This warning was put into writing and is said to have multiplied Lambert's eventual damages tenfold. [5]

Meanwhile, the House of Commons was debating the renewal of the BBC's Charter, following the publication of the Ullswater Report. BBC observers in the gallery were startled when Sir Stafford Cripps launched a violent attack on Reith's dictatorial

[1] Murray was dismissed by the Board on 31 March 1936. He appealed, was eventually granted Grace Leave and was appointed General Manager of the new Canadian Broadcasting Corporation before the dismissal took effect.

[2] Lambert, op.cit., p.236.

[3] R.C. Norman to Major G.C. Tryon, the Postmaster-General, 19 May 1936.

[4] J.C.W. Reith, *Diary*, 6 March 1936.   [5] Lambert, op.cit., p.251.

staff policies in general and the BBC's pressure on Lambert to call off his action in particular. This he called 'a grave scandal'. He condemned Reith's methods of staff recruitment, the compensation paid to individuals forced to resign because of incompetence, the absence of settled salaries and grades for different posts, the supervision over the private lives of staff, including the summary dismissal of so-called guilty parties to divorce proceedings, and the absence of machinery to air grievances. [1]

Lambert was given Grace Leave, part of which was spent at the Nuremberg Rally as 'Hitler's guest'. [2] The case of *Lambert v. Levita*, known as the Talking Mongoose Case, began on 4 November 1936. The jury awarded damages of £7500. Reith described them as 'amazing and monstrous'. [3]

The Chairman had hoped in vain to give the court his side of the story. When he was not called, he wrote to the Prime Minister (Stanley Baldwin) saying that because the BBC was not a party to the action he had had no chance to correct erroneous impressions of his conduct as Chairman of the BBC. He suggested an official enquiry. [4] Baldwin immediately convened a three-man board under the chairmanship of Sir Josiah Stamp to look into the various allegations concerning the BBC which had emerged in court.

The Inquiry's findings, published on 16 December 1936, just after King Edward VIII's abdication, exonerated Norman and Brown of the Board and Reith and Tallents of the Executive from the imputation of exerting undue pressure, but also demonstrated that formal warnings to Lambert had been expressed without sufficient regard to the strength of his case. It declared that it did not follow that because the Governors and BBC officials 'were honest in what they did, they were also wise'. [5] It also said of one memo which Lambert had sent to Reith, 'we have not often read one more unfortunately phrased'. [6]

The Press reaction to the Stamp Report was mixed. The *Daily Telegraph* noted 'the Committee distributes its censure evenly enough', [7] and the other papers tended to seize on the passages they preferred. Thus, the *Daily Mail* said the gist of the report was

[1] *Hansard*, vol. 311, cols. 974–80, 29 April 1936.
[2] Lambert, op. cit, p.263.   [3] Reith, *Diary*, 6 Nov. 1936.
[4] R.C. Norman to S. Baldwin, 9 Nov. 1936 (Post Office Archives).
[5] Cmd 5337 (1936), *Report of the Special Board of Inquiry*, p.22.
[6] Ibid.   [7] *Daily Telegraph*, 17 Dec. 1936.

'the Corporation has not yet learned to handle tactfully officials in its employ', [1] while the *Morning Post* said 'nothing that has come to light reflects in any way on the integrity and honour of any individual member of the BBC' [2]. The *News Chronicle* thought Lambert's position had been justified. He had not always been wise or tactful, 'but that is neither an explanation nor an excuse for the extraordinary manner in which his case was handled by the BBC'. [3] The *Daily Herald* found it difficult 'to imagine a more astonishing or unfortunate document', [4] and the *New Statesman* declared 'the hierarchy in control of the BBC are signally deficient in a sense of human values and humour alike . . . a misguided attempt has been made to run Broadcasting House on semi-military lines'. [5]

The Stamp Report had concluded by drawing a sharp distinction between the BBC and the Civil Service though both were servants of the public. Nevertheless, the Committee felt that the BBC might well learn with advantage from the Civil Service practice in dealing with staff matters. This was already a matter of great interest in Labour Party and trade-union circles. Baldwin later recorded his satisfaction 'that the Corporation welcome this offer of assistance'. [6]

Lambert himself wrote of the affair in general terms: 'Soon, the murky atmosphere that had enveloped Broadcasting House for so long began to clear, and improvements were made on every side. Methods of appointing new staff were regularised, by advertising vacancies and setting up selection boards, including a Treasury Commissioner. The old staff-contract form was revised and made less one-sided. Grades and salary scales were defined, and every employee informed where he stood. After a tussle behind the scenes, divorce ceased to be a ground for punishing an employee, either by enforced resignation, or by transfer to another part of the service. . . . Members of the Board of Governors began to mix freely with members of the staff, and acquire for the first time first-hand knowledge of how the Corporation's work was carried on. And finally, the apparently still-born pro-

[1] *Daily Mail*, 17 Dec. 1936.
[2] *Morning Post*, 17 Dec. 1936.
[3] *News Chronicle*, 17 Dec. 1936.
[4] *Daily Herald*, 17 Dec. 1936.
[5] *New Statesman*, 19 Dec. 1936.
[6] Cmd 5405 (1937), *Minute by the Prime Minister*.

ject for a Staff Association was revived, and slowly and cautiously carried forward towards a concrete result.'[1]

Lambert emigrated to Canada early in the war.

5 Party Manners 1950

On 12 June 1950 the Home Service broadcast *Party Manners*, a play written by Val Gielgud, the Head of Drama, during his Grace Leave. It was a lighthearted comedy with political overtones, and concerned an Old Etonian Labour politician and the secret of the atomic bomb. There were objections only from three listeners – two that it showed *left* wing bias, and one that it laid too much emphasis on the role of alcohol in politics. On 1 October *Party Manners* was transmitted to the then much smaller television audience. During this phase in broadcasting history, before good video-recording, the Sunday television play was normally repeated live on Thursday while the scenery was readily available and the actors still remembered their parts.

The Labour Party annual conference was being held that week in Margate. Ernest Whitfield, the blind Governor, attended, and informed the Chairman, Lord Simon of Wythenshawe, that *Party Manners* had caused great offence to the Labour leadership.[2] The *Daily Herald* demanded that 'this crude, silly and insulting "comedy" should not be repeated in Thursday's programme'.[3]

Meanwhile, Lord Simon had already taken personal action. Without securing the approval of other members of the Board, and overriding the objections of the Director-General (Haley), he cancelled the repeat of *Party Manners* on the grounds of upholding democracy. He went on to issue a Press statement of his own saying that the play was capable of being misunderstood, and because of this it could not be in the public interest.[4] Simon, described by a business colleague as an 'autocratic head' – 'for autocrat he was, if he seldom acted autocratically'[5] – had two years earlier arbitrarily cancelled a radio repeat of a Third Programme talk by Malcolm Muggeridge on Beatrice Webb's

[1] Lambert, op.cit., p.302.
[2] Information from Sir William Haley.
[3] *Daily Herald*, 3 Oct. 1950.
[4] BBC Press Handout, 10 Oct. 1950.
[5] Ian Hey, Chairman of Henry Simon (Holdings) Ltd, in a privately printed book to mark Lord Simon's 80th birthday on 9 October 1959, p.10.

diaries.[1] This time he found himself in the political fire. Few journalists believed his assertion that the cancellation of the repeat was not the result of political pressure. *The Recorder* likened it to Hitler's burning of the books,[2] and the House of Lords scheduled a debate.

The Governors, deep in the problem of whether to appoint Norman Collins or George Barnes to the new post of Director of Television, discussed *Party Manners* at four separate meetings. Barbara Wootton, who personally disliked the play, said it was 'a matter of principle that Governors should not interfere in detailed programmes' and that 'the BBC must not only be impartial but must manifestly be seen to be impartial. There was, in this case, no political pressure, but no one will ever believe that, least of all in the middle of the Labour Party Conference.'[3]

Simon tried to defend his action in two critical debates, though he defended it lamely. The first was a debate in the General Advisory Council where the attack was opened by Duncan Sandys. He demanded to know whether the Chairman had had external protests about *Party Manners*, whether he had consulted the Director-General before banning its repeat, and whether the Board had subsequently endorsed the Chairman's action. Simon plaintively asked the GAC Chairman, Lord Halifax, whether he had to answer these damaging questions. He managed to avoid doing so.[4]

Two weeks later Lord Hailsham made a devastating maiden speech in the debate in the House of Lords. 'If Mr Val Gielgud were now to rewrite the play,' he said, 'in such terms as to portray a member of the Labour Party, newly converted to the creed, appointed to a public board, not now an atomic board but the British Broadcasting Corporation, who suppresses a document, not now a report on atomic energy but a popular comedy, not on the ground that it is intrinsically immoral or obscene but in the face of a violent attack, not now from the Cabinet (as in the existing version of the play) but from the official organ of the Labour Party, and on the ground that it might bring his Party into ridicule, I can only say that the noble Lord, Lord Simon of

[1] 'The Webb Partnership', note by L. Miall, 3 Aug. 1977.

[2] *The Recorder*, 7 Oct. 1950.

[3] Board of Governors, *Papers*, Letter from Prof. Wootton to the Chairman, 12 Oct. 1950.

[4] General Advisory Council, *Verbatim Report*, 24 Oct. 1950.

'Would you mind repeating that last line, Mr Shakespeare?'

Wythenshawe, would have only himself to blame.'[1] After light-hearted comments on various satires from Shakespeare through W.S. Gilbert to Bernard Shaw, Hailsham told Simon, 'There is only one way of upholding democracy – if that be, as I believe, the aim of the noble Lord – and that is by being democratic. You do not do it by humourless sensitivity to criticism.'[2]

Simon's action was defended by Lord Strabolgi, who described *Party Manners* as pernicious. Lord Jowitt, the Lord Chancellor, found the play 'sorry stuff', but warned the House against any Parliamentary interference with the BBC. The debate was wound up by Lord Simon himself with another rather feeble apology. 'I did not foresee the hurricane which arose. I think it is clear that I made a serious underestimate – I made a mistake – in taking that action . . . For the same reason I made a second mistake . . . if it had occurred to me for one moment that it would be suggested that I had read the *Daily Herald* article, and that I, as a member of the Labour Party, had been influenced by that, and that therefore I was bringing Party politics into the BBC, it would have been utterly inconceivable for me to act without consulting the other Governors.'[3]

Simon's final reflection came in his book *The BBC from Within*, published a year after he ceased to be Chairman. 'Personally (of

[1] *House of Lords Official Report*, vol. 169 no. 4, col. 158, 7 Nov. 1950.
[2] Ibid., col. 163.   [3] Ibid., col. 193.

course I may be prejudiced) I still hold that the play was an undesirable one and that my action was right; though I no doubt made a mistake in the method of my action. But that is not the point. What is important is that when it was thought that the chairman had taken advantage of his position to act arbitrarily in "banning" a play, a storm was raised so violent that quite obviously no chairman will ever dream of doing anything of the sort again.'[1]

Lord Woolton drew a different conclusion. The Chairman's action, he told Harman Grisewood, was decisive in convincing him that the monopoly should be terminated.[2]

6 Suez 1956

The most serious threat to the BBC as an institution occurred a year after the start of commercial television. But it came from the Government of Sir Anthony Eden, not from the competitor. On 26 July 1956, President Gamal Abdel Nasser nationalised the Anglo-French Suez Canal Company, one of whose directors was Sir Alexander Cadogan, the BBC Chairman, who had also served long and faithfully as Eden's right-hand man at the Foreign Office.

The immediate reaction of the Labour Party was sharply anti-Nasser. Thus, Hugh Gaitskell, the Leader of the Opposition, denounced the Egyptian President as another Hitler, and Herbert Morrison called him the 'pocket dictator in Cairo'.[3] On 8 August, during this period of political harmony, Eden made what then was only the second Ministerial broadcast on television. It was delayed twenty-four hours so that it could also be relayed by ITV. It was simultaneously broadcast by domestic radio and on shortwave by the General Overseas Service. It was also relayed by all four radio networks in the United States, in all Dominions and in many Colonies.[4] The Prime Minister warned the world against appeasing dictators and said that Nasser had created 'a very grave situation'.

Thereafter, for a number of reasons, the Labour Opposition

[1] Lord Simon, *The BBC from Within* (1953), p.329.
[2] Note by Harman Grisewood, 17 March 1979.
[3] Anthony Nutting, *No End of a Lesson* (1967), p.47.
[4] G. Mosley, 'The Suez Crisis and the BBC', July 1961.

became increasingly critical of the Eden Government's stand, and the changing political situation was reflected by a special balanced discussion on Suez broadcast on 10 August by the Television Service. Radio, however, made no immediate comparable effort to include anti-Government views.[1] Meanwhile, Eden was strongly backed by Robert Menzies, the Prime Minister of Australia, who arrived in London, and at lunch with Eden agreed to a suggestion that he should broadcast on the BBC about Australia's support for the British Government.[2]

Menzies was surprised, and Eden angry, when this offer to broadcast was declined by John Green, Controller of Talks (Sound), on grounds of political imbalance.[3] Green was acting for Harman Grisewood (who was in hospital) as the BBC's liaison with the political parties. He felt that Menzies would make another 'semi-ministerial' broadcast, and noted that Selwyn Lloyd, the Foreign Secretary, had claimed a radio Ministerial for about the same time. Green was concerned that radio appeared to be presenting a one-sided account of the Government's position.[4] He ignored what was happening on television.

The Prime Minister then telephoned his old friend the Chairman, taking strong exception to Green's rejection of the Menzies offer, and Cadogan agreed that it was absurd.[5] 'This is really nonsense', he recorded in his diary, and telephoned Sir Ian Jacob to say that Menzies must be allowed to speak 'no matter what our traditions and inhibitions might be'.[6] The Menzies broadcast was accordingly accommodated in the Television Service.[7]

The incident disturbed Harman Grisewood, the Chief Assistant to the Director-General, on his return from hospital. He was worried not so much by the contact between the Prime Minister and the Chairman, as by the danger that, influenced by the Prime Minister, Cadogan would assume more of an executive responsibility inside the BBC than seemed to Grisewood practical or constitutionally proper.[8]

[1] G. Wyndham Goldie, *Facing the Nation* (1977), p.178.
[2] R. Menzies, *Afternoon Light* (1967), p.151.   [3] Wyndham Goldie, op.cit., pp.178–81.
[4] J. Green to L. Wellington, 13 Aug. 1956.
[5] A. Eden, *Full Circle* (1960), p.448.
[6] D. Dilks (ed.), *The Diaries of Sir Alexander Cadogan* (1971), p.797.
[7] In *Highlight*, 13 Aug. 1956.
[8] H. Grisewood, *One Thing at a Time* (1968), pp.196–7.

Meanwhile, the Board as a whole was concerned about political balance at the top level. By agreement between the Parties Ministerial broadcasts were 'meant' to be confined to non-controversial measures: they were to be used to make factual pronouncements, to explain legislation approved by Parliament, or to appeal to the public to co-operate in national policies. If the Opposition considered that a Ministerial broadcast had transgressed into party controversy, it could claim a reply through the 'usual channels', the Chief Whips, and if after three days the Government would not yield a reply, the Opposition could appeal to the BBC Board to arbitrate.[1] In such circumstances the Board would then be faced with an essentially political decision which the Governors did not welcome.

By mid-September the Suez question had become highly controversial, and there were sharp differences of approach on the part of Government and Opposition. The House of Commons had been recalled, and Gaitskell was demanding an opportunity to present the Labour Party's viewpoint on television.[2] Cadogan and Jacob doubted whether Ministers or Opposition leaders would wish to broadcast about Suez in a party political context, and expected that there might be a request from Downing Street for a further television Ministerial which could hardly fail to raise further controversy.[3] The Board was thus being steadily driven into a difficult political position in which existing machinery would not work. As Jacob put it later, 'the procedures which govern political broadcasting were designed for domestic controversy of the kind that normally accompanies political life; a national emergency when Government action was not nationally supported presented a new problem'.[4]

The Board accordingly authorised Cadogan and Jacob to discuss this problem with both Government and Opposition,[5] and a meeting was held on 14 September 1956 with R.A. Butler (Lord Privy Seal) and Gaitskell. This resulted in an invitation to Gaitskell to appear in *Press Conference* on 21 September, in other words in a normal BBC television programme rather than in the context of a Party Political or a Ministerial Reply. A similar

[1] Aide-Memoire on Political Broadcasting, 6 Feb. 1947, revised July 1948.
[2] Board of Governors, *Minutes*, 13 Sept. 1956.
[3] Ibid.
[4] Sir Ian Jacob, 'The Suez Crisis and the BBC', *Ariel*, Jan. 1957.
[5] Board of Governors, *Minutes*, 13 Sept. 1956.

invitation went to Selwyn Lloyd to be interviewed in *Panorama* on 24 September.

After secret Anglo-French-Israeli consultations near Paris, suspected but hotly denied at the time, and now admitted,[1] Israeli forces entered Egypt on 29 October, and attacked positions in the Sinai desert. The next day Britain and France sent an ultimatum both to Egypt and Israel to cease hostilities and withdraw, and on 31 October the RAF and the French Air Force began to attack Egyptian airfields. This was military action, but there had been no declaration either of war or of a state of emergency.

As often happens in such circumstances, leading personalities were missing. Jacob was by then on his way to a Commonwealth Broadcasting Conference in Australia, and Cadogan was not immediately available. It was the Vice-Chairman, Sir Philip Morris, therefore, who after a long conversation with Grisewood agreed that there should be 'no changes as regards programmes, editorial objectivity or relationships between staff and normal contact outside'. In Morris's words this 'occasioned surprised reactions outside the BBC, particularly at No. 10 and the Foreign Office and to some extent, within the BBC'.[2]

A further request for a television Ministerial then came from Eden's public relations adviser, William Clark, who was told that if Gaitskell went on to request a right of reply the Board would probably concede it. Clark said this was understood and expected by the Prime Minister.[3] Eden duly broadcast from 10 Downing Street, therefore, on the evening of Saturday 3 November, explaining why the Government had decided to bombard Egypt: 'What we did do, was to take police action at once.' The broadcast was also carried by ITV. Gaitskell immediately telephoned the BBC demanding the right to reply the next day. There was some delay while the formalities were observed and the request was forwarded through the 'usual channels' of Opposition Chief Whip (Herbert Bowden) to Government Chief Whip (Edward Heath).[4] Heath told Bowden that Eden's broadcast had been the least controversial it could be in the circumstances, adding that though the Government felt that no reply should be conceded, if

[1] Selwyn Lloyd, *Suez 1956: a Personal Account* (1978), pp.180–7.
[2] Sir Philip Morris to Sir Hugh Greene, 26 Dec. 1975.
[3] Mosley, loc.cit.
[4] Grisewood, op.cit., p.202.

the Board of Governors decided to allow Labour to reply no objection would be made.[1] By then it was after midnight and Grisewood refused to awaken Cadogan. It was not until the following morning that Cadogan granted Gaitskell a television reply that evening, Sunday 4 November. The Board unanimously endorsed the Chairman's action.[2]

The House of Commons earlier that week had reflected the mood of a country which was far from united. As the Deputy Editor of *The Times* later recalled: 'At each word the whole of the Labour benches rose like a wall, no longer shouting. They were howling with anger and real anguish . . . The Speaker could no longer be heard . . . I just saw him wave as a sign that the sitting was suspended, and out the Members trooped, still shouting and shaking their fists.'[3]

In this atmosphere Gaitskell's television reply intensified the passionate divisions, particularly when he appealed to 'those Conservatives who, like us, are shocked and troubled by what is happening' and undertook to 'support a new Prime Minister in halting the invasion of Egypt, in ordering the ceasefire and complying with the decisions and recommendations of the United Nations'.

From No. 10 Clark telephoned the BBC urging that the more inflammatory parts of Gaitskell's broadcast should not be transmitted in the BBC's Arabic Service,[4] and later he passed on an informal but strongly worded request that not too much prominence should be given to the domestic opposition to the Prime Minister's policy merely because the *Manchester Guardian* expressed it well.[5]

Clark was to resign, quietly, from his Downing Street service as soon as the Suez action ended. When he came to write 'an inside story' of Suez in *The Observer* twenty years later, he mentioned that Eden was worried that the BBC's overseas services, extensively heard in Egypt, gave 'comfort to the enemy by reporting domestic divisions, thus weakening the credibility of our threats'. He then added 'These worries resulted in innumerable schemes to discipline the BBC,' without attempting to specify what these

[1] Ibid.
[2] Board of Governors, *Minutes*, 8 Nov. 1956.
[3] Iverach McDonald, *Tonight*, 'The Suez Affair Part III', 10 Nov. 1976.
[4] Mosley, loc.cit.   [5] Ibid.

'schemes' were.[1] Clark had been encouraged by Eden to take a holiday in the second half of October 1956 and was in Spain when he received an urgent message to return on 29 October, the day of the Israeli attack on Sinai.[2] His more specific statement, made soon after his return, that the Prime Minister had actually instructed the Lord Chancellor, Lord Kilmuir, to prepare an instrument which would take over the BBC altogether and subject it wholly to the will of the Government[3] has been widely discussed, and even debated in the House of Commons.[4] But it lacks any independent confirmation and relates to a time when Clark himself was abroad.

The Board had indeed been facing exceptionally heavy pressure from Whitehall on the External Services based in Bush House. Between Munich and Suez, Great Britain had not been divided by any fundamental issue in foreign affairs. Eden in 1956 expected the BBC to rally to a nation virtually at war, as it had rallied in 1939; indeed, he saw striking parallels between the two situations. For many Governors, however, there was a conflict between what seemed to be the Government's immediate interests and the long-term credibility of BBC broadcasting. There had to be both veracity and consistency. Eight years earlier Haley had defined the problem thus: 'The BBC does not attempt to have one story for its own people and another for the rest of the world . . . That has been our policy all through. In some ways, curiously enough, it is an easier policy to sustain in war than in peace. In war, the perils are so great that you dare to tell the truth and everyone applauds. In peacetime . . . specious arguments are sometimes put forward to prove that it is in the long-term interest to be not quite so meticulous.'[5]

Such an argument was put forward by the Foreign Office in relation to the Bush House daily summary of press opinion which had continued to include extracts from editorials critical of Government policy. Just before his departure for Australia Jacob had been summoned to the Foreign Office and told that it was proposed to reduce the Government Grant-in-Aid which financed

[1] William Clark, 'Suez: an Inside Story' in *The Observer*, 3 Oct. 1976.
[2] Record of Conversation between Clark and Miall, 10 April 1976.
[3] Grisewood, op.cit., p.199.
[4] *Hansard*, vol. 764, cols. 173–82, 6 May 1968.
[5] W. Haley, 'The Responsibilities of Broadcasting', *Lewis Fry Memorial Lecture*, Bristol University, May 1948.

the External Services by one million pounds and to divert the money to other overseas information purposes. It was made clear that this was a punitive action.[1]

Cadogan and Jacob saw R.A. Butler the next day, and as a result of the meeting the threatened cut was reduced by one half. Yet at both these meetings it was proposed that a special Foreign Office liaison officer should be stationed at Bush House as a watchdog.[2] On 31 October, the day the Anglo-French bombardment began, the Foreign Office decided the time had come to place this liaison officer in Bush House. He was to be Lanham Titchener, an ex-BBC television producer, then *en poste* in Teheran. Pending his return Duncan Wilson[3] was installed. He immediately let it be known that his task was to vet BBC news bulletins in Arabic to see whether they were suitable for re-broadcasting by a radio station in Cyprus which the Governor had just requisitioned for British Government purposes and which had been renamed 'The Voice of Britain'.[4]

After Jacob's departure for Australia the Director of Administration, Sir Norman Bottomley, was the Acting Director-General during the more acute stages of the Suez crisis. Bottomley was then 65, and in the last weeks of his BBC career. He had previously been Deputy Chief of the Air Staff, Air Officer Commanding-in-Chief Bomber Command, under 'Bomber' Harris, and Inspector-General of the RAF. He proved nonetheless to be a stalwart proponent of BBC independence throughout a period of heavy pressure from Whitehall and of continuing debate, often bitter debate, in the country.

The *Manchester Guardian* had denounced the Anglo-French action as soon as it took place as 'an act of folly without justification in any terms but brief expediency',[5] and J.B. Clark, the Director of External Broadcasting, with a long record of dedication to accurate reporting, pointed out that no honest press review could ignore the *Guardian* leader. Bottomley referred the matter to Cadogan, who ruled that scheduled press reviews should continue in the normal manner. The Board subsequently

[1] Mosley, loc.cit.   [2] Ibid.
[3] Later British Ambassador to Moscow and Master of Corpus Christi College, Cambridge.
[4] Mosley, loc.cit. See also E. Watrous, Report on the Near East Arab Broadcasting Station, Sharq al Adna', 23 Oct. 1956.
[5] *Manchester Guardian*, 31 Oct. 1956.

endorsed the Chairman's action.[1] The Foreign Office, however, took strong exception to the BBC following its normal policy. Paul Grey, the Under-Secretary concerned, stated vehemently to Bottomley that in such a situation as the military action against Egypt it was not necessary to tell the whole truth, and argued that certain news items should be suppressed in Arabic bulletins. The Acting Director-General and the Chairman spoke separately to the Paymaster-General, Sir Walter Monckton, recalling the Government's proclaimed long-term policy that treatment of an item in an Overseas news bulletin must never differ materially from its treatment in domestic news,[2] and the Chairman told the Board he believed the Paymaster-General would support the BBC in the matter of news objectivity.[3]

Meanwhile, BBC news objectivity was being attacked from another quarter. On 7 November Peter Rawlinson, Conservative MP for Epsom, telegraphed Bottomley demanding an immediate enquiry into the selection of news during the Suez crisis, and in an adjournment debate a week later he and Charles Ian Orr-Ewing, Conservative MP for North Hendon, charged the BBC with making deliberate distortions in news bulletins, press reviews and other current affairs programmes, and with partial presentation by omission, exaggeration or the use of voice tone and an unrepresentative choice of people for interview. Bottomley told the Board these criticisms were probably unprecedented.[4] They made a great many specific allegations against the competence of BBC news and impugned the integrity of BBC parliamentary correspondents.[5]

The BBC staff prepared lengthy reports examining each charge which had been made in the adjournment debate, and on 22 November the Board inspected in great detail the evidence, side by side with the allegations.[6] It concluded, with minor reservations, that in the field of news bulletins and press reviews 'a successful and creditable result had been generally achieved'

[1] Board of Governors, *Minutes*, 22 Nov. 1956.
[2] Cmd 6852 (1946), *Broadcasting Policy*, para. 59.
[3] Board of Governors, *Minutes*, 8 Nov. 1956.
[4] Bottomley, 'Debate in the House of Commons, Nov. 14th, BBC Broadcasts: Political Balance', 28 Nov. 1956 (posted on all BBC noticeboards).
[5] Board of Governors, *Papers*, 'Debate in the House of Commons, 14 Nov. 1956, BBC News Broadcasts', 21 Nov. 1956.
[6] Bottomley, loc.cit.

during a period of great difficulty, 'and that this result fulfilled the BBC's obligation for impartiality, objectivity and for telling the truth'.[1]

By that time, however, the international situation had changed; there had been a serious run on the pound and the British Government had had to accept the United Nations' demand for a cease-fire. There was a crisis in Eastern Europe also, and the Russians had sent tanks into Budapest. Eisenhower had been re-elected for a second term as President and Eden was flying to Jamaica to recuperate from a serious illness. The Suez crisis was over. As the Vice-Chairman of the BBC put it: 'The action of the United Nations brought relief all round and it remained only for the Governors to deal with various reports on what had happened during the crisis. The discussion was considerable, as it was bound to be between eight/nine people with no common view on the events themselves as distinct from the BBC's behaviour in relation to them.'[2] The role of broadcasting during the crisis continued to provoke argument. There was a sense, indeed, in which it was never resolved even after the Suez crisis itself had passed into history.

7 That Was the Week That Was 1962–3

That Was the Week That Was had its first transmission at 10.50 p.m. on Saturday 24 November 1962. It was an entirely new kind of television programme: highly topical, 'with new sketches, new songs, new and barbed portraits of leading political figures and new lyrics which embodied sharp comments on the contemporary social scene'.[3] Its young anchorman was David Frost, recently recruited from ITV, nurtured at Cambridge by both *Granta* and the Footlights. *TWTWTW* did not rely on established comedians. Its versatile resident team of Millicent Martin, William Rushton, Lance Percival, Roy Kinnear, David Kernan, Kenneth Cope and the talented cartoonist Timothy Birdsall (whose early death was greatly mourned) brought new faces to television. The most readily recognisable one belonged to Bernard Levin. *TWTWTW* had its own jazz group and made

[1] Board of Governors, *Minutes*, 22 Nov. 1956.
[2] Morris to Greene, 26 Dec. 1975.
[3] G. Wyndham Goldie, *Facing the Nation* (1977), p.224.

"Stop laughing, you fool—they're taking the mickey out of people like us."

much use of both the studio audience and the bare studio walls. Cameras seen in shot were no disgrace. The television studio became a club or cave in which nothing was hidden.

TWTWTW was started in the wake of the Vassall affair. Before its first series ended the country was engrossed in the more lurid details of the Profumo scandal. The tone of the new programme was iconoclastic, anti-Establishment. As Angus Wilson wrote: 'The audience know the actors are with them against authority, the people who push them round, or try to stop them enjoying themselves; to laugh with *TW3* gives you certainty you're laughing at the bullies, the fakes and the killjoys.' [1]

That Was the Week That Was was bred in the *Tonight* stable, not in the Light Entertainment Group. Its director, Ned Sherrin, had a flair for fast-moving impromptu programmes. It was originally expected to appeal mainly to a small sophisticated audience of between two and three million. Soon, however, its audience was between eight and ten million. Many liked its vitality, wit and absence of cant. Many others were shocked by blasphemy, schoolboy sexual jokes and lavatory humour.

From the start the Director-General involved the Governors in this new enterprise. At a Board meeting two days before the first

---

[1] Quoted by Kenneth Adam in *The BBC Book of That Was the Week That Was* (1963).

edition, with Sir James Duff the Vice-Chairman presiding, Greene said the project was a difficult one to realise successfully. It might need time to find its feet.[1]

The programme soon ran into political trouble. To be anti-establishment tended to mean being anti-Government, which at that time meant being anti-Conservative.

The Board gave the programme long and anxious attention. During 1963 scarcely a meeting passed without some comment on *TW TW TW*. On 10 January Greene told the Board that its audience had risen to some six and a half million viewers, 'an exceptionally high figure for a late evening programme'.[2] A fortnight later the Board took note of 'the mainly appreciative comment on the programme by members of the General Advisory Council' and Greene said problems of timing and overlong items were being watched.[3] By the beginning of April the Board noted that *TW TW TW* was 'wearing somewhat thin in Westminster circles' and Sir David Milne was deprecating lapses in taste.[4] At the end of the month Sir Ashley Clarke warned the Board that some Government Ministers were inclined to be sensitive, and Sir Arthur fforde suggested that the Board should carefully review the plans for reviving *TW TW TW* after its summer break.[5]

This review took place at Television Centre on 4 July 1963. The Director of Television, Kenneth Adam, summarised for the Board the programme's strengths and weaknesses: on the one hand audience appeal, the attraction of new writers to television and the creation of a new image of Britain overseas, with evidence of political and social maturity; on the other the excessive length of some editions, too many personal attacks not always well directed, too much smut and too much use of Bernard Levin.[6] A lengthy minute recorded the Board's attitude to *TW TW TW* at the time:

The members of the Board recalled the pleasure they had found in the programme and the support they had given to it. They had appreciated its exploitation of the 'amateur' enthusiasm of its performers; of technical improvisation in the studio; and of the element of unpredictability.

[1] Board of Governors, *Minutes*, 22 Nov. 1962.
[2] Ibid., 10 Jan. 1963.   [3] Ibid., 24 Jan. 1963.   [4] Ibid., 4 April 1963.
[5] Ibid., 25 April 1963.   [6] Ibid., 4 July 1963.

Their admiration had been tempered towards the end by the introduction of adolescent smut; by the items offensive to sincere religious feeling . . . by the unrelieved iconoclasm of its constituent elements, and by the snide sneer and the personal attack which turned the subject into a monster not credible in terms of the original or to which the subject could not reply. The mummery surrounding the Crown, for example, was fair game, but not the Queen or the Royal family as persons. The Board expressed some uncertainty as to the rightness of the weekly frequency of the series and the occasionally excessive length of past editions. Events, they recognised, were bound to dictate a large measure of the content, and if the events of the week were distasteful the programme would have to apply itself to the problem of balance. The difficulty of control, both as to content and performance, seemed to be the predictable hazard of the business . . . A difficult programme of this kind was bound to make mistakes, but it ought to continue to learn from them. The Board attached great importance to the prospect of new programmes opened up by the emergence of *TWTWTW*, and hoped that the *élan* and catalytic effect produced by the series would be maintained. They were much reassured by what they had heard.[1]

The programme returned in late September 1963 to a mixed reception both from the Press and from the Board. The Board regretted that the first programme had contained items which offended against the canons they had suggested in their discussion on 4 July, and found it difficult to understand how the producer could have failed to appreciate the significance of the Board's views after they had been so fully communicated to him. Sir Arthur fforde hoped that the programme would 'survive at the level of its best achievements'. What he would deplore would be 'its withdrawal in circumstances which might look like a surrender to public pressure'.[2]

Sir James Duff, however, was becoming increasingly disenchanted with *TWTWTW*, and both Sir Hugh Greene and Sir Robert Lusty have subsequently disclosed that if the programme had not been taken off Duff would probably have resigned. Greene recorded: 'In November '63 I happened to be laid up for a week with an attack of 'flu and had time to lie in bed and think and I came to the conclusion that it was in the general interest, in the interests of the BBC that the programme should not go on,

[1] Ibid.   [2] Ibid., 10 Oct. 1963.

". . . ANYWAY, WE DON'T **NEED** ANY SATIRICAL COMICS IN ELECTION YEAR!

any sort of resignation from the Board of Governors on an issue like that would have done immense damage to the BBC, so at the next meeting of the Board of Governors after I'd got up from bed I said that I had come to the conclusion that the programme should come off the air at the end of the year and there was really a deep sigh of relief round the table, sad though I was to be killing this programme.'[1]

Greene made his announcement to the Board on 7 November 1963. Less than three weeks later *TWTWTW* achieved perhaps its finest hour when it scrapped all existing plans, rewrote a whole programme overnight, and broadcast a moving tribute to President Kennedy, assassinated the day before.

8 Yesterday's Men 1971

Yesterday's Men, a television documentary about the impact of losing office on the Labour Party, was broadcast on 17 June 1971 and resulted in 'the biggest and most furious row that a television programme in the English language has ever provoked'.[2]

[1] Sir Hugh Greene, interview with Frank Gillard, 19 March 1977.
[2] Anthony Smith, *New Statesman*, 16 June 1972.

The idea of producing a documentary film on the Opposition was first mooted by David Dimbleby, a reporter under contract, soon after the 1970 general election. He prepared a synopsis, headed *Yesterday's Men*. It would consider the job of Opposition as ex-Ministers saw it. It would cover enquiries as to what it was like to lose high office suddenly and unexpectedly, and it would include their comments on matters which were being made public in memoirs. Permission to proceed on this basis was given.[1]

Several members of the Shadow Cabinet were filmed, and on 11 May 1971 Dimbleby put various questions to the Leader of the Opposition, Harold Wilson, in a filmed interview. There was a sharp disagreement on the appropriateness of certain questions about how much money Wilson had received for the publication and serialisation of his memoirs. The BBC subsequently undertook to destroy a part of the film. There was a further disagreement on the extent of the film which this undertaking covered.

Yesterday's Men can be considered from many different angles, some concerned with the complicated relationships in a current affairs programme between the reporter, the producer and the broadcasting organisation,[2] some with the sensitivities of English politicians. Were the reporter's questions to Harold Wilson proper, even if delivered with a smile Wilson failed to see? Why did Wilson flare up at questions he had previously answered without demur?[3] Had Dimbleby and the producer Angela Pope misled the participants by not disclosing the title *Yesterday's Men*[4] (taken from the Labour Party's description of the Conservatives in its 1970 general election campaign) and by commissioning the pop group The Scaffold to provide satirical and incidental music? Was television trivialising politics?[5] Was there proper editorial control? Should *Yesterday's Men* have been scheduled to precede a totally different kind of programme on the Conservatives at the same time the following day? Should the political establishment be given deferential treatment? The list could go on much longer. All the questions were in a context far removed from that of the

[1] '*Yesterday's Men*: a statement by the Board of Governors', 8 July 1971.
[2] See David Dimbleby's account in *The Listener*, 16 Nov. 1972.
[3] *The Listener*, 15 July 1971.
[4] Compare the Labour Party Political Broadcast of 7 December 1977 which did not reveal to participants that they were being filmed for a Party Political.
[5] *The Times*, 19 June 1971.

"Thank you, Mr. Prime Minister, and now in conclusion, and to balance the programme 'Yesterday's Men'..."

1930s when Malcolm Muggeridge had complained of the BBC 'patiently wearing away angular opinions; like the waves on a beach, ebbing and flowing, transforming rocks and stones into smooth round pebbles'.[1]

There were also complicated legal aspects, including the threat of an action for defamation. Damages were demanded and refused. There was a conflict of recollection as to what John Crawley, Chief Assistant to the Director-General, had promised Joe Haines, the Press Adviser to the Leader of the Opposition.[2] For the purpose of this essay the important aspect is the role the Board of Governors played.[3]

A few hours before *Yesterday's Men* was transmitted it was seen by the Chairman and several members of the Board. Sir Charles Curran, the Director-General, argued later to the Board of Management that the Board had not previewed and authorised the showing of *Yesterday's Men*. Rather it had been asked to approve a particular editing decision recommended by the

---

[1] Quoted by H. Fairlie, 'The BBC: Voice of the Establishment', in *Encounter*, vol. 13, No. 2, Aug. 1959. He said the criticism was true of 1959 too.

[2] Crawley was hauled out of a shower bath on the Finnish boat *Bore III* in Leningrad harbour to take a telephone call from Broadcasting House seeking confirmation of his version (Crawley Papers, note dated 23 June 1971).

[3] For a more general view see Michael Tracey 'Yesterday's Men – a case study in political communication', in J. Curran, M. Gurevitch and J. Woollacott, *Mass Communication and Society* (1977).

Director-General. Some Governors had viewed it as individuals informing themselves and not formally as a Board.[1] Sir Hugh Greene, however, speaking as both a former Governor and a former chief executive, declared in his 1972 Granada Lecture, 'The Chairman [Lord Hill] insisted that the Board should see the programme before it was broadcast. Not only did the Board do this, but they let the fact that they had done so be publicly known.'[2]

A preview of *Yesterday's Men* had been arranged for lobby correspondents and television critics at Television Centre. They were due to see it at 11 a.m. on 17 June 1971, the day of transmission. The Governors' Finance Committee also met at Television Centre the morning of that same Thursday, at 9.30. Sir Robert Bellinger was in the chair. He had an appointment after the Finance Committee and did not stay for the full Board meeting. Sir Ralph Murray and Lord Dunleath attended the Finance Committee as did Lord Hill and the new Vice-Chairman Lady Plowden. The Governors on the Finance Committee were later joined by Dame Mary Green, Sir Hugh Greene and Paul Wilson. *Yesterday's Men* was shown to them on closed circuit, and they went on to discuss it at the Board meeting proper. (Professor Glanmor Williams, Lady Avonside, Tom Jackson and Lord Constantine were absent as well as Bellinger.)

The Director-General gave the Board an outline of the circumstances which had led to the dispute with the Leader of the Opposition. Curran and Huw Wheldon, Managing Director of Television, had called on Lord Goodman, Wilson's legal adviser, in the small hours of that morning. Goodman, threatening legal action, had made three demands, on behalf of Wilson, for alterations in the documentary. The first was that the BBC should remove all the questions asked by Dimbleby about the former Prime Minister's remuneration from the sale of his memoirs to the *Sunday Times* (which Wilson claimed was in breach of the undertaking given by Crawley on the BBC's behalf to Haines). The second was that the title *Yesterday's Men* must be changed. The third was that three still photographs of Wilson's houses should be removed from the programme. The Board held a long

---

[1] Board of Management, *Minutes*, 3 May 1976.
[2] Sir Hugh Greene, 'The Future of Broadcasting in Britain', *1972 Granada Guildhall Lecture*.

'So when they ask you again how much you got out of your book . . .'

discussion on these three points as well as on the general merits of the programme. It was eventually agreed to meet the first of Wilson's demands but to reject the other two.[1]

Lady Plowden then said that she would be interested to know how the situation discussed by the Board had come about. The question in her mind was the purpose served by Governors when, as on that morning, they were faced with a situation over which they could exercise little real control. Greene said that Governors could not exercise editorial controls, while Dame Mary Green thought that the business of Governors was to delegate responsibility to the staff whom, after due care, they had appointed. The Chairman said that Governors could not hope to oversee the whole of a vast output, but they were brought into discussions of specific issues of importance, as they had been that morning.[2]

Greene subsequently observed: 'In the past the Board would not have seen the programme in advance and any statement they subsequently made could have been accepted as an impartial judgement – as in this case it was not so accepted and indeed could not be.'[3] Demands for a Broadcasting Council followed, both in the General Advisory Council and in the correspondence columns of *The Times*.[4] The pressure to create a broadcasting

[1] Board of Governors, *Minutes*, 17 June 1971.   [2] Ibid.
[3] Greene, 'The Future of Broadcasting in Britain', but see above p.123–4.
[4] General Advisory Council, *Minutes*, 14 July 1971; Board of Management, *Minutes*, 19 July 1971.

council was only partially dispelled by the appointment of a Programmes Complaints Commission.[1]

The Press gave the programme a mixed reception. *The Times* said it was too shallow to be tolerated and added 'it is much more dangerous to trivialise than it ever is to criticise politicians'.[2] The *Daily Telegraph* found it 'an entertaining and not altogether uninstructive programme', and said 'though we certainly would not criticise the BBC for refusing to withdraw the title "Yesterday's Men", it was in itself undesirable'. The *Telegraph* thought Mr Wilson was 'making too much of the affair. Nevertheless television interviewers do owe to eminent public men at least the sort of courtesy which is usually called good manners.'[3]

Anthony Smith commented a year later in the *New Statesman*: 'The Whitley Document says clearly that the role of the Governors is "to safeguard broadcasting in the national interest. Their functions are not executive, their responsibilities are general and not particular." That definition was finally buried and laid to rest by the *Yesterday's Men* affair. A constitutional pattern was overturned and its destruction is now as irreversible as the smile which Mr Wilson didn't see.'[4]

John Crawley reflected privately: 'Looking back over the whole *Yesterday's Men* affair, I conclude that it did us great harm. Most who wrote about it never saw the programme, and wrote about it as though it was a cheat on the Shadow Cabinet by virtue of the way the interviews were cut. Not true; but it *was* a cheat because they would never have agreed to take part if they had known that the title and the commissioned song was going to give it the flavour of malice that ruined it. But most commentators (and nearly all politicians, of both parties) concluded that we could not be trusted, and it will take ages to live it down.'[5]

Some read into the Labour Government's White Paper,[6] published after the Annan Report, evidence that it had still not been lived down.

[1] *BBC Handbook 1972*, p.10. The Programmes Complaints Commission was established in October 1971.

[2] *The Times*, 19 June 1971.

[3] *Daily Telegraph*, 19 June 1971.

[4] *New Statesman*, 16 June 1972.

[5] Crawley Papers, note dated 8 Aug. 1971.

[6] Cmnd 7294 (1978), *Broadcasting*.

9 The Question of Ulster 1972

The Question of Ulster — an Enquiry into the Future was a three-hour television programme broadcast live on BBC1 on 5 January 1972. The Home Secretary, Reginald Maudling, had publicly urged the BBC not to transmit it. It is, therefore, important as a case history of disagreement between the BBC and the Government of the day, but not of disagreement between the Board and the professional executive. The Chairman (Lord Hill) and later the full Board were involved in the detailed planning of the programme and the decision to transmit it. Both Waldo Maguire, Controller Northern Ireland, and the television service Current Affairs Group had long felt that 'a long cool programme of talk, not action, would do something to complement the day-to-day news film of violence and disorder' in Northern Ireland.[1] Under the leadership of Richard Francis, then an Assistant Head of Current Affairs Group, Television, a small team planned what was perhaps unfortunately described as a television 'tribunal of enquiry'. One of the copies typed by a producer on location included the word 'Tribunal' with a capital T. It was this, as much as anything, that was to cause trouble later on.[2]

The chairman chosen for the live programme was Lord Devlin, formerly a Lord Justice of Appeal and a former chairman of the Press Council. With him would be two senior politicians with relevant experience: Lord Caradon (Labour), a former Governor of Cyprus, and Sir John Foster, QC, MP (Conservative), a leading international lawyer. The programme would open with a short historical setting of the scene, after which eight political representatives of the different Irish sectional interests – including two from Eire – would each make a statement of policy. Expert witnesses would also be available for questions on matters of fact. At the end the chairman and his colleagues would sum up their views on the propositions they had heard, not judging among them but setting them in perspective.[3]

As Lord Hill noted, the word 'tribunal' caused controversy. It was alleged that the programme infringed the Government's

---

[1] R. Francis, 'The Question of Ulster', (unpublished) draft article for the *EBU Review*, 10 May 1972.
[2] Ibid.
[3] Lord Hill, op.cit., pp.217–18.

sphere by trying to set itself up in judgement on solutions to Ulster's problems. [1]

The first alarm bell rang on 9 December 1971 when the Prime Minister of Northern Ireland, Brian Faulkner, wrote to Charles Curran, the Director-General, expressing his reservations about the wisdom of the programme while people were being killed. He was critical of the proposed casting on the ground that the eight proposed Irish speakers included only one Ulster Unionist, Robin Baillie, the Minister of Commerce. [2] Nevertheless, if the programme were to go ahead, clearly it would be necessary for the Stormont Government's case to be stated strongly, and Baillie would be a suitable man to do so. [3]

At this stage, the Home Secretary, who had specific responsibility for Northern Ireland, asked the Chairman and Director-General to visit him. They went to the Home Office on 13 December. Both the *Daily Telegraph* and Hill have published fairly full accounts of it. Maudling was 'seriously disquieted by the project, which he regarded as potentially dangerous, quite apart from the fact that it had a built-in bias'. [4]

On 11 December 1971 the Board discussed the proposed programme in detail. One Governor expressed the fear that there might be discussions, even negotiations, going on between the Governments of which the BBC and the parties in the programme might be unaware. [5] In that respect the Board ran a risk. However, the Board decided to proceed, leaving open how the Unionist viewpoint might best be put.

On 23 December it was learnt that no Stormont representative would take part in *The Question of Ulster* and on Christmas Eve the Peterborough column in the *Daily Telegraph* published a strong attack on the proposed programme. 'Hill and Curran tried in vain to persuade the Government of its usefulness in assessing possible solutions', it reported. 'The Home Secretary blew his top, objecting to the choice of participants seven to one against Internment, and to the BBC setting itself up as a Court of Inquiry.' Peterborough continued: 'So viewers are to be entertained with a kind of "Famous trials" enactment of a contemporary situation, in which fellow citizens are being bombed

[1] Ibid., p.218.   [2] Ibid., p.219.   [3] Francis, loc.cit.
[4] Hill, op.cit., p.219; *Daily Telegraph*, Peterborough Column, 24 Dec. 1971.
[5] Board of Governors, *Minutes*, 11 Dec. 1971.

and murdered. It is scarcely surprising that some MPs believe there are no limits to the irresponsibility of the Corporation.'[1]

Over Christmas there were discussions involving the Chairman, the Director-General and those working on the programme. Faulkner reiterated that no representative of the Northern Ireland Government would take part. The Rev. Ian Paisley, MP, also dropped out. He could not afford to be seen consorting with politicians of the South unless the Ulster Unionists were seen to be doing the same. It looked as though the programme would have to be cancelled through censorship by abstention.

With just three days to go before the billed transmission date, the last Ulster Unionist MP at Westminster, Jack Maginnis, was tracked down on his farm in County Armagh. A farmer, and former sergeant in the Royal Ulster Constabulary, he was much an independent man. He was loyal to Faulkner, and fairly orthodox in his Ulster Unionist views. But he had heard all about the programme, was adamant that the Unionist case should be heard, and was eager to take part. Paisley rejoined the programme.

Hill called a special meeting of five available Governors with others at Broadcasting House on Monday 3 January. Subject to consultation with absent Governors by telephone, the decision was taken to go ahead with the programme. Hill revealed in his memoirs that of the twelve Governors, nine were in favour, two were unavailable and one abstained.[2]

The next day the BBC announced that the programme would go out as planned on 5 January. It also defined exactly what the enquiry entailed and what it did not, and the Press announcement confirmed there would be prerecorded statements of the Westminster Government and Opposition positions, and the Stormont Government policy before the 'enquiry' started. Immediately Faulkner issued a statement accusing the BBC of 'plumbing the depths of absurdity', and disowned Maginnis and the use of any news archive film of himself which purported to represent his policies.[3]

Formal invitations were issued simultaneously to the Home Office and to Harold Wilson's office (Wilson was then Oppo-

[1] *Daily Telegraph*, 24 Dec. 1971.
[2] Hill, op.cit., p.221.   [3] Francis, loc.cit.

"Switch it off Mick—now we've got the telly judges' verdict we'd better get back to work."

sition spokesman on Northern Ireland as well as Leader of the Opposition). Maudling responded with a letter sent by hand to the Chairman, and later given to the Press. It declared that the programme 'in the form in which it had been devised could do no good and could do serious harm'. Hill's reply, also prominently published the next morning, said: 'If we shared your fears that such a programme would worsen the situation in Ulster we would not dream of proceeding with it. On the contrary we hope and believe that it will be of value in widening understanding of the issues involved.' Maudling refused to let anyone from the Home Office appear. Wilson accepted with alacrity and publicised the fact immediately.

On 5 January, the day of transmission, the Belfast *Newsletter* led the hysterical wing of the Press with the headline: 'The Full United Kingdom is Now in Peril.' At 9.20 pm $7\frac{1}{2}$ million viewers were tuned in to BBC1, including nearly two-thirds of the population of Ulster. Telefis Eireann relayed the programme live through Eire. 'What they saw,' Francis reported, 'was a cool, at times laborious, examination of eight different solutions to the problems of Ulster. Inevitably it was an anti-climax, but more than half the viewers who started stayed through to the summing up at a quarter past midnight. As Lord Caradon put it, "We may have been dull, but not dangerous!" Whereas telephoned calls to the BBC were 10–1 against the programme beforehand they were 5–1 in favour afterwards. Some critics ate their words, several right-wing politicians admitted in private that the Ulster

Unionists had misjudged the whole thing and should have been represented officially at a senior level. And with so many people watching, the streets of Northern Ireland had one of the quietest nights for weeks.' [1]

Since *Yesterday's Men* and *The Question of Ulster* there have been no comparable confrontations between the BBC Board and the Westminster front benches, although Ulster has continued to present a political problem for the Government and a broadcasting problem for the Governors. In November 1976 a Board Meeting was held in the newly opened studio block in Belfast. Afterwards the Board gave a dinner party for thirty at the Culloden Hotel to celebrate the occasion. The guests included Roy Mason, the Secretary of State for Northern Ireland, and Major-General David Young, Commander of the Land Forces.

According to later Press accounts [2] Sir Michael Swann, Chairman, Mark Bonham Carter, Vice-Chairman, and the other Governors and Northern Ireland staff present were 'amazed' when Mason charged the BBC with being disloyal, supporting the rebels and purveying their propaganda. He then bluntly reminded the Governors that the Charter and Licence were coming up for renewal, that they wanted the licence income increased, and that these were matters over which he and other Ministers had control. He also mentioned the possibility of instituting a three-month special system of D Notices. Reports of the occasion, referred to in the *Daily Mail* as 'the Second Battle of Culloden', [3] caused a number of Ulster journalists to demand that Mason should repudiate his suggestion of censorship, and in a letter to the Belfast branch of the National Union of Journalists he conceded that 'the answer to this problem . . . is not censorship; it is the continued exercise of judgement in balancing the public's interest with the public's right to know'. [4]

Meanwhile, from the vantage point of Dublin, an editorial in the *Irish Times* declared that the accusation that the BBC was disloyal and supported the rebels was absurd, and that the BBC

[1] Ibid.
[2] See *Daily Mail*, 6 Jan. 1977, *The Times*, *Daily Mirror*, *Guardian*, *Irish Times*, 7 Jan. 1977, *Daily Telegraph*, 8 Jan. 1977.
[3] *Daily Mail*, 6 Jan. 1977.
[4] *The Times*, 14 Jan. 1977.

"Would you chaps mind getting shot again — this time for colour TV!"

purveyed the rebels' propaganda was untrue. 'It is well known that the BBC performs a very careful sifting of Northern Ireland news with the object of ensuring that it does not inadvertantly make propaganda for para-military groups,' the *Irish Times* commented. 'If the BBC occasionally declines to accept the advice of the British authorities on what should or should not be published, it, like any other responsible news gathering organisation, is only carrying out its proper function in rejecting pressure to slant the news. It is disquieting that Mr Mason appears to equate the normal exercise of professional judgement with support for the rebels.' [1]

The BBC has never published its own account of what happened at that dinner, although there was a brief reference in the 1978 *Handbook* to the 'long and frank talk with the Secretary of State for Northern Ireland' which had caused the Governors to re-examine editorial policy in the context of 'the continuing struggle against terrorism in the Province'. [2] It is possible that the Press heightened the drama and missed some of the nuances in what was said at the dinner. In any event the Governors went on to declare in the Introduction to that year's *Handbook*: 'The public trusts us, and we wish to continue to deserve that trust. We

[1] *Irish Times*, 11 Jan. 1977.   [2] *BBC Handbook 1978*, p.6.

will not deserve it if we ever give up our proper journalistic role and resort to what some people call patriotic self-censorship, or make ourselves a propaganda weapon in the hands of any group.' [1]

In his Foreword to the same *Handbook* Swann turned to a more pressing subject. He noted that the Annan Report had 'decisively reinforced the unity, strength and independence of the BBC', but the Government had 'for the first time in history, imposed a licence fee settlement deliberately designed to last for only one year'. [2] Since then there has been a second time in history, and the attention of the Governors has had increasingly to be focused on the matters mentioned in Belfast, the renewal of a Charter which provided constitutional independence, and the establishment of a licence fee adequate for the task.

[1] Ibid.
[2] Ibid., Foreword.

CHAPTER V

INTO THE UNKNOWN

During the long wait between the publication of the Annan Report and the Government's official reaction to it, there was much speculation about the future of the fourth television channel and of the pattern of local broadcasting. These were interesting themes which raised large questions of principle and pointed to substantial practical difficulties in policy implementation. There was little public expectation, however, given the story told in this essay, that there would be any challenge to the position of the Governors of the BBC.

As it was, Cmnd 7294, published in July 1978 with the simplest of all titles – 'Broadcasting', passed more quickly than the Annan Report had done from praise of the BBC's performance and reputation to criticism that the Corporation was 'too monolithic, too impervious to criticism and too bureaucratic'. Looking more precisely than the Annan Report itself had done at the balance of opinion within the Committee, the White Paper noted that as many as six members of the Committee had considered that the answer to criticisms made of the BBC was a division of the Corporation into two – one dealing with television and one with radio. Most, if not all, the members of this group had held this opinion before the enquiry began. That there were powerful arguments against such a division of public services, as there had been at the time of the publication both of the Beveridge and of the Pilkington Reports, was not given equal prominence. The argument of the minority, strongly supported by sections of the Government, was given the greater weight.

The White Paper, however, like most official documents on broadcasting, including those which brought into existence the Independent Television Authority in 1954,[1] showed many signs of compromise. Historians will probably be able to trace the origins and significance of all of these only in the very distant future, when official papers become available. There was certainly no consensus in Home Office and Cabinet Committee discussions, and it may well have been because there was no agreement about 'dividing the BBC' that the Cabinet decided to

[1] See A. Briggs, *Sound and Vision* (1979), p.4 and *passim*.

focus attention on the Governors. While not recommending a division of the BBC, as some members of the Committee and the Government wished, the White Paper suggested a fundamental change in the position of the Governors. Because they were dealing both with supervision and management, it was argued, they should in future be 'distanced' from management, as the members of the Independent Broadcasting Authority were said to be. In addition, however, and it was an odd addition, it was suggested that there should be a 'measure of decentralisation for each of the BBC's three services (Television, Radio and External Services)' in order to 'encourage greater creativity and diversity of approach in programme making, including the presentation of news and current affairs on the domestic services'. The words 'of course' stood out in the next clause – 'subject, of course, to the fulfilment of the general obligations laid on broadcasting authorities'.[1] What weight did they carry?

Whether or not the 'distancing' of Members of the Independent Broadcasting Authority from the operations of the commercial companies is a constitutional device appropriate for imitation is itself a matter of argument. The operational patterns of public and commercial broadcasting are quite different. Moreover, the Government seems to have been completely unaware of the steps taken towards 'decentralisation' inside the BBC.[2] Yet these were not the main points taken up in most Parliamentary and Press comment on the Government's proposals. What was criticised – and criticised strongly and almost universally – was the particular way in which it was suggested that the 'distancing' should take place and the Corporation become more 'decentralised'.

The White Paper proposed that there should be separate Service Management Boards for each of the three services – a Television Service Management Board, a Radio Service Management Board and an External Services Management Board. By delegating to these Boards many of the management functions which now were said, with some exaggeration, to rest with the Governors, it was claimed that the Governors would be enabled to follow in the wake of the IBA and concentrate on their supervisory and public accountability functions.

[1] Cmnd 7294 (1978), *Broadcasting*, Ch. 5 'The BBC', paras. 45–9, pp.18–20.
[2] See above, p.184.

Each Service Management Board would be responsible to the Board of Governors collectively for supervising the programme strategy and management of its service. News gathering, engineering, personnel management and finance would continue to be provided as common services, but the new arrangement would ensure diversity. Co-ordination would be achieved by the provision that the Chairman of each Service Management Board would be a member of the Board of Governors, although he would be appointed to the Board specifically as such. So much for 'distancing'. Accountability would be further strengthened by the proposal that half the members of each Service Management Board would be people appointed by the Home Secretary after consultation with the Chairman of the Board of Governors. So much for giving the Governors greater detachment in their regulatory role. The concept of 'professionalism' was criticised more in the White Paper than it had been in the Annan Report, and the non-professional members would be people 'of standing and independence with experience or qualifications which fit them to make a positive and distinctive contribution to the work of the Boards'.[1] If the Governors were to be thought of as angels – and we have seen what high qualities successive Committees of Enquiry and Governments had expected of them – the outside members of the Service Management Boards were to be a little lower than the angels. But they would have direct contact with mortals in that the Managing Directors of the relevant BBC services would also be members of the Boards and that they would be able to invite other people to their meetings, including, for example, members of the National Broadcasting Councils. The latter would be appointed by the Home Secretary after consultation with both the Chairman of the Board of Governors and the Secretary of State for Scotland or Wales, but thereafter would be given more 'autonomy'.[2]

The Director-General would be expected to attend all meetings, and the Governors would continue to be expected to act as Trustees for the whole system. Yet the White Paper rejected the Annan Committee's view that there should be a reduction in the number of Governors, a view which had been backed by many of the most knowledgeable witnesses seen by the Committee. Indeed, it noted instead that in the light of the proposed rearrange-

[1] Cmnd 7294 (1978), para. 49, p.19.   [2] Ibid., para. 61, p.23.

ments there would have to be more! At the same time it maintained that the new machinery would not add to costs or 'significantly increase the numbers employed by the BBC'. This op-
timistic belief was in line with the assumption which seems to
have been held by at least some people in Government at least
from the time of Reginald Bevins onwards – and even in the
1930s – that the BBC could 'save money' if it genuinely tried. Yet
there was no cross-reference at this point to relative costs in public
and commercial broadcasting.

The Government's bundle of proposals had a very bad reception immediately and later, mainly on two grounds – first,
that the Home Secretary directly or indirectly was being given a
substantial amount of new patronage at a time when Government patronage was already being dangerously extended and
widely criticised, and, second, that the independence of the BBC,
treasured in the most difficult periods of history but always
vulnerable, would be threatened through the presence of the
appointed members. The very first reaction in the *Evening Standard*, for example, placarded that day on newspaper stands outside Broadcasting House, was that 'BBC chiefs may lose some
powers'. 'A subtle move' was being made, according to some
politicians, Robert Carvel said, to enable 'any government to
lean more on the BBC and thus weaken its resistance to political
pressure.' 'The BBC hierarchy', he went on with some under-
statement, 'is far from enthusiastic about such changes.' [1]

There was, in fact, an immediate and sharp critical reaction
from 'the BBC hierarchy'. Welcoming the endorsement of the
Annan Committee's recommendation about the independence
of broadcasting and accepting the need to make big public bodies
more decentralised and publicly accountable, it resisted the idea
of Home Office nominees. 'It would be a pity if the search for
accountability and diversity weakened the ability of the Corporation to fulfil that particular independent role which is endorsed
within the White Paper itself.' [2]

This was milder language, however, than that used in the
widest possible range of newspapers from the *Daily Telegraph* to
the *Morning Star*. And it was milder language, too, than that
employed in the House of Commons by the Conservative
Shadow Home Secretary, William Whitelaw, who replying to

[1] *Evening Standard*, 26 July 1978.   [2] BBC Press Statement, 26 July 1978.

*" Stands to lose a marginal seat and
four Quangos "*

the Home Secretary, Merlyn Rees, stated both that there would
be a proliferation of Quangos (quasi autonomous national
governmental organisations) and that he feared that 'the independence of the BBC would be threatened'. [1] He added in a later
interview that 'the whole character of the BBC would be jeopardised'. [2] There was almost as much public comment on the
proposals as there was on the recommendation that the fourth
channel should be handed over to a new authority, the recommendation which had hitherto been most widely discussed in the
Press and at conferences on broadcasting.

The Guardian was as critical of the 'Quangoid tendencies' in the
White Paper as the *Daily Telegraph,* and the *Evening News* went
further than the *Evening Standard.* 'In an organisation already
over loaded with red tape, the scheme to put in new "management boards" for TV, radio and the World Service is idiotic.
While the plan to staff them with people appointed by the Home

[1] *Hansard,* vol. 954, col. 1565, 26 July 1978. For the beginnings of Quango literature,
see R. Taylor, 'How Quango rewards the great and the good' in *The Observer,* 9 May
1976. The article followed the publication of *A Directory of Paid Public Appointments made
by Ministers* (HMSO, April 1976). See also *Daily Telegraph,* 8 Sept. 1976, *The Guardian,*
9 April 1977.
[2] *Television,* March–April 1979.

'And now, a political broadcast on behalf of the BBC'

Office is downright sinister.'[1] 'Editorial independence must be protected against encroachment by politicians,' wrote the *Financial Times*; 'the plan to partly split up the present corporation, and run it under separate Boards staffed by Home Office appointees, not only has serious implications from a democratic point of view,' wrote the *Morning Star*, 'it could help to weaken the BBC in the face of commercial broadcasting interests.'[2] 'The proposal to elevate the present BBC Governors to an Olympian role' would in no sense 'enable the general public to express their pleasure or dismay at particular editorial decisions', the *Daily Telegraph*'s leader said. 'It will simply strengthen the influence of politicians and their hangers-on.'[3] *The Times* thought that 'the remedy would intensify not cure the disease' and introduced the useful term 'mini-governors' to describe the appointed members of the Service Management Boards. Would not 'both they and the Governors claim to speak for the public interest?' it asked.[4]

[1] *The Guardian, Evening News*, 27 July 1978.

[2] *Financial Times*, 27 July 1978; *Morning Star*, 28 July 1978.

[3] *Daily Telegraph*, 27 July 1978.

[4] *The Times*, 27 July 1978. Cf. the *News of the World*, 30 July 1978: 'The proposal in the Government's off-White Paper to intimidate the proud BBC into craven impotence is no laughing matter. It is malicious. It is sinister. It is appalling. It will succeed at our peril.'

Nor were there London voices only in a swelling chorus. *The Scotsman*, while welcoming the greater degree of Scottish autonomy, criticised all the managerial proposals. So, too, did the *Glasgow Herald*. 'The delicacy of the Corporation's relationship with Government must produce scepticism about ministerial capacity for disinterested appointment,' *The Scotsman* argued.[1] 'There would be little point in opening up the TV waves,' the *Glasgow Herald* added, 'if officialdom at the same time laid the foundations for a Corporate State, with Ministers deciding who was and was not fit to take broadcasting decisions.'[2]

A number of outsiders went deeper than the editorials, although few pointed to possible divisions within the Government. Peter Fiddick, for example, claimed that the broadcasters themselves had every reason to be just as suspicious as the Governors of a plan to draw in non-professional members of the Service Management Boards *before* programmes were made and that both broadcasters and Governors could legitimately object to the introduction of a new lawyer of control in the name paradoxically of less bureaucracy.[3] 'What it will mean in practice,' Philip Purser added, 'is that the Governors will be driven into a purely censorious role while the professional heads of radio, television and Bush House are lumbered with gangs of amateurs querying everything down to Angela Rippon's dress allowance.'[4]

Two ex-Director-Generals expressed their views firmly. In *The Observer* Sir Hugh Greene spoke bluntly of 'this threat to the BBC's freedom' and went on to deal with some of the obvious, but not widely publicised, oddities of the proposed structure. Three stood out. First, 'the chairman of a management board must in the nature of things have some executive functions, much more than any Governor has at present. So much for "distancing".' Second, 'would the new structure be efficient from an administrative point of view? Think of it. Management by a mixed body of professionals and political appointees presided over by a Governor. The utmost confusion, constant disagreement, majority votes would be guaranteed, and there would be

[1] *The Scotsman*, 27 July 1978.
[2] *Glasgow Herald*, 'Opening the Box', 27 July 1978.
[3] P. Fiddick, 'Stand by for Trethowan versus Rees', in *The Guardian*, 27 July 1978.
[4] P. Purser, 'Enter the TV Sponsor?', in the *Sunday Telegraph*, 30 July 1978.

no clear line of responsibility.' Third – and here Greene spoke
with the full weight of experience behind him – 'What about the
Director-General? He, poor devil, would be a member of all
three Boards, as well as presiding over the central board of
management and attending meetings of the Board of Governors.
He would spend his life tearing from one meeting to another and
all his authority as editor-in-chief of the BBC would disappear
into limbo.'[1]

Sir Charles Curran's notes were not published in a newspaper,
but they were just as forthright. And he spoke in the light of more
recent history than Greene. 'The management problem of the
BBC – and indeed the editorial problem' – had not been to
secure decentralisation. It had been 'to ensure reasonable co-
ordination between the three major services without excessively
limiting their programme independence'. Curran made two
other basic points. 'Creativity comes from individual producers
operating in freedom. That is the experience of fifty years of
broadcasting. It does not come by direction from management
committees, however distinguished.' Second, even as far as the
committees were concerned, there would be in-built conflicts at
many points. The Chairman of each Service Management
Board, himself a Governor, might find himself obliged to desert
his Service Board colleagues or to be reduced to a minority voice
among the Governors. And he would have problems with
his Managing Director also. Where would 'the firm voice of
Authority', so much demanded in the late 1960s, be heard?[2]

Both Greene and Curran, successive but in some respects
contrasting Director-Generals, rejected the presupposition of the
White Paper that Governors had been 'confused' in their tasks.
For Greene, they had seldom, if ever, got involved in management in any detailed way, even if there had been 'a slight lurch
when Lord Hill was chairman . . . more a matter of huffing and
puffing than of anything real'.[3] For Curran, there had been
growing pains which did not necessarily call for new top structures, and the proposed new structures would leave both the
Director-General and the Chairman in an extremely difficult
position. It was not only that the former would be expected to

[1] Sir Hugh Greene, 'This threat to the BBC's freedom' in *The Observer*, 30 July 1978.
[2] Sir Charles Curran, 'Notes on the White Paper Proposals', 1978.
[3] Greene, loc.cit.

attend all three Boards: the latter would attend none. He would
not be as well informed as he was within the present system, and
he could easily find himself outflanked.

'The central point of the argument,' Curran concluded, 'must
remain the proper execution of the task of the Board of Governors
– to act as trustees of the national interest in broadcasting.' All
that was needed was for the Government to reaffirm the primary
concern of the Governors with their public trusteeship duties,
and for the right calibre of Governors to be insisted upon. The
White Paper undermined the Governors' authority by seeking to
establish alternative centres of power. Its proposals had a long
pedigree: they would have the effect not of increasing efficiency
but of threatening all that the BBC stood for.[1]

For once in the history of the BBC no one mentioned Reith.
The context really had changed. As the Governors set about
seeking to deal with the implications of the White Paper, they
were aware that their situation was genuinely new. There had
been threats before and not all of them had been pushed very far,
but given the combination of constitutional and financial pressures in 1978, there seemed an all too obvious danger that the
BBC might lose not only its reputation – under attack on more
than one front – but its distinctive identity. The national political
situation was itself so uncertain, however, in 1978 that there were
still doubts as to how urgent the danger was. The Government
seemed at risk at the next general election – and with it the
White Paper or any legislation based upon it; and there were differences behind the scenes within the parties as well as between
them, as there had been so often in the history of broadcasting.
There was in any case a separate danger that if the internal organisation of the BBC became a matter of party controversy, that
controversy itself could threaten its long-term independence.

Powerful support was given to the BBC on one of the critical
points by two members of the Annan Committee – the chairman
and Dipak Nandy, who had been one of the influential minority
of six. Speaking for the minority, Dipak Nandy objected to 'the
insertion of at least twelve Government appointees between the
Governors and the staff', and asserted plainly that 'the BBC are
right to complain of the threat to their independence in the name
of accountability'. If the Corporation was 'outraged', it was

[1] Curran, loc.cit.

'right' to be outraged. 'None of my colleagues envisaged, intended or would have agreed to anything remotely approaching this proposal. Accountability is not an absolute goal, any more than editorial independence, and in this instance I would cast my vote in favour of independence from political control.' Given the fact that the BBC was having to argue every step of the way about a necessary increase in the licence fee, if the White Paper became law 'a temporary dilemma will have been institutionalised into permanent paralysis'.[1]

Lord Annan's language was less strong, although he, too, complained that if the nominees of the Home Secretary were appointed on a representative basis there would be trouble, that the proposed consultation with the Chairman of the BBC about appointments would be an insufficient guarantee, and that another tier would be added to 'a bureaucracy which our committee thought was already too complex'. Finally, he remarked that there was not a word in the White Paper about the Committee's recommendation that if the public expected the Governors to work as hard as it was demanding and also to take the flak that was fired at them, month in, month out, then they deserved to be paid more.[2]

Although, apart from the Chairman, they were not paid more, the Governors worked very hard during the autumn of 1978, when there were other difficult problems involving Government (including BBC salaries and wages), to seek answers of their own to some of the Annan criticisms which were picked up in the White Paper, while informing the Government and the public of the extent of the existing decentralisation. Their answers were duly passed on to the Home Office, along with the reminder that as things stood they were Crown appointees and not appointees of the Home Secretary. Their aim, the Governors stated, was to carry existing tendencies within the Corporation further, not to substitute an entirely new pattern, and in so doing to preserve the essential independence of the institution of which they were determined to remain the trustees.

The Board of Governors have decided to make important changes in their method of working in order to improve their effectiveness in the

---

[1] Dipak Nandy, 'The Best System in the World?' in the *Sunday Times*, 30 July 1978.
[2] Lord Annan, 'Much as We said' in *The Listener*, 3 Aug. 1978.

control of programme policy. They are establishing special programme policy committees consisting both of Governors and senior management, to which people from outside the BBC will be invited in order that they may give the BBC the benefit of an additional range of opinion and experience. These people will in the main be drawn from the Advisory Bodies of the BBC (whose work is praised in the White Paper) and who will in this way be asked to make a new and significantly greater contribution. The Governors also intend further to develop Regional involvement in their work.

The BBC's purpose is the production of programmes and the Board's prime function the overall responsibility for those programmes. The Governors are therefore to remove from the agenda of the full Board detailed discussion of those other issues – such as finance, property and appointments – which can be more economically dealt with by small groups of Governors. This will create more time for consideration of programme strategy, policy and content in the special committees.

On the management of the BBC, the Governors intend to encourage diversity and decentralisation within the essential unity of the Corporation. Directorate management groups already run Television, Radio and External Broadcasting on a day-to-day basis.

It is the intention of both the Board of Governors and of the Board of Management that the different creative units of the BBC, at both national and regional levels, shall be given the greatest possible managerial freedom and responsibility to get on with the job, with the minimum need to refer to higher management or to the centre. We intend to maintain the independence of the BBC and to govern and to manage, within our essential unity, a diverse, creative and ultimately accountable staff so that their skills can be used most efficiently and responsibly to continue to make good programmes.[1]

The press release which contained these paragraphs had the same title as this essay, 'Governing the BBC'. The title of this essay, however, was chosen before! The Governors' deliberations were more speedy than those of the Government, which did not produce any bill in the autumn of 1978. 'We intend to legislate on the basis of the White Paper following discussions with various interests', the Home Secretary stated in September 1978, promising that he would take account of those critics of the Government's proposals who had alleged that they strengthened

[1] BBC Press Release, 15 Nov. 1978.

ministerial patronage. Doubtless there were many other broadcasting issues which delayed legislation – notably the organisation
of an Open Broadcasting Authority and the future pattern of
local radio; but while the delay continued – and there was no
adequate increase in licence fees – the distinctive features of
British public broadcasting, so long admired in other parts of the
world, were in danger of being destroyed as much by erosion as
by confrontation. It is not surprising that Sir Michael Swann,
meditating on the continuing uncertainty, urged that there
should be no further inquiries into broadcasting 'without a substantial measure of agreement between the political parties'. It
was in this context that he emphasised that the BBC was 'not
indestructible' and that 'the plant might one day die'.[1]

Few politicians on either side thought in botanical terms: few
bothered to look backwards across historical vistas. Yet necessary
information about the role of the Governors must be information
in depth, covering more than one period in broadcasting history.
Much of the argument in 1978 was crude and uninformed and
the perspectives were far too narrow. It is sometimes said that we
are prisoners of history in this country – and certainly at times
during the 1920s and 1930s there was a danger that we were
becoming so. Now there is a danger that we may ignore history.
We may ignore too the crucial relationships, difficult to analyse,
between 'structures' and 'quality' of programmes. Broadcasting
in doubt or under threat has become more cautious than it was
during the 1960s; in another botanical phrase – this time of
Anthony Smith in a book about to be published – 'caution has
grown over broadcasting like lichen over standing stones'.[2]

The first chapters of this essay explained why it is impossible to
consider 'governing the BBC' simply in terms of formulae, ap-
plicable to all time, however tempting it is to choose formulae like
'the Chairman should have more power than the Director-
General' or that 'management knows best'. The nine cases considered in Chapter IV dealt with problem situations, some of
which have passed into the folklore of national history. Would
any of the weaknesses in the BBC's handling of these problem
situations have been avoided or lessened if there had been a
different 'system' of broadcasting, including a devolved system

[1] Ariel, 15 Nov. 1978. See also above, p.185.
[2] A. Smith (ed.), Television and Political Life.

separating radio and television, or a system supervised by a special Ministry for Broadcasting or a Council concerned with both BBC and the commercial companies?

Turning to the future, whatever form any new 'systems' might take, it is certain that there will continue to be tensions in the relationships between executives and Governors and between Government and broadcasters; and if a new system were designed to constrain or check the BBC's 'independence', such tensions would probably be more disturbing than those which have existed in the past. There have been many moments and periods of tension in the United States, where a market system is in operation and where there are no Governors at all; and there have been difficulties likewise even in countries where broadcasting is 'controlled' by government. There would certainly be more such tensions if in a free and pluralistic British society (with a Parliamentary Opposition and open public debate) the power of a particular Government penetrated directly or indirectly into the daily operations of broadcasting. Indeed, the power of broadcasting itself could be used by 'authority', as it often has been used elsewhere, to impose an order on society. Freedom and pluralism are part of our inheritance, but they cannot be taken for granted.

Some past difficulties have been clearly concerned less with the 'system' than with the abilities, attitudes and activities of the individuals in charge of it. Lord Simon in the case of *Party Manners* failed to appreciate how the system worked and suffered in consequence; and in earlier times Reith sometimes overplayed his hand, as he did in the case of the U-Boat Commander. He refused the Government's request only to find that his Chairman had accepted it. There might have been even more trouble during the 1960s about *That Was the Week That Was*. If the Chairman and the Director-General (people of different interests and gifts who usually worked well together) had insisted on continuing the programme, they would have upset the triangular relationship with the Board. As it was, they avoided a possible collision, the kind of collision which some critics of the BBC would have welcomed.

There are some 'system' difficulties, however, although they are difficulties inherent in the political as well as the broadcasting system. *Yesterday's Men* may have vindicated editorial independence, but it led to a distrust among Labour politicians which has affected all subsequent BBC attitudes to documentary production. There is inevitable institutional defensiveness and equally inevitable transfer of discussion to committees. The 'institutional' form of the BBC equally inevitably creates BBC interests – vis-a-vis IBA, for example – and it is important not to equate those automatically with the 'national' interest. If the politicians or the public perceive of BBC interests as 'particular' and 'vested', then the BBC will be in genuine danger. Ultimately in the British system the electorate chooses – subject increasingly to pressures outside the ballot box and the operation of the electoral system. If the BBC were to be estranged from the public, it could not survive as an independent body.

The range and quality of broadcasting output, which is the ultimate test of the British broadcasting 'system', depends on the right appointments being made both to executive posts and to places on the Board, and the proper balance between them. It is vital that those who make the top appointments – politicians and Governors – should realise this. Appointments 'lower in the hierarchy' are important, too, in that the public judges more through what producers – and their Controllers – do than through what Governors do. It is unfortunate that at all levels there is more gossip about personalities than discussion of the necessary qualities in people holding key positions. Meanwhile, through political and social change the broadcasting operation continues, a competitive operation which to be successful will require not only skill and imagination but courage and morale.

APPENDIX I

BBC GOVERNORS 1927–77

Age on BOG:

ADAMSON, John
Governor 1.1.1947–31.7.1952
Born: 23.1.1886   Died 29.10.1969   60–66

ALLAN, Robert, DSO, OBE, RD (Lord Allan of
Kilmahew 1973)
Governor 1.7.1971–30.6.1976
Born: 11.7.1914   Died: 4.4.1979   56–61

ALLEN OF FALLOWFIELD, Lord, CBE
Governor 16.12.1976–
Born: 7.7.1914   62–

AVONSIDE, Lady, OBE
National Governor for Scotland 1.5.1971–30.4.1976
Born: 31.5.1917   53–58

BAIRD, Lady, CBE, BSC, MB, CHB, LLD
National Governor for Scotland 30.11.1965–29.11.1970
Born: 14.5.1901   64–69

BALFOUR, Earl of, FRSA
National Governor for Scotland 1.7.1956–26.10.1960
Born: 31.12.1902   Died: 27.11.1968   53–57

BELLINGER, Sir Robert, GBE
Governor 15.2.1968–30.6.1971
Born: 10.3.1910   57–61

BENTHALL, Sir Edward, KCSI
Governor 1.8.1955–31.1.1960
Born: 26.11.1893   Died: 5.3.1961   61–66

BONHAM CARTER, Lady Violet, DBE (Baroness Asquith
of Yarnbury 1964)
Governor 4.4.1941–24.7.1945 and 5.9.1945–3.4.1946
Born: 15.4.1887   Died: 19.2.1969   53–58

BONHAM CARTER, Hon. Mark
Vice-Chairman 16.6.1975–
Born: 11.2.1922   53–

BRIDGEMAN, Viscount, PC, DL, JP
Governor 1.1.1933–Chairman 29.3.1935–14.8.1935
Born: 31.12.1864   Died: 14.8.1935 (in office)   68–70

BRIDGEMAN, Caroline, Viscountess, DBE
Governor 25.10.1935–5.9.1939
Born: 30.6.1873   Died: 26.12.1961   62–66

BROWN, Harold G., BA, LLB   Age on BOG:
Governor 1.1.1932–Vice-Chairman 25.10.1935–
  31.12.1936
Born: 24.12.1876   Died: 12.11.1949   55–60
CADOGAN, Rt Hon. Sir Alexander, OM, GCMG
Chairman 1.8.1952–30.11.1957
Born: 25.11.1884   Died: 9.7.1968   67–73
CAZALET-KEIR, Mrs Thelma, CBE
Governor 1.7.1956–30.6.1961
Born: 28.5.1899   57–62
CHAPPELL, Philip, CBE
Governor 24.7.1976–
Born: 12.6.1929   47–
CLARENDON, Earl of, KG, PC, GCMG, GCVO
Chairman 1.1.1927–May 1930
Born: 7.6.1877   Died: 13.12.1955   49–52
CLARKE, Sir Ashley, GCMG, GCVO
Governor 1.10.1962–30.9.1967
Born: 26.6.1903   59–64
CLARKE, Mrs Stella, JP
Governor 1.2.1974–
Born: 16.2.1932   41–
CLYDESMUIR, Lord, PC, GCIE, TD
Governor 1.1.1950–National Governor for Scotland
  1.8.1952–31.10.1954
Born: 13.2.1894   Died: 31.10.1954 (in office)   55–60
COKE, Gerald, CBE, JP, DL
Governor 2.8.1961–1.8.1966
Born: 25.10.1907   53–58
CONSTANTINE, Sir Learie, MBE (Lord
  Constantine 1969)
Governor 13.7.1968–1.7.1971
Born: 21.9.1901   Died: 1.7.1971 (in office)   66–69
DUFF, Sir James, MA, MED
Governor 14.9.1959–Vice-Chairman 1.7.1960–
  Chairman 26.2.1964–Vice-Chairman 14.5.1964–31.7.1965
Born: 1.2.1898   Died: 24.4.1970   61–67
DUNLEATH, Lord, TD, DL
National Governor for Northern Ireland 1.8.1967–29.5.1973
Born: 23.6.1933   34–39
FEATHER, Victor, CBE (Lord Feather 1974)
Governor 25.5.1973–28.7.1976
Born: 10.4.1908   Died: 28.7.1976 (in office)   65–68

Age on BOG:

FFORDE, Sir Arthur, GBE
Chairman: 1.12.1957–31.1.1964
Born: 23.8.1900   57–63

FISHER, Rt Hon. H.A.L., OM, FRS
Governor 29.3.1935–5.9.1939
Born: 21.3.1865   Died: 18.4.1940   70–74

FRASER, Sir Ian, CH, CBE (Lord Fraser of Lonsdale 1958)
Governor 1.1.1937–5.9.1939 and 25.4.1941–24.4.1946
Born: 30.8.1897   Died: 19.12.1974   39–42, 43–48

FRY, Miss Margery, MA, JP
Governor 1.1.1938–5.9.1939
Born: 11.3.1874   Died: 21.4.1958   63–65

FULLER, Professor Roy, CBE, MA, FRSL
Governor 1.1.1972–
Born: 11.2.1912   59–

FULTON, Sir John (Lord Fulton 1966)
Vice-Chairman 19.9.1965–Governor 11.6.1966–
   Vice-Chairman 15.2.1968–18.9.1970
Born: 27.5.1902   63–68

GAINFORD, Lord, PC, JP, DL
Vice-Chairman 1.1.1927–31.12.1932
Born: 17.1.1860   Died: 15.2.1943   66–72

GODWIN, Dame Anne, DBE
Governor 1.7.1962–30.6.1968
Born: 6.7.1897   64–70

GREEN, Dame Mary, DBE
Governor 13.7.1968–12.7.1973
Born: 27.7.1913   54–59

GREENE, Sir Hugh, KCMG, OBE
Governor 1.7.1969–31.8.1971
Born: 15.11.1910   58–60

GREENHILL, Sir Denis, GCMG, OBE (Lord Greenhill
   of Harrow 1974)
Governor 8.11.1973–7.11.1978
Born: 7.11.1913   60–65

HALSBURY, Earl of, FRS
Governor 11.5.1960–30.6.1962
Born: 4.6.1908   51–54

HAMILTON, Mrs Mary Agnes, CBE
Governor 1.1.1933–31.12.1937
Born: 1884   Died: 10.2.1966   48–53

HANCOCK, Dame Florence, DBE
Governor: 1.7.1956–30.6.1962
Born: 25.2.1893   Died: 14.4.1974   63–69

HILL OF LUTON, Lord, PC, MA, MD, DPH, LLD   Age on BOG:
Chairman 1.9.1967–31.12.1972
Born: 15.1.1904   63–68

HOWARD, George A.G., DL
Governor 15.2.1972–
Born: 22.5.1920   51–

HUGHES, Dr Glyn Tegai, MA, PhD
National Governor for Wales 1.11.1971–
Born: 18.1.1923   48–

INMAN, Lord, PC, JP
Chairman 1.1.1947–22.4.1947
Born: 12.6.1892   54–

JACKSON, Tom
Governor 15.2.1968–14.2.1973
Born: 1.4.1925   42–47

JOHNSTON, Rt Hon. Thomas, CH, LLD
National Governor for Scotland 1.1.1955–29.6.1956
Born: 1881   Died: 5.9.1965   73–75

JONES, Mrs Rachel
National Governor for Wales 1.7.1960–30.6.1965
Born: 4.8.1908   51–56

LLOYD, Rt Hon. Geoffrey, (Lord Geoffrey-Lloyd 1974)
Governor 5.4.1946–31.12.1949
Born: 17.1.1902   44–47

LUSTY, Robert F. (Sir Robert 1969)
Governor 30.11.1960–29.11.1965
Vice Chairman 11.6.1966–Acting Chairman
   16.6.1967–Vice-Chairman 1.9.1967–31.1.1968
Born: 7.6.1909   51–58

MACDONALD OF GWAENYSGOR, Lord, PC, KCMG
National Governor for Wales 1.8.1952–30.6.1960
Born: 17.5.1888   Died: 20.1.1966   64–72

MCKEE, J. Ritchie
National Governor for Northern Ireland
   1.7.1958–30.6.1962
Born: 25.10.1900   Died: 26.2.1964   57–61

MALLON, Dr J.J., CH, LLD
Governor 1.1.1937–5.9.1939 and 4.4.1941–3.4.1946
Born: 1875   Died: 12.4.1961   61–64, 65–70

MANN, Arthur H., CH
Governor 4.4.1941–3.4.1946
Born: 7.7.1876   Died: 23.7.1972   64–69

MILLIS, C.H.G., DSO, OBE, MC
Vice-Chairman: 8.6.1937–31.12.1946
Born: 1894   43–52

	Age on BOG:
MILNE, Sir David, GCB	
National Governor for Scotland 30.11.1960–29.11.1965	
Born: 1896 Died: 4.2.1972	64–69
MORGAN, A.W.C. (Tony)	
Governor 1.1.1972–31.12.1976	
Born: 24.8.1931	40–45
MORRIS, Sir Philip, KCMG, CBE	
Governor 1.8.1952–Vice-Chairman 1.7.1954–	
30.6.1960	
Born: 6.7.1901	51–58
MULHOLLAND, Bt, Rt Hon. Sir Henry,	
National Governor for Northern Ireland	
1.8.1952–30.6.1958	
Born: 20.12.1888 Died: 5.3.1971	63–69
MURRAY, Sir Ralph, KCMG, CB	
Governor 1.10.1967–30.9.1973	
Born: 3.3.1908	59–65
NAIRNE, Bt, Sir Gordon	
Governor 1.1.1927–31.12.1931	
Born: 4.1.1861 Died: 9.2.1945	65–70
NICOLSON, Hon. Harold, CMG (Sir Harold, KCVO, 1953)	
Governor 22.7.1941–21.7.1946	
Born: 21.11.1886 Died: 1.5.1968	54–59
NORMAN, R.C.	
Vice-Chairman 1.1.1933–Chairman 3.10.1935–	
18.4.1939	
Born: 15.11.1873 Died: 5.12.1963	59–65
NORMANBROOK, Lord, PC, GCB	
Chairman 14.5.1964–15.6.1967	
Born: 29.4.1902 Died: 15.6.1967 (in office)	62–65
O'HARA, Bill	
National Governor for Northern Ireland	
25.10.1973–24.10.1978	
Born: 26.2.1929	44–49
PECK, Air Marshal Sir Richard, KCB, OBE	
Governor 4.4.1946–31.12.1949	
Born: 2.3.1893 Died: 12.9.1952	53–56
PIM, Sir Richard, KBE, VRD, DL	
National Governor for Northern Ireland	
1.7.1962–30.6.1967	
Born: 10.7.1900	61–66
PLOWDEN, Lady, DBE	
Vice-Chairman 12.11.1970–12.2.1975	
Born: 5.5.1910	60–64

Age on BOG:

POWELL, Sir Allan, GBE, DL
Chairman 19.4.1939–31.12.1946
Born: 3.2.1876   Died: 24.1.1948   63–70

READING, Dowager Marchioness of, GBE
(Baroness Swanborough 1958)
Governor 25.4.1946–Vice Chairman 1.1.1947–
31.12.1950
Born: 6.1.1894   Died: 22.5.1971   52–56

RENDALL, Dr Montague J., CMG, MA, LLD, JP
Governor 1.1.1927–31.12.1932
Born: 6.5.1862   Died: 5.10.1950   64–70

RHYS WILLIAMS, Lady, DBE
Governor 1.8.1952–30.6.1956
Born: 17.12.1898   Died: 18.9.1964   53–57

ROCHDALE, Lord, OBE, TD, DL
Governor 1.7.1954–30.6.1959
Born: 5.6.1906   48–53

SEROTA, Baroness, JP
Governor 1.8.1977–
Born: 15.10.1919   57–

SIMON OF WYTHENSHAWE, Lord, LLD, MICE,
MIMECHE
Chairman 9.6.1947–31.7.1952
Born: 9.10.1879   Died: 3.10.1960   67–72

SNOWDEN, Mrs Ethel (Viscountess Snowden 1931)
Governor 1.1.1927–31.12.1932
Born: 1881   Died: 22.2.1951   45–51

STEDEFORD, I.A.R. (Sir Ivan 1954), GBE
Governor 1.1.1951–30.6.1955
Born: 28.1.1897   Died: 1.2.1975   53–58

SWANN, Sir Michael, MA, PHD, FRS, FRSE
Chairman 1.1.1973–
Born: 1.3.1920   52–

TEDDER, Marshal of the Royal Air Force, Lord, GCB
Governor 1.1.1950–Vice Chairman 1.1.1951–
30.6.1954
Born: 11.7.1890   Died: 3.6.1967   59–63

THOMPSON, Professor Alan E., MA, PHD
National Governor for Scotland 1.5.1976–
Born: 16.9.1924   51–

TROWER, John, CBE, FCA
Governor 15.11.1966–30.1.1968
Born: 30.1.1913   Died: 30.1.1968 (in office)   53–55

WARD, Miss Barbara, DBE (Baroness Jackson of   Age on BOG:
  Lodsworth 1976)
Governor 4.4.1946–31.12.1949
Born 23.5.1914   31–35
WHITFIELD, Dr Ernest, PHD (Lord Kenswood 1951)
Governor 22.7.46–31.12.1950
Born: 5.9.1887   Died: 21.4.1963   58–63
WHITLEY, Rt Hon. J.H., DCL, LLD, JP
Chairman 2.6.1930–3.2.1935
Born: 8.2.1866   Died: 3.2.1935 (in office)   64–68
WILLIAMS, Francis, CBE (Lord Francis-
  Williams 1962)
Governor 1.1.1951–31.7.1952
Born: 10.3.1903   Died: 5.6.1970   47–49
WILLIAMS, Professor Glanmor, MA, DLITT
National Governor for Wales 4.8.1965–3.8.1970 and
  1.10.1970–31.10.1971
Born: 5.5.1920   45–51
WILSON, Paul N., OBE, DSC, MA, JP (Lord Wilson of
  High Wray 1976)
Governor 15.2.1968–14.2.1972
Born: 24.10.1908   59–63
WOOTTON, Professor Barbara, CH, MA
  (Baroness Wootton of Abinger 1958)
Governor 1.1.1950–30.6.1956
Born: 14.4.1897   52–59

APPENDIX II

BOARDS OF GOVERNORS

as at 1 January

FIRST CHARTER 1 January 1927 (five governors)

	Director-General	Prime Minister	Postmaster-General
1927 Earl of Clarendon 49 *Chairman* Lord Gainford 66 *Vice-Chairman* Sir Gordon Nairne 65 Dr M.J. Rendall 64 Mrs Ethel Snowden 45 *Average age 57.8*	Reith	Baldwin (Con.)	Mitchell-Thomson
1928 Earl of Clarendon 50 *Chairman* Lord Gainford 67 *Vice-Chairman* Sir Gordon Nairne 66 Dr M.J. Rendall 65 Mrs Ethel Snowden 46 *Average age 58.8*	Reith	Baldwin	Mitchell-Thomson
1929 Earl of Clarendon 51 *Chairman* Lord Gainford 68 *Vice-Chairman* Sir Gordon Nairne 67 Dr M.J. Rendall 66 Mrs Ethel Snowden 47 *Average age 59.8*	Reith	Baldwin	Mitchell-Thomson
1930 Earl of Clarendon 52 *Chairman* Lord Gainford 69 *Vice-Chairman* Sir Gordon Nairne 68 Dr M.J. Rendall 67 Mrs Ethel Snowden 48 *Average age 60.8*	Reith	MacDonald (Lab.)	Lees-Smith

1931 J.H. Whitley 64 *Chairman* Lord Gainford 70 *Vice-Chairman* Sir Gordon Nairne 69 Dr M.J. Rendall 68 Mrs Ethel Snowden 49 *Average age 64*	Reith	MacDonald	Lees- Smith
1932 J.H. Whitley 65 *Chairman* Lord Gainford 71 *Vice-Chairman* Dr M.J. Rendall 69 Viscountess Snowden 50 Harold G. Brown 55 *Average age 62*	Reith	MacDonald (Nat. Govt)	Ormsby- Gore
1933 J.H. Whitley 66 *Chairman* R.C. Norman 59 *Vice-Chairman* Harold G. Brown 56 Viscount Bridgeman 68 Mrs M.A. Hamilton 48 *Average age 59.4*	Reith	MacDonald	K. Wood
1934 J.H. Whitley 67 *Chairman* R.C. Norman 60 *Vice-Chairman* Harold G. Brown 57 Viscount Bridgeman 69 Mrs M.A. Hamilton 49 *Average age 60.4*	Reith	MacDonald	K. Wood
1935 J.H. Whitley 68[1] *Chairman* R.C. Norman 61 *Vice-Chairman* Harold G. Brown 58 Viscount Bridgeman 70 Mrs M.A. Hamilton 50 *Average age 61.5*	Reith	MacDonald	K. Wood

[1] On 3 February 1935 Whitley died. He was succeeded by Viscount Bridgeman who died on 14 August 1935. Norman became Chairman in succession to Bridgeman, whose widow then joined the Board.

1936 R.C. Norman 62	Reith	Baldwin	Tryon
Chairman		(Nat. Govt)	
Harold G. Brown 59			
Vice-Chairman			
Mrs M.A. Hamilton 51			
H.A.L. Fisher 70			
Caroline, Viscountess			
Bridgeman 62			
Average age 60.8			

SECOND CHARTER I January 1937 (seven Governors)

	Director-General	Prime Minister	Postmaster-General
1937 R.C. Norman 63	Reith	Baldwin	Tryon
Chairman			
(vacancy)			
Vice-Chairman			
Mrs M.A. Hamilton 52			
H.A.L. Fisher 71			
Caroline, Viscountess			
Bridgeman 63			
Sir Ian Fraser 39			
Dr J.J. Mallon 61			
Average age 58.2			
1938 R.C. Norman 64	Reith[1]	Chamber-lain	Tryon
Chairman		(Nat. Govt)	
C.H.G. Millis 43			
Vice-Chairman			
H.A.L. Fisher 72			
Caroline, Viscountess			
Bridgeman 64			
Sir Ian Fraser 40			
Dr J.J. Mallon 62			
Margery Fry 63			
Average age 58.3			

[1] Sir John Reith (48) resigned as Director-General on 30 June 1938. He was succeeded by F.W. Ogilvie (45) on 1 October 1938.

1939	R.C. Norman 65 [1] *Chairman* C.H.G. Millis 44 *Vice-Chairman* H.A.L. Fisher 73 Caroline, Viscountess Bridgeman 65 Sir Ian Fraser 41 Dr J.J. Mallon 63 Margery Fry 64 *Average age 59.3*	Ogilvie	Chamber- lain	Tryon
1940	Sir Allan Powell 63 *Chairman* C.H.G. Millis 45 *Vice-Chairman* *Average age 54*	Ogilvie	Chamber- lain	Tryon
1941 [2]	Sir Allan Powell 64 *Chairman* C.H.G. Millis 46 *Vice-Chairman* *Average age 55*	Ogilvie	Churchill (Coalition)	W.S. Morrison
1942	Sir Allan Powell 65 *Chairman* C.H.G. Millis 47 *Vice-Chairman* Dr J.J. Mallon 66 Lady Violet Bonham Carter 54 A.H. Mann 65 Sir Ian Fraser, MP 44 Hon. Harold Nicolson, MP 55 *Average age 56.6*	Ogilvie [3]	Churchill	W.S. Morrison

[1] Norman retired 18 April 1939 and was immediately succeeded by Sir Allan Powell. On 5 September 1939 the Board was reduced by Order in Council to two.

[2] A five-Governor Board was reconstituted by Order in Council on 4 April 1941. Mallon returned and was joined by Lady Violet Bonham Carter and A.H. Mann. Subsequent Orders in Council on 25 April 1941 added Sir Ian Fraser, MP, and on 22 July 1941 the Hon. Harold Nicolson, MP.

[3] F.W. Ogilvie (48) resigned as Director-General on 27 January 1942 and was immediately succeeded by R.W. Foot (52) and Sir Cecil Graves (49) as Joint Directors-General.

1943	Sir Allan Powell 66 *Chairman* C.H.G. Millis 48 *Vice-Chairman* Dr J.J. Mallon 67 Lady Violet Bonham Carter 55 A.H. Mann 66 Sir Ian Fraser, MP 45 Hon. Harold Nicolson, MP 56 *Average age 57.6*	Foot & Graves[1]	Churchill	Crookshank
1944	Sir Allan Powell 67 *Chairman* C.H.G. Millis 49 *Vice-Chairman* Dr J.J. Mallon 67 Lady Violet Bonham Carter 56 A.H. Mann 67 Sir Ian Fraser, MP 46 Hon. Harold Nicolson, MP 57 *Average age 58.6*	Foot[2]	Churchill	Crookshank
1945	Sir Allan Powell 68 *Chairman* C.H.G. Millis 50 *Vice-Chairman* Dr J.J. Mallon 67 Lady Violet Bonham Carter 57 A.H. Mann 68 Sir Ian Fraser, MP 47 Hon. Harold Nicolson, MP 58 *Average age 59.6*	Haley	Churchill	Crookshank

[1] Graves (51) resigned on 6 September 1943 leaving Foot (54) as sole Director-General.

[2] Foot (54) resigned as Director-General on 31 March 1944 and was immediately succeeded by W.J. Haley (42).

1946 Sir Allan Powell 68   Haley   Attlee   Listowel
         Chairman   (Lab.)
         C.H.G. Millis 51
         Vice-Chairman
         Dr J.J. Mallon 68
         Lady Violet Bonham
           Carter 58
         A.H. Mann 69
         Sir Ian Fraser, MP 48
         Hon. Harold Nicolson 59
         Average age 60.6

THIRD CHARTER 1 January 1947 (seven Governors)

		Director-General	Prime Minister	Postmaster-General
1947	Lord Inman 54 [1] *Chairman* Lady Reading 52 *Vice-Chairman* Barbara Ward 32 Sir Richard Peck 53 Geoffrey Lloyd 44 Dr Ernest Whitfield 59 John Adamson 60 *Average age 50.6*	Haley	Attlee	Listowel
1948	Lord Simon of Wythenshawe 68 *Chairman* Lady Reading 53 *Vice-Chairman* Barbara Ward 33 Sir Richard Peck 54 Geoffrey Lloyd 45 Dr Ernest Whitfield 60 John Adamson 61 *Average age 53.4*	Haley	Attlee	Paling

[1] Lord Inman resigned on 22 April 1947 to become Lord Privy Seal.

1949 Lord Simon of Haley Attlee Paling
Wythenshawe 69
Chairman
Lady Reading 54
Vice-Chairman
Barbara Ward 34
Sir Richard Peck 55
Geoffrey Lloyd 46
Dr Ernest Whitfield 61
John Adamson 62
Average age 54.4

1950 Lord Simon of Haley Attlee Paling
Wythenshawe 70
Chairman
Lady Reading 55
Vice-Chairman
Dr Ernest Whitfield 62
John Adamson 63
Lord Clydesmuir 55
Lord Tedder 59
Prof. Barbara Wootton 52
Average age 59.4

1951 Lord Simon of Haley Attlee Ness
Wythenshawe 71 Edwards
Chairman
Lord Tedder 60
Vice-Chairman
John Adamson 64
Lord Clydesmuir 56
Prof. Barbara Wootton 53
I.A.R. Stedeford 53
Francis Williams 47
Average age 57.7

1952 Lord Simon of Haley[1] Churchill De La
Wythenshawe 72 (Con.) Warr
Chairman
Lord Tedder 61
Vice-Chairman
John Adamson 65
Lord Clydesmuir 57
Prof. Barbara Wootton 54
I.A.R. Stedeford 54
Francis Williams 48
Average age 58.7

[1] Sir William Haley (51) resigned as Director-General on 30 September 1952 to become Editor of *The Times*. He was succeeded on 1 December 1952 by Sir Ian Jacob (53).

FOURTH CHARTER 1 July 1952 (nine Governors including National Governors)

		Director-General	Prime Minister	Postmaster-General
1953	Sir Alexander Cadogan 68 *Chairman* Lord Tedder 62 *Vice-Chairman* Lord Clydesmuir 58 *Scotland* Lord Macdonald 64 *Wales* Sir Henry Mulholland 64 *N. Ireland* Prof. Barbara Wootton 55 I.A.R. Stedeford 55 Lady Rhys Williams 54 Sir Philip Morris 51 *Average age 59*	Jacob	Churchill	De La Warr
1954	Sir Alexander Cadogan 69 *Chairman* Lord Tedder 63 *Vice-Chairman* Lord Clydesmuir 59 *Scotland* Lord Macdonald 65 *Wales* Sir Henry Mulholland 65 *N. Ireland* Prof. Barbara Wootton 56 I.A.R. Stedeford 56 Lady Rhys Williams 55 Sir Philip Morris 52 *Average age 60*	Jacob	Churchill	De La Warr

1955 Sir Alexander Cadogan 70   Jacob   Churchill   De La
   Chairman   Warr
   Sir Philip Morris 53
   Vice-Chairman
   Lord Macdonald 66
   Wales
   Sir Henry Mulholland 66
   N. Ireland
   Thomas Johnston 73
   Scotland
   Prof. Barbara Wootton 57
   Sir Ivan Stedeford 57
   Lady Rhys Williams 56
   Lord Rochdale 48
   Average age 60.7

1956 Sir Alexander Cadogan 71   Jacob   A. Eden   Hill
   Chairman   (Con.)
   Sir Philip Morris 54
   Vice-Chairman
   Lord Macdonald 67
   Wales
   Sir Henry Mulholland 67
   N. Ireland
   Thomas Johnston 74
   Scotland
   Prof. Barbara Wootton 58
   Lady Rhys Williams 57
   Lord Rochdale 49
   Sir Edward Benthall 62
   Average age 62

1957 Sir Alexander Cadogan 72[1]   Jacob   A. Eden   Hill
   Chairman
   Sir Philip Morris 55
   Vice-Chairman
   Lord Macdonald 68
   Wales
   Sir Henry Mulholland 68
   N. Ireland
   Earl of Balfour 54
   Scotland
   Lord Rochdale 50
   Sir Edward Benthall 63
   Mrs Thelma Cazalet-Keir 57
   Dame Florence Hancock 63
   Average age 61.1

[1] Sir Alexander Cadogan retired on 30 November 1957 and was immediately succeeded by Sir Arthur fforde.

1958	Sir Arthur fforde 57 *Chairman* Sir Philip Morris 56 *Vice-Chairman* Lord Macdonald 69 *Wales* Sir Henry Mulholland 69 *N. Ireland* Earl of Balfour 55 *Scotland* Lord Rochdale 51 Sir Edward Benthall 64 Mrs Thelma Cazalet-Keir 58 Dame Florence Hancock 64 *Average age 60.3*	Jacob	Macmillan (Con.)	Marples
1959	Sir Arthur fforde 58 *Chairman* Sir Philip Morris 57 *Vice-Chairman* Lord Macdonald 70 *Wales* Earl of Balfour 56 *Scotland* J. Ritchie McKee 58 *N. Ireland* Lord Rochdale 52 Sir Edward Benthall 65 Mrs Thelma Cazalet-Keir 59 Dame Florence Hancock 65 *Average age 60*	Jacob[1]	Macmillan	Marples
1960	Sir Arthur fforde 59 *Chairman* Sir Philip Morris 58 *Vice-Chairman* Lord Macdonald 71 *Wales* Earl of Balfour 57 *Scotland* J. Ritchie McKee 59 *N. Ireland* Sir Edward Benthall 66 Mrs Thelma Cazalet-Keir 60 Dame Florence Hancock 66 Sir James Duff 61 *Average age 61.9*	Greene	Macmillan	Bevins

[1] Sir Ian Jacob (60) retired as Director-General on 31 December 1959 and was immediately succeeded by Hugh Carleton Greene (49).

1961 Sir Arthur fforde 60   Greene   Macmillan   Bevins
         Chairman
         Sir James Duff 62
         Vice-Chairman
         J. Ritchie McKee 60
         N. Ireland
         Sir David Milne 64
         Scotland
         Mrs Rachel Jones 52
         Wales
         Mrs Thelma Cazalet-Keir 61
         Dame Florence Hancock 67
         Earl of Halsbury 52
         Robert Lusty 51
         Average age 58.8

1962 Sir Arthur fforde 61   Greene   Macmillan   Bevins
         Chairman
         Sir James Duff 63
         Vice-Chairman
         J. Ritchie McKee 61
         N. Ireland
         Sir David Milne 65
         Scotland
         Mrs Rachel Jones 53
         Wales
         Dame Florence Hancock 68
         Earl of Halsbury 53
         Robert Lusty 52
         Gerald Coke 54
         Average age 58.9

FOURTH CHARTER EXTENDED 1 July 1962

1963 Sir Arthur fforde 62   Greene   Macmillan   Bevins
         Chairman
         Sir James Duff 64
         Vice-Chairman
         Sir David Milne 66
         Scotland
         Mrs Rachel Jones 54
         Wales
         Sir Richard Pim 62
         N. Ireland
         Robert Lusty 53
         Gerald Coke 55
         Dame Anne Godwin 65
         Sir Ashley Clarke 59
         Average age 60

1964	Sir Arthur fforde 63 [1]	Greene	Douglas-	Bevins
	Chairman		Home	
	Sir James Duff 65		(Con.)	
	Vice-Chairman			
	Sir David Milne 67			
	Scotland			
	Mrs Rachel Jones 55			
	Wales			
	Sir Richard Pim 63			
	N. Ireland			
	Robert Lusty 54			
	Gerald Coke 56			
	Dame Anne Godwin 66			
	Sir Ashley Clarke 60			
	Average age 61			

FIFTH CHARTER 30 July 1964 (nine governors)

		Director-	*Prime*	*Postmaster-*
		General	*Minister*	*General*
1965	Lord Normanbrook 62	Greene	Wilson	Benn
	Chairman		(Lab.)	
	Sir James Duff 66			
	Vice-Chairman			
	Sir David Milne 68			
	Scotland			
	Mrs Rachel Jones 56			
	Wales			
	Sir Richard Pim 63			
	N. Ireland			
	Robert Lusty 55			
	Gerald Coke 57			
	Dame Anne Godwin 67			
	Sir Ashley Clarke 61			
	Average age 61.7			

above:

[1] Sir Arthur fforde resigned on grounds of ill health on 31 January 1964. Sir James Duff was appointed Chairman from 26 February 1964 to 14 May 1964 when Lord Normanbrook was appointed to the chairmanship.

opposite:

[2] On 11 June 1966 Sir John Fulton was appointed to head the Committee on the Civil Service. He temporarily ceased to be Vice-Chairman but remained an ordinary Governor. Robert Lusty was recalled to the Board as Vice-Chairman.

[3] Lord Normanbrook died on 15 June 1967. He was succeeded on 1 September by Lord Hill of Luton. The Board was increased to 12 members by Order in Council of 28 July 1967.

1966 Lord Normanbrook 63   Greene   Wilson   Benn
   Chairman
   Sir John Fulton 63 [2]
   Vice-Chairman
   Sir Richard Pim 64
   N. Ireland
   Lady Baird 64
   Scotland
   Prof. Glanmor
    Williams 45
    Wales
   Gerald Coke 58
   Dame Anne Godwin 68
   Sir Ashley Clarke 62
   (vacancy)
   Average age 60.9

1967 Lord Normanbrook 64 [3]   Greene   Wilson   Short
   Chairman
   Robert Lusty 57
   Vice-Chairman
   Sir Richard Pim 65
   N. Ireland
   Lady Baird 65
   Scotland
   Prof. Glanmor
    Williams 46
    Wales
   Lord Fulton 64
   Dame Anne Godwin 69
   Sir Ashley Clarke 63
   J.H. Trower 53
   Average age 60.7

1968 Lord Hill of Luton 63   Greene   Wilson   Short
   Chairman
   Robert Lusty 58
   Vice-Chairman
   Lady Baird 66
   Scotland
   Prof. Glanmor
    Williams 47
    Wales
   Lord Dunleath 34
   N. Ireland
   Lord Fulton 65
   Dame Anne Godwin 70
   J.H. Trower 54
   Sir Ralph Murray 59
   (3 vacancies)
   Average age 57.3

1969	Lord Hill of Luton 64	Greene[1]	Wilson	Stonehouse
	Chairman			
	Lord Fulton 66			
	Vice-Chairman			
	Lady Baird 67			
	Scotland			
	Prof. Glanmor			
	Williams 48			
	Wales			
	Lord Dunleath 35			
	N. Ireland			
	Sir Ralph Murray 60			
	Sir Robert Bellinger 58			
	Tom Jackson 43			
	P. N. Wilson 60			
	Dame Mary Green 55			
	Sir Learie Constantine 67			
	(vacancy)			
	Average age 56.6			
1970	Lord Hill of Luton 65	Curran	Wilson	Stonehouse
	Chairman			
	Lord Fulton 67			
	Vice-Chairman			
	Lady Baird 68			
	Scotland			
	Prof. Glanmor			
	Williams 49			
	Wales			
	Lord Dunleath 36			
	N. Ireland			
	Sir Ralph Murray 61			
	Sir Robert Bellinger 59			
	Tom Jackson 44			
	P. N. Wilson 61			
	Dame Mary Green 56			
	Lord Constantine 68			
	Sir Hugh Greene 59			
	Average age 57.7			

[1] Sir Hugh Greene (58) resigned as Director-General on 31 March 1969 and was immediately succeeded by Charles Curran (47). Greene was appointed a Governor with effect from 1 July 1969.

1971 Lord Hill of Luton 66   Curran   Heath   Chataway
Chairman   (Con.)
Lady Plowden 60
Vice-Chairman
Prof. Glanmor
 Williams 50
 Wales
Lord Dunleath 37
 N. Ireland
(vacancy) *Scotland*
Sir Ralph Murray 62
Sir Robert Bellinger 60
Tom Jackson 45
P.N. Wilson 62
Dame Mary Green 57
Lord Constantine 69
Sir Hugh Greene 60
Average age 57

1972 Lord Hill of Luton 67   Curran   Heath   Chataway
Chairman
Lady Plowden 61
Vice-Chairman
Lord Dunleath 38
 N. Ireland
Lady Avonside 54
 Scotland
Dr G. Tegai Hughes 48
 Wales
Sir Ralph Murray 63
Tom Jackson 46
P.N. Wilson 63
Dame Mary Green 58
Robert Allan 57
Roy Fuller 59
Tony Morgan 40
Average age 54.5

1973	Sir Michael Swann 52	Curran	Heath	J. Eden

      Chairman
      Lady Plowden 62
      Vice-Chairman
      Lord Dunleath 39
      N. Ireland
      Lady Avonside 55
      Scotland
      Dr G. Tegai Hughes 49
      Wales
      Sir Ralph Murray 64
      Tom Jackson 47
      Dame Mary Green 59
      Robert Allan 58
      Roy Fuller 60
      Tony Morgan 41
      George Howard 52
      Average age 53.1

1974	Sir Michael Swann 53	Curran	Heath	J. Eden[1]

      Chairman
      Lady Plowden 63
      Vice-Chairman
      Lady Avonside 56
      Scotland
      Dr G. Tegai Hughes 50
      Wales
      Bill O'Hara 44
      N. Ireland
      Lord Allan of Kilmahew 59
      Roy Fuller 61
      Tony Morgan 42
      George Howard 53
      Lord Feather 65
      Lord Greenhill of Harrow 60
      (vacancy)
      Average age 55.1

[1] Broadcasting matters were transferred to the Home Secretary on 29 March 1974.

Home
Secretary

1975 Sir Michael Swann 54   Curran   Wilson   R. Jenkins
        Chairman   (Lab.)
        Lady Plowden 64
        Vice-Chairman
        Lady Avonside 57
        Scotland
        Dr G. Tegai Hughes 51
        Wales
        Bill O'Hara 45
        N. Ireland
        Lord Allan of Kilmahew 60
        Roy Fuller 62
        Tony Morgan 43
        George Howard 54
        Lord Feather 66
        Lord Greenhill of Harrow 61
        Mrs Stella Clarke 42
        Average age 54.9

1976 Sir Michael Swann 55   Curran   Wilson   R. Jenkins
        Chairman
        Hon. Mark Bonham
        Carter 53 *Vice-Chairman*
        Lady Avonside 58
        Scotland
        Dr G. Tegai Hughes 52
        Wales
        Bill O'Hara 46
        N. Ireland
        Lord Allan of Kilmahew 61
        Roy Fuller 63
        Tony Morgan 44
        George Howard 55
        Lord Feather 67
        Lord Greenhill of Harrow 62
        Mrs Stella Clarke 43
        Average age 54.9

FIFTH CHARTER EXTENDED 1 August 1976

1977	Sir Michael Swann 56 *Chairman* Hon. Mark Bonham Carter 54 *Vice-Chairman* Dr G. Tegai Hughes 53 *Wales* Bill O'Hara 47 *N. Ireland* Prof. Alan Thompson 52 *Scotland* Roy Fuller 64 George Howard 56 Lord Greenhill of Harrow 63 Mrs Stella Clarke 44 Philip Chappell 47 Lord Allen of Fallowfield 62 (vacancy) *Average age 54.4*	Curran[1]	Callaghan (Lab.)	M. Rees
1978	Sir Michael Swann 57 *Chairman* Hon. Mark Bonham Carter 55 *Vice-Chairman* Dr G. Tegai Hughes 54 *Wales* Bill O'Hara 48 *N. Ireland* Prof. Alan Thompson 53 *Scotland* Roy Fuller 65 George Howard 57 Lord Greenhill of Harrow 64 Mrs Stella Clarke 45 Philip Chappell 48 Lord Allen of Fallowfield 63 Baroness Serota 58 *Average age 55.6*	Trethowan	Callaghan	M. Rees

AVERAGE AGE OF BOARDS ON 1 JANUARY 58.3

[1] Sir Charles Curran (55) resigned as Director-General on 30 September 1977 and was immediately succeeded by Ian Trethowan (54).

APPENDIX III

PUBLIC ENQUIRIES INTO DOMESTIC BROADCASTING

SYKES COMMITTEE

Appointed 24 April 1923
Date of Report (Cmd 1951) 25 August 1923

MEMBERS	AGE ON APPOINTMENT
Sir Frederick Sykes, MP	45
Major the Hon. J.J. Astor, MP	36
F.J. Brown	58
Sir Henry Bunbury	46
Viscount Burnham	60
W.H. Eccles	47
Sir Henry Norman, MP	64
J.C.W. Reith	33
Field-Marshal Sir William Robertson	63
Charles Trevelyan, MP	52

Cost: £320

CRAWFORD COMMITTEE

Appointed 20 July 1925
Date of Report (Cmd 2599) 2 March 1926

MEMBERS	
Earl of Crawford	53
Lord Blanesburgh	63
Capt. Ian Fraser, MP	27
Rt Hon. William Graham, MP	38
Sir William Henry Hadow	65
(Rudyard Kipling – resigned)	59
Rt Hon. Ian MacPherson, MP	45
Lord Rayleigh	49
Sir Thomas Royden	54
Dame Meriel Talbot	59

Cost: £106 7s 1d

SELSDON TELEVISION COMMITTEE

Appointed 14 May 1934
Date of Report (Cmd 4793) 14 January 1935

MEMBERS	AGE ON APPOINTMENT
Lord Selsdon	57
Sir John Cadman	56
Col. A.S. Angwin	50
Noel Ashbridge	44
O.F. Brown	
Vice-Admiral Sir Charles Carpendale	59
F.W. Phillips	54

Cost: £965

ULLSWATER COMMITTEE

Appointed 17 April 1935
Date of Report (Cmd 5091) 31 December 1935

MEMBERS	
Viscount Ullswater	80
Major the Hon. J.J. Astor, MP	48
Major the Rt Hon. C.R. Attlee, MP	52
E. Clement Davies, MP	51
Lord Elton	43
Sir William McLintock	61
Marchioness of Reading	41
Lord Selsdon	58
H. Graham White, MP	54

Cost: £564 10s

HANKEY TELEVISION COMMITTEE

Appointed September 1943
Date of Report 29 December 1944

MEMBERS	AGE ON APPOINTMENT
Lord Hankey	66
Sir Stanley Angwin	59
Sir Edward Appleton	51
Sir Noel Ashbridge	53
Sir Raymond Birchall	55
Prof. J.D. Cockcroft	46
(R.W. Foot until March 1944)	54
W.J. Haley (from April 1944)	42
R.J.P. Harvey	39

Cost not given

BEVERIDGE COMMITTEE

Appointed 21 June 1949
Date of Report (Cmd 8116) 15 December 1950

MEMBERS	
(Lord Radcliffe)	50
Lord Beveridge	70
A.L. Binns	58
J. Crawford (from 23 Feb. 1950)	53
Earl of Elgin	68
Lady Megan Lloyd George, MP	47
Selwyn Lloyd, MP	44
W.F. Oakeshott	45
J. Reeves, MP	61
I.A.R. Stedeford (from 27 Sept. 1949)	52
Mary Stocks	57
Dr Stephen Taylor (from 20 March 1950)	39
(Sir William Coates resigned)	
(James Bowman resigned)	
(E.A.J. Davies, MP resigned)	

Cost: £15,415

PILKINGTON COMMITTEE

Appointed 13 July 1960
Date of Report (Cmnd 1753) 1 June 1962

MEMBERS	AGE ON APPOINTMENT
Sir Harry Pilkington	55
H. Collison	51
Elwyn Davies	51
Joyce Grenfell	50
Richard Hoggart	41
E.P. Hudson	57
Prof. F.H. Newark (from March 1961)	53
J.S. Shields	57
R.L. Smith-Rose	66
Mrs Elizabeth Whitley	44
W.A. Wright	36
(J. Megaw resigned 5 Jan. 1961)	
(Peter Hall resigned 27 Jan. 1961)	
(Sir Jock Campbell resigned 2 Feb. 1961)	

Cost: £45,450

ANNAN COMMITTEE

Appointed 10 April 1974
Date of Report (Cmnd 6753) 24 February 1977

MEMBERS

Lord Annan	57
Peter Goldman	49
Prof. Hilde Himmelweit	54
Tom Jackson	49
Antony Jay	44
Marghanita Laski	58
Mrs Hilda M. Lawrence	50
A. Dewi Lewis	63
Sir James MacKay	67
The Hon. Mrs Charles Morrison	39
Dipak Nandy	37
John G. Parkes	55
John Pollock	48
Prof. Geoffrey Sims	47
Phillip Whitehead, MP	36
Sir Marcus Worsley	49

Cost: £315,000

APPENDIX IV

STAFF AND LICENCES, 1922-77

Note: Figures from 1922–38 as at 31 December of each year, thereafter as at 31 March.

YEAR	BBC STAFF NOS.	Radio (R)	Monochrome TV and Radio (M)	Colour TV (C)	Total	Fees
1922	4	35,774				R 10s
1923	177	595,496				
1924	465	1,129,578				
1925	658	1,645,207				
1926	773	2,178,259				
1927	989	2,395,183				
1928	1,064	2,628,392				
1929	1,109	2,956,736				
1930	1,194	3,411,910				
1931	1,287	4,330,735				
1932	1,512	5,263,017				
1933	1,747	5,973,758				
1934	2,031	6,780,569				
1935	2,518	7,403,109				
1936	3,350	7,960,573				
1937	3,673	8,479,900				
1938	4,060	8,908,900				
1939	5,100	8,968,338				
1940	6,445	8,951,045				
1941	10,504	8,752,454				
1942	11,849	8,683,098				
1943		9,242,040				
1944	11,657	9,554,838				
1945	10,727	9,710,230				
1946	11,132	10,395,551				R £1 M £2
1947	12,286	10,763,144	14,560		10,777,704	
1948	11,512	11,134,112	45,564		11,179,676	
1949	11,730	11,620,881	126,567		11,747,448	
1950	12,413	11,875,566	343,882		12,219,448	
1951	12,552	11,605,086	763,941		12,369,027	
1952	12,267	11,304,246	1,449,260		12,753,506	
1953	12,688	10,749,779	2,142,452		12,892,231	
1954	12,834	10,187,901	3,248,892		13,436,793	M £3
1955	13,524	9,476,730	4,503,766		13,980,496	
1956	14,519	8,521,958	5,739,593		14,261,551	
1957	15,242	7,558,843	6,966,256		14,525,099	M £4*
1958	15,472	6,556,347	8,090,003		14,646,350	
1959	16,108	5,480,991	9,255,422		14,736,413	
1960	16,889	4,535,258	10,469,753		15,005,011	
1961	17,515	3,908,984	11,267,741		15,176,725	
1962	18,012	3,538,507	11,833,712		15,372,219	

* Including £1 excise duty not receivable by BBC.

YEAR	BBC STAFF NOS.	Radio (R)	Monochrome TV and Radio (M)	Colour TV (C)	Total	Fees	
1963	18,940	3,256,185	12,442,802		15,698,991		M £4	
1964	20,836	2,999,348	12,885,331		15,884,679			
1965	22,128	2,793,558	13,253,045		16,046,603	R £1 5s	M £5	
1966	22,758	2,611,066	13,567,090		16,178,156			
1967	22,898	2,505,934	14,267,271		16,773,205			
1968	22,933	2,557,314	15,068,079	20,428	17,645,821			C £10
1969	23,753	2,463,872	15,396,642	99,419	17,959,993		M £6	C £11
1970	23,854	2,301,191	15,609,131	273,297	18,183,719			
1971	24,761	abolished	15,333,221	609,969	15,943,190		M £7	C £12
1972	24,857		15,023,691	1,634,760	16,658,451			
1973	24,882		13,792,623	3,331,996	17,124,619			
1974	25,131		11,766,424	5,558,146	17,324,570			
1975	26,080		10,120,493	7,580,322	17,700,815		M £8	C £18
1976	25,963		9,148,732	8,639,252	17,787,984			
1977	25,719		8,098,386	9,957,672	18,056,058		M £9	C £21

INDEX

ABC Television, 106
Accountability, in BBC, 21, 46, 136, 237
Acland, Sir Francis, 200
Adam, Kenneth, 116, 120, 219
Adamson, John, 96, 153
Addison rules, 31–2
Administrative Division, 78
Adult Education Advisory Committee, 199–201
Advertising, on BBC, 126–7, 138
Advisory Councils, 92, 136
Aldington, Lord, 29
Allan, Robert, 165, 166
Allen of Fallowfield, Lord, 166
Allighan, Garry, 60
Annan, Lord, 47, 138–9
  and 1978 White Paper, 244
Annan Committee, 138–42, 171–2, 235
  and communications studies, 183
  and Governors, 44–5, 46, 139, 169
  members, 138, 278
  and *That Was the Week That Was*, 189–90
Asquith of Yarnbury, Baroness, *see* Bonham Carter, Lady Violet
Associated-Rediffusion, 105, 107
Associated Television, 105
Attlee, Clement, 63–4, 86, 170
Audiences, BBC and ITV, 105, 106
  for *That Was the Week That Was*, 218, 219
Avonside, Lady, 165, 224
Aylestone, Lord, *see* Bowden, Herbert

BBC From Within, The, 93, 208
Baillie, Robin, 228
Baird, Lady, 124, 163
Baldwin, Stanley, 146, 191, 196, 200, 204

Balfour, Harold, 198
Balfour, Earl of, 159
Barker, Sir Ernest, 181
Barnes, George, 73, 98, 207
Bartlett, Vernon, 189, 194–7
Bellinger, Sir Robert, 133, 164, 224
Benn, Anthony Wedgwood, 21, 38, 125–6, 127, 178–9, 182
Benthall, Sir Edward, 159
Bett, Michael, 184
Betterton, Sir Henry, 191
Betting odds, *see* Horseracing
Beveridge, Lord, 95, 96, 189
  on Governors, 29
  and the monopoly, 88–9
Beveridge Committee, 87, 89–92, 95, 189
  members, 277
Bevins, Reginald, 114–15, 119, 177, 238
Billington, Kevin, 124
Blakenham, Lord, 177
Board of Governors, *see* Governors
Board of Management, 87–8, 93, 99
  and Haley, 167
  minutes, 130
  origin, 26
Bonham Carter, Mark, 33, 166, 231
Bonham Carter, Lady Violet, 78, 82, 83, 85, 86, 89
  appointment, 70, 72–3, 152
Bottomley, Sir Norman, 215, 216
Bowden, Herbert, 126, 164, 190, 212
Brabazon, J. T. C. Moore-, 149
Bracken, Brendan, 69, 71, 73, 74, 76, 77, 79
Brand, R. H., 149
Bridgeman, Viscount, 33, 34, 65, 148
Bridgeman, Caroline, Viscountess, 33, 148, 149
British Broadcasting Company, 49, 53–4